The meaning of DREAMS

The meaning of
DREAMS

Unlock the messages from your subconscious

Rose Inserra

Illustrations by Ivan Hissey

HINKLER
BOOKS

Contents

HINKLER
BOOKS

The Meaning of Dreams
First Published in 2008 by Hinkler Books Pty Ltd
45–55 Fairchild Street
Heatherton VIC 3202 Australia
www.hinklerbooks.com

ISBN 978 1 7418 2142 0

Designed and produced for Hinkler Books Pty Ltd
by The Bridgewater Book Company Ltd.

Text: Rose Inserra
Illustrations: Ivan Hissey
Cover Design: Hinkler Books Studio
Cover images: © Melgama/Dreamstime.com
Internal Design: Fineline
Project Manager: Susie Behar
Editor: Judith Chamberlain-Webber
Internal Art Director: Michael Whitehead

Printed and bound in China

Preface

Vanessa woke clutching her stomach, her heart pounding. It was the same dream. For five nights she had dreamed that she was standing barefoot on grass when she felt something cold on her feet. Looking down, a snake passed over her toes and moved on. Within moments, she felt pain and a miscarriage began. But when she woke up the baby seemed fine.

Was something wrong with the baby? Was this an omen? Or, as her husband suggested, was it just her subconscious fears expressed through her dreams?

Can dreams tell us something about the future? Are some dreams more significant than others? Is it possible to learn the language of dreams and unlock their messages?

Dreams offer useful information about our unconscious mind. For centuries people have believed in the power of dreams to heal, offer spiritual insight, foretell the future and solve problems and daily dilemmas. The emphasis in this book is on trying to unlock the code to the messages that our dreams beam to us through images. In dreaming, our unconscious minds are aware of aspects of our personalities that our conscious minds do not want to acknowledge. Dreams are a way of bringing up issues that our waking selves would otherwise continue to ignore at the risk of our emotional and physical health.

Interpreting dreams can, therefore, help us better understand ourselves through learning more about our true feelings, thoughts, behaviour, motivations and values. It can also help us to solve problems. People in creative fields, such as artists, writers, actors and inventors, often get their ideas from dreams. The most important things to keep in mind are that dreams reflect our innermost thoughts and feelings, and that all events that happen in our dreams are personal to us.

Introduction

Technically speaking, a dream is an hallucination. A dream is also a fantasy journey in our sleep that either reduces our stress or enables us to live out our greatest fears in the safety of sleep. When we sleep, we get rest and relief from our waking days. In this sense, dreams are a way of relaxing and letting our minds drift away into distant worlds. In this state we can interact in a non-physical sense with people, places and both living and non-living things. How many of us are sad when we wake up from a beautiful dream?

When we are in tune with our waking lives, dreams can help us to understand ourselves better. If we interpret them correctly, we can find a treasure trove of hidden secrets. Who do we wish would 'vanish into thin air?' Who or what are we running away from in a chase scenario? If our teeth are falling out, should we be paying the dentist a visit or is it all to do with losing our grip on things? These are common images and scenes that are locked in our subconscious. Isn't it about time you unlocked the message of your dreams?

There are three main theories explaining why we dream.

- Sigmund Freud said that the function of dreams was to preserve sleep; but that theory is contradicted by modern studies showing that dreams happen very regularly—at least four to five times per night during the most active part of sleep, known as REM (rapid eye movement) sleep.

- Carl Jung, another famous dream theorist, claimed that the reason we dream is to compensate for those parts of the psyche or total personality that are underdeveloped in waking life.

- Other dream theorists tell us that dreams have a problem-solving purpose. Dreams are supposed to deal with problems we can't solve in waking life and to offer some kind of solution.

CHAPTER ONE

Unlocking the

How many times have you woken from a dream feeling worried by what you have just experienced or simply wondered what on earth it was all about? Though dreams often seem completely unfathomable, you might be surprised to see how much you can learn about yourself and your behaviour by carefully studying all the aspects of the dream. This chapter helps you understand the nature of sleep and different types of dreams, and gives you some tips on how to recall your dreams and then interpret them.

messages

The land of make-believe

Some people can actually control what happens in their dreams. This state or ability is called 'lucid dreaming'. A lucid dream is where the unreality of the dream makes the dreamer realise that it can't be real. For example, if you are breathing underwater without the help of oxygen or dancing in midair, you know it can't be true. The dreamer not only knows that a dream is taking place, but also can somehow control the dream and maintain this empowering state for some time.

The strange fact is that the dreamer is in a rational state and can act voluntarily in the dream while still remaining sound asleep in an incredibly real dream world. Lucid dreaming can occur during the end of a nightmare, when the dreamer realises that it is only a dream and decides to see it through till the end, as one does in a horror movie.

Have you ever had a dream where you said, 'This isn't real, so I'm not going to run away and be scared'? If you have, it was a lucid dream.

Accounts of lucid dreaming date back to Aristotle, who recorded his experience and dismissed the whole thing as a sign of madness or a message from the gods. Researchers specialising in lucid dreams found that lucid dreamers can control parts, but not all, of their dreamscape. An experiment found that when subjects were asked to turn a light on in the dream, the light switch would either not work or the bulb would blow.

How long does a dream last?

Most dreams are in colour, but the images soon change into black and white and within about ten minutes the dream completely fades unless we conveniently wake up and make an effort to remember. That is why we tend to remember only the last dream we had before we wake up. Some dreams can last up to half an hour, although they seem to go on forever in the dream. Oddly enough, within seconds of suddenly waking from a dream we are usually alert and responsive. However, if we are suddenly awoken from the deep stage of non-dreaming sleep, we can experience confusion and lack of coordination.

Can you feel emotions in dreams?

Do you sometimes wake from a nightmare feeling shaky and sweaty?

Do you ever get hurt in a dream and go through the motions of pain without experiencing any real pain? The reason the dreamer experiences an emotional detachment from events in the dream, and becomes more of an observer, is because parts of the brain controlling the emotions shut down during the dreaming sleep. That is lucky for the dreamer. Imagine the pain you would feel when attacked by a crocodile or falling down an abyss in a dream if you were to experience the actual sensation.

Sometimes when we wake from a nightmare we may be feeling physically shaky or sweaty, and this is a residue from the emotions felt in the dream. Nightmares are the end result of a frightening dream. Night terrors, on the other hand, suddenly appear out of deep, non-dreaming sleep. In a night terror, the dreamer sits up and suddenly screams, often experiencing some kind of horrifying experience. The terror and sense of panic can last for up to ten minutes and is a grave concern to parents whose children suffer this state of fear. Unlike their parents, however, children will have little if any recollection of this experience the next morning on waking up.

13

Understanding sleep

Nearly every animal sleeps in some way. It is evident that sleep performs some important function for the nervous system. Many theories have been suggested, but the most practical seems to be the one put forward by Nobel Prize winner Francis Crick. He claims that the purpose of sleep is to allow the brain to 'take out trash'—to undo daily events that don't need to be stored for long-term memory. Basically, as humans we need to get rid of unimportant mental items clogging our brains and recharge during sleep so that nerve cells can be re-engaged the next day to face a new set of tasks.

Experiments in sleep deprivation have shown that it is not lack of sleep that causes people to be disturbed, but 'dream' deprivation. Dreams are likely to be the result of the brain sorting through its short-term memory of the day's events, storing some in the long-term memory and then getting rid of the rest.

Who dreams?

Science tells us that everyone dreams—even animals and birds. Some of us can dream in vibrant colours and recall every detail the next morning, while a few claim they never dream at all. There are also those of us who dream some of the time and can remember the dream in sketchy detail.

Did you know that we spend one third of our lives sleeping? Not only that, but we spend two to three hours per night dreaming. That means that by the time we're 75, we have slept for 25 years and dreamed for about 10!

So, when do we dream? There are four stages of sleep:

Stage 1

The first stage of sleep is a very light sleep. You can easily be woken and might deny having been asleep on awakening. Ever heard someone say, 'I wasn't asleep! I only had my eyes closed'?

That's because the brainwaves are going from a waking frequency (beta) to a more relaxed phase, known as alpha state. This is when the body temperature, heart and pulse rate drop slightly and the eyes begin to roll. Drifting thoughts and floating sensations, as well as vivid pictures flow through the brain. Stage 1 may last for five to ten minutes.

Stage 2

In stage 2, the brainwaves keep on slowing down. This is a much deeper sleep than stage 1 and is when dreams start to brew. Although there are no clear images, thoughts and ideas float in and out of the sleeper's mind. The brain frequency has now reached a level called theta.

Snoring is common at this stage and there's a decreased heart rate, pulse, blood pressure and temperature. Breathing can be shallow and irregular. Ever had that twitch or jerk but still felt unable to shake yourself awake? This is the stage at which it happens.

More importantly, the eyes now move back and forth rapidly beneath the closed eyelids. This is known as REM (rapid eye movement) sleep, and lasts for a few minutes the first time it occurs. If one wakes at this time, the dream can usually be remembered.

Stage 3

This is a deep sleep stage, with stage 4 being more intense than stage 3. These stages are known as slow-wave or delta sleep. These long, regular delta waves produce a deep dreamless sleep. The sleeper's muscles are totally relaxed and the heart rate and blood pressure has slowed down. Breathing is steady and even, and it's going to be very difficult to wake up. Delta waves can last up to an hour before the dreamer goes into the deeper sleep of stage 4.

Stage 4

This is the deepest sleep. It is virtually impossible to wake up from this stage of sleep. The sleeper's blood pressure and heart rate fluctuate. There is an increased secretion of growth hormone (this is to restore body tissues). That is why it is so important for infants and children to get as much of this sleep as possible.

This is the stage when dreams occur and REM is at its best because the brain is in an active state. The first REM period will last approximately ten minutes. After that, the sleeper goes back into a deep stage 4 sleep. Then it's back into REM stage after a short time and the cycle is repeated until the sleeper wakes up. The final REM stage lasts about one hour.

These four phases of sleep repeat four or five times during the night, approximately every 90 to 120 minutes. So a person may complete up to five cycles in a typical night's sleep. The REM stage lasts longer the more one sleeps. The longest uninterrupted period of dreaming occurs in the early morning and may last up to one hour. That's why you remember dreams most vividly on awakening.

'I wasn't asleep!

I only had

my eyes

closed.'

What happens when we sleep?

The discovery of REM sleep proved that sleep is not a dormant state for the body, but a mentally active period during which dreaming occurs. During REM sleep there is intense activity in the brain and rapid bursts of eye movement under the eyelids. Your body is still during this stage but your brain is very active. Scientists also discovered that the body is paralysed during REM sleep and the brain at its most active. To imagine this paralysis when one is not dreaming is a horrible notion, since in many cases dreams can be violent and active.

Interestingly, the paralysis is absent during non-dreaming sleep. Here, sleepwalking and sleep talking can take place usually in the deepest stage of non-dreaming sleep. Have you ever tried to wake a sleepwalker or make sense of what they are saying? Sleepwalkers are difficult to arouse, even more than dreamers in REM sleep are. The best course of action is simply to usher them back to bed without trying to wake them. They will feel disoriented and confused. They may sometimes act in a violent manner. Be warned.

'While we sleep, our senses no longer function in the same manner as when we are awake.'

While we sleep, our senses of hearing, touch, taste, sight and sound no longer function in the same manner as when we are awake. We are only able to utilise these senses in an emergency. For example, you may be able to smell the toast burning or you'll hear a loud thunderstorm. Generally, while we sleep our sleeping systems are working free of input from the outside world. And amazingly, people have vivid dreams—many of which involve all the senses.

From research on brain patterns during sleep, scientists have begun to understand and develop treatments for sleep disorders. Sleep disorders affect the quality and duration of sleep. Change of sleep schedule, stress, environment and illness can all affect the sleep cycle. Medical and psychological conditions such as depression shorten the duration of REM.

So why can't you sleep?

You can increase REM sleep naturally by doing the following just before going to bed:

- Eating foods that contain the amino acid tryptophan such as turkey, milk, bananas and cheese

- Having a warm bath

- Not doing strenuous activities

- Meditating or relaxing

Did you know that the frequency of REM sleep is highest during early childhood years? It drops during adolescence and young adulthood and decreases in old age. Total sleep time becomes shorter during childhood and increases in adolescence. Older people get less total sleep but a lengthening of REM stage.

What the dream experts say

Dream analysts believe that in dreams our unconscious minds are providing clues to help us understand ourselves better and provide solutions to our problems. Not many of us realise that we are being productive while we sleep. The problem is remembering the dream vividly so that you can unlock its message and apply it to whatever is affecting you in waking life.

The earliest examples of dream interpretation come from the Bible. The most famous biblical dream is Pharaoh's dream about the seven fat and thin cattle and the seven fat and thin ears of corn, which Joseph interpreted as a prophecy of seven years of abundance and seven years of famine. Joseph's interpretation had a huge impact not only on Egypt but also on the future of dream analysis.

Greek philosophers improved on the early theories of dream interpretation. Plato called dreaming 'the between state', an actual place where the soul went to meet with the gods. Aristotle spoke of the illusion of 'sense-perception'. He suggested that the malfunctioning of the senses allowed dreams to occur and that dreams, therefore, were formed by these imbalances of the body.

'The purpose of dreams is to allow us to satisfy in fantasies the instinctual urges that society judges unacceptable.'

Not until modern times did two of the greatest pioneers in dream analysis come along: Sigmund Freud and Carl Jung. Their dream theories contributed significantly to current explanations of dreams and their functions.

Sigmund Freud (1856–1939) is known as the 'father' of psycho-analysis. He believed that the analysis of dreams was a powerful tool in uncovering hidden thoughts and desires and, as a result, his work focused on finding the causes of dreams. Freud's psychoanalytical approach theorised that dreams are created by unconscious desires, especially sexual urges and hidden fears. He believed that our conscious minds are disgusted by our hidden desires and they repress these urges because we are ashamed or afraid of what others might think. He claimed that 'the purpose of dreams is to allow us to satisfy in fantasies the instinctual urges that society judges unacceptable'.

Freud created a method called 'free association' in which the patient describes thoughts and feelings as they come to mind. For example, if the therapist said 'blue', the dreamer would have to reply with the first word that came to mind. This method was used to discover the real issue behind the dreams. According to Freud, there was a repressed sexual motive behind most dreams. A snake, bird or pencil represented the male genitals while a wineglass, cave, glove or tunnel represented the female genitals. Flying, falling, ascending and descending stairways all represented sex.

Today, dream therapists do not strictly follow Freud's teachings. What are fascinating to analysts today are the revelations of the unconscious mind—thought to be more honest and representative of our true selves than our conscious mind.

While Freud was interested in finding the causes of dreams, his student, Carl Jung, looked to the purpose of dreams. Carl Jung (1875–1961) was a psychotherapist, a philosopher and a scholar of mythology. He believed in the 'collective unconscious'—archetypal images shared by people all around the world, regardless of their religions and cultures.

'Plato called dreaming **'the between state'**, *an actual place where the soul* *went to* ***meet with the gods.*'***

Symbols & images

'Archetypes' are universal symbols that are common to everyone because they represent something that relates to the universal principles of life, or themes lived by each one of us. Archetypal characters and symbols can come from religious teachings and images, myths, fairytales, folk tales and legends.

Here are some of Jung's most common archetypes that appear in dreams:

The divine child

The innocent, playful 'child' represents the true self. If you dream of a baby or young child, you may be starting a new activity or are ready for a new beginning. Perhaps you are looking for more childlike qualities to apply to your life, such as spontaneity, a new perspective, more trust and playfulness.

The divine/earth mother

The nurturing, loving female represents growth, generosity and wisdom. Dreaming of a mother figure can mean that there are areas in life you need to nurture.

The shadow

The 'shadow' represents those parts of you that are deeply buried because they are seen as bad and rejected by your conscious. These parts scare you or trigger unpleasant emotions and are usually the opposites of what you consciously project. Paying attention to the shadow means having to accept the 'dark side' of your personality and dealing with the issues involved.

The anima and animus

The 'anima' is the hidden feminine part of a man's personality—the feminine side. The 'animus' is the masculine part of a woman's personality. When you lose touch with these personalities, your life is not in a state of perfect balance. It would make sense, therefore, to take note of them in your dreams and apply their symbolic meaning to your everyday life.

The wise old man

The 'wise old man' can be represented by any authority figure whom you respect. It could be a king, judge, priest or an older person whom you wish to take advice from—whether the advice that you are given is encouraging or disapproving.

The hero and the hero's journey or quest

As in any hero story or epic, the 'hero' must encounter challenges, hardships, villains, temptations and danger. To begin the hero's journey, you must first be cut off from your roots and be mistreated or misunderstood. Then you can begin the adventure and discover your true self, which only comes after encounters with all the challenges listed above. Finally, you experience an understanding and acceptance of your heroic self and reach your goal. It is time, then, to go back to the past— back to the time when you were misunder- stood or mistreated—and enlighten those who caused you to feel this way. This process is one of spiritual growth and essential for development and enlightenment.

The fool or seeker

If you see yourself as the 'fool', or not efficient, in your dreams, the dream is suggesting that you have an important lesson to learn. The 'seeker' is looking for knowledge and experience and if the dreamer feels immature or naïve, it shows that he or she is unprepared and needs to gain knowledge.

Monsters

Monsters represent your worst fears or the parts of your personality that are usually kept hidden away. The best way to deal with these monsters is to face them and ask them what they want from you. This method helps you to deal with issues that are too scary for you to deal with in normal life.

Death and rebirth

Myths and legends describe heroes and creatures that die and come back to life. Even the Bible tells us of Jesus Christ who comes back from the dead. And nature gives us examples of this, such as the caterpillar that hides in its cocoon and emerges as a butterfly. When you dream of death, it is usually an indication of personal growth and suggests that after death there is rebirth and transformation. It is a positive dream you should embrace.

21

Typical dreams

These are dreams which most people have had at some point such as flying or being chased. But it's a myth that if you hit the bottom in a falling dream you will have died in your sleep...

Falling

Many people have dreamed that they have hit bottom in a fall and they are still alive to tell the story! Falling is a common theme, which often indicates that in your real life you are feeling a little out of control and insecure. You may be experiencing a lack of support and grounding. In your waking life you may be feeling unsupported, unsafe or weighed down. The circumstances of the fall in the dream are important to notice. Were you pushed or did you jump willingly? Could it point to a situation in real life where you are trying to escape something, someone or a situation that you either cannot cope with or don't wish to face?

The place of falling is also important. If you are in a falling dream, do you clutch onto something to break your fall or do you close your eyes and fall directly below? If you can control your landing in a fall and perhaps have a soft landing, it could mean that the crisis you are having in real life might not be as difficult as you imagined.

*Were you **pushed** or did you **jump willingly?***

Flying

Sigmund Freud claimed that flying represented dreams of a sexual nature. Most likely they are dreams of a longing for freedom or of letting go, as well as dreams of journeying. You need to pay attention to the details in your flying dreams so that you can interpret correctly the way in which you see yourself journeying through life. When you fall in a dream, you experience a lack of support and grounding. In real life you may be feeling unsupported, unsafe, or heavily burdened with a wish to be freer and lighter.

*Most likely they are dreams of a **longing for freedom** or of letting go.*

Naked in public

It can be a nightmare to feel embarrassed in a recurring anxiety dream where you are the only one naked. Ask yourself in which areas of your life you feel embarrassed, incompetent or lacking in confidence. Generally, being naked in front of others represents a fear of being exposed in waking life.

Driving

Driving was another of Freud's famous dream images. He believed driving fast in a dream was associated with sexual prowess and power. It may well be that sex is a 'driving' force in your life; however, it can also represent the desire for power or success. Losing control when driving, or being on the wrong side of the road, suggest that you may not be in control of your real life. Perhaps life is too hectic, so slowing down and not being so controlling are reflections of real-life needs.

It's important to notice the scenery and other persons in the car or around you in the dream so that you can explore your life in more detail and take control of situations. If you are a passenger, perhaps you should ask yourself why you're not the driver and who has control of the car. Driving can also represent a personal journey. Problems such as loss of control can be indicative of the obstacles or struggles experienced during that journey. The other symbols in the dream will give clues about the reason for the journey.

Swimming or drowning

Water is a symbol of emotion and your spiritual life. If you are swimming in a dream, the surrounding circumstances could tell you about your emotional and spiritual state of being. You may be in a vast sea or lake, trapped in a pond or being swept downstream by a fast flowing river. How you cope in these situations may indicate your real-life drama. Can you swim safely to shore? If so, it's a positive sign that you're going to overcome your emotional ups and downs and be able to reach your goal.

'Can you swim safely to shore?'

If you're feeling overwhelmed, and begin to drown, then emotions are too strong for you and you're unable to cope. Dark, muddy water is also pointing out that you are stuck or are confused about an emotional issue.

Stuck in slow motion

Of all nightmarish dreams this one can be the most frustrating of all, particularly if you dream of being chased and can't get away. This could well indicate that you are stuck in real life, unable to get anywhere fast enough, or to voice your true feelings.

'You have to ask yourself who is chasing you and why?'

Being injured

If part of your body is being dismembered and you are feeling pain, it may well be that you are neglecting or mistreating aspects of yourself in real life.

Being chased or attacked

This common dream is one of the most frightening and can be disturbing. You have to ask yourself who is chasing you and why. The person doing the chasing usually represents a major fear—your shadow, or hidden self—that has grown to a huge proportion and causes terror and a feeling of being a victim. To find out what this fear or aspect of yourself is, ask the pursuer in the nightmare why they are chasing you. By facing your fear, you are standing your ground. This can in turn help you to stand up for yourself in your conscious life and take charge.

Recurring & anxiety dreams

Almost everyone has experienced dreams that contain anxiety or fear. These experiences can be traumatic and sometimes they haunt us by recurring repeatedly.

Typical nightmare themes include:

- falling
- being chased or attacked
- walking into a meeting or a class unprepared
- being stuck in slow motion
- being trapped and unable to move or scream
- drowning or choking
- being naked in public

Experiences of this sort are unpleasant and usually tell us that we are not making progress in solving our real-life conflicts. Some theorists believe that recurring dreams are due to lack of action in the dreamer's waking state. One of the reasons for dream interpretation is to solve these problems.

What is a nightmare?

A nightmare is a distressing dream, which can cause us to partially awaken. How many of us have sat upright from a nightmare, our hearts thumping with fear and glad to be awake? Did you feel negative emotions in the nightmare such as guilt, sadness, anger and especially fear and anxiety? The most frightening and common nightmare is probably being chased. Anxiety is heightened when we can't move, are trapped in slow motion or are paralysed and keep falling down.

Nightmares are regarded as a warning about current behaviour patterns or imbalances that we need to solve if we don't want such unpleasant dreams to repeat themselves. Some people try to block nightmares and those who have recurring nightmares usually try to change the outcome. However, if we block them or ignore these messages from the subconscious for too long, the nightmare may begin to show up in our real life—not as in the dream but as accidents, illnesses and relationship difficulties.

What causes nightmares?

A number of factors may cause nightmares, including:

- medication
- illness
- suffering a traumatic event
- undergoing a great deal of stress in one's life, such as surgery, loss of a loved one, an accident, a divorce, moving house, change of job, pregnancy and concerns about financial or other matters

The most **frightening** *and common nightmare is probably being* **chased.**

Children forget their nightmares soon after waking.

Young children tend to have nightmares as they struggle to learn about dealing with the usual childhood fears and insecurities. It is normal for the majority of children to have nightmares between the ages of three and eight.

Carl Jung observed that parts of an individual's whole personality may become 'disowned' and these are frequently projected outward in dreams. These take the form of devils, monsters, intimidating people or animals, or even natural events such as tidal waves, floods and tornadoes. These symbolic forms are what Carl Jung referred to as 'the shadow'. If we become any of these elements of our shadow through nightmares, then 'accepting' these disowned portions of ourselves will help us reveal the message of the nightmare.

On the positive side, nightmares provide a release for the psyche as they can bring us valuable insight into what is causing the most stress in our lives.

Resolving nightmares

What can be done about nightmares? Young children should be encouraged to discuss their nightmares with an adult if it is a recurring nightmare. Usually, children forget their nightmares soon after waking. Adults' nightmares offer the opportunity to understand what is going on in their waking lives. With practice you can learn to unlock the code of the symbolic language of the nightmare and see how it relates to your real-life fear. Usually the dream connects to your life, and sometimes to your past, by evoking a specific feeling.

If you are distressed about a recent nightmare, redesign a different ending to the dream. Choose something that leaves you feeling empowered, instead of helpless, as you did with your original nightmare outcome. Then apply this new happy outcome to areas in your life that you feel need attention.

What are night terrors?

Night terrors are sudden, dramatic interruptions in our sleep and are quite different to nightmares. They occur during the first hour or two of sleep—the deep non-REM sleep—and sufferers have no recollection of the dream. They can last anywhere from ten to thirty minutes.

They're most common in children, causing them to bolt out of bed, thrash around and scream or run wildly though the house. Their eyes may be wide open, but they are not awake; neither are they aware of anybody around them. Night terrors can also cause children to sleepwalk and/or to urinate in bed. Other symptoms include sweating, rapid heart rate and confusion. Night terrors, sleepwalking and sleep talking are all disorders of arousal, called parasomnias. They are usually caused by stress.

Extraordinary dreaming

There are have been countless numbers of accurate dreams predicting future events. These are known as precognitive dreams. It seems that we are able to pick up information through a faculty other than our five physical senses.

Famous prophetic dreams

- Several people predicted President Kennedy's assassination a few days before it took place.

- A few days before his assassination, President Abraham Lincoln dreamed of his own corpse, laid out in a room in the White House.

- Several passengers, having dreamed that the Titanic sank, decided to cancel their trip at the last minute and lived to tell the tale.

- Joan of Arc dreamed that God instructed her through dream visions to save France from the English.

Other less famous and well-known events have been predicted by people all over the world, but there seems to be no scientific explanation for why this is so. However, it is wise to listen to warnings and omens as they may be pointing to things that need fixing in our lives, such as our health and well-being.

Forecasting dreams

When the body consciousness senses an imbalance, a warning of disharmony sounds throughout the body. That warning signal works its way up though the brain as we sleep and registers in the conscious mind as a forecasting dream—that is, a dream that forecasts a potential physical problem.

If you dream of a specific part of your body that is at risk, pay particular attention to it. If you dream of problems such as your car radiator overheating, it may be something to do with your overactive emotional state. Cars and houses often symbolise your body. For example, if the brakes won't work, you may be feeling out of control and stretched for time. If the car won't start, perhaps you're lacking energy and need to refuel. A house renovation indicates that major work needs to be done on the body—whether it's exercise, rest or a health-check. If your house is on fire, you may be feeling feverish or perhaps have too many blankets on.

Insects are also another good indication of what's going on in your body. Dreaming of insects in general denotes infection; while maggots, worms and moths suggest that there is some sickness or emotional state that's 'eating away at you'.

Creative dreaming

Writers, artists, musicians, dancers and inventors have all found inspiration and reached their full creative potential by having lucid dreams or 'dream incubation' (see below). Lucid dreaming takes place when we are aware that we are dreaming while still asleep and in the dream. Have you ever said, 'Is this a dream?' while you were dreaming? Or perhaps you're familiar with the dream and decide to change the ending or sequence of the dream. This means that you are manipulating the dream so that you affect its outcome.

Famous creative dreams include the following:

- Mary Shelley wrote *Frankenstein* after she had a vivid dream.

- The novelist, Stephen King, is said to find inspiration for his novels in his nightmares.

- Robert Louis Stevenson got the idea for *Dr. Jekyll and Mr. Hyde* from a dream.

Other artists who credit dreams as a source of inspiration include Mozart, Beethoven, William Blake, screenwriter Ingmar Bergman and many others. Inventors are also highly inspired by their dreams. Otto Leowi's dream resulted in the chemical mediation of nerve impulses. Others include Elias Howe's invention of the sewing machine and many of Thomas Edison's inventions.

Experiencing a lucid dream

Lucid dreams are the ultimate virtual realities where anything is possible and the dreamer has some element of control, masterminding adventure, science fiction, romance, or gravity-defying stunts with no physical limitations. We can perform amazing feats in which the boundaries of the imagination are the only limits. Tibetan monks use lucid dreaming as a spiritual tool on the path to enlightenment.

How many of us can fly with owls and birds, swim with dolphins and dive underwater like seals or climb like mountain goats on the giant slopes of the Himalayas? This feeling of exhilaration, or being able to do anything, can translate itself into a creative process and be a great tool for anyone who wants to develop this side of their personality. Dreams offer the chance to have fun, adventure and to explore one's creativity, as well as being used for healing or gaining insight.

Sleep on it—dream incubation

Dream incubation involves consciously asking the dream for guidance in solving an actual problem in waking life. There is an old saying that if you have a decision to make, it is best to 'sleep on it' beforehand. That way, you'll find a solution that isn't based on emotion or just a gut reaction.

To incubate a dream you must, before you go to sleep, have your question or problem clearly in your mind and then ask yourself that question. For example, you may ask 'Is this relationship good for me?' In the morning, record the dream and your thoughts about it and try to work out the meaning.

Using subconscious images

These are some common elements in dreams that can help you with dream interpretation. Try to remember how you felt in the dream or where the dream took place.

Mood

The mood of a dream can help you to interpret the meaning more accurately. It may be totally opposite to how you would feel if you were in a real-life situation. Are you feeling confident facing lions in the Colosseum when in real life you would be terrified? Make a note of the mood, the people and place and action to help you work out why you felt that mood or emotion. Perhaps the dream is telling you that you are more confident than you give yourself credit for.

Activity

Physical and mental activities in dreams can actually make you feel exhausted when you wake up. Perhaps your life needs more action or you should put yourself in an unfamiliar situation where you can use skills that are presently underdeveloped.

Setting

The place you find yourself in a dream is also an important clue to the message of your dream. The scenery usually represents the inner self, while weather conditions can suggest your mood.

Perhaps the dream is telling you that you are more confident than you give yourself credit for.

Buildings may be a setting for the story of the dream or may be important keys in themselves. School could mean you should study something carefully in real life; an office represents status; a bar reflects your social life; a train station is about direction and a bridge could mean that two aspects of your life need to be linked.

The house represents the dreamer's inner self. Each room within a house symbolises a particular part of self. A room high up in the house represents the spiritual self or higher states of consciousness. Basements represent the primal or the emotional self. The bedroom is indicative of passion and rest.

Mountains can represent your aspiring self—reaching for success or spiritual goals. Freud, however, saw mountain peaks as phallic symbols, representing sexual desires.

Water represents your emotions. Whether it's ocean, lake or river, the appearance of the water is significant in your dream. Clear water gently lapping against the shore is usually a good sign, while stormy waves engulfing the swimmer is a sign of the dreamer being overwhelmed by emotion. A murky pool, or being stuck in mud, is also a reflection of being emotionally stagnant in your waking life.

Characters

Sometimes you dream of people you know or have known, while other times they may be strangers or famous personalities. The people in your dream can represent different aspects of your own personality. It's important for you to question your reaction to how they behaved in the dream. Do you see uniforms? Is it because you're a rebel or that you wish to conform? Perhaps you have a meeting with the president. What does this suggest about your attitude to things or people in real life? Are you traditional in your view? Do you 'rule' people? Animals can either represent themselves, people you know or even different aspects of your own personality. Birds usually stand for freedom; cats are independent; dogs are loyal; farm animals are productive; bees are hard workers; spiders are creative.

31

Recall & interpretation

Do you have problems remembering your dreams? The problem of dream recall and lucid dreaming is that waking and dreaming memory aren't connected very well. This means that as the dreamer you have to make a consistent effort to remember and record your dreams.

Here are some tips to help you remember your dreams.

- Before you fall asleep, remind yourself that you want to remember your dreams. This desire to remember will provide motivation for your memory to respond to in your waking hours.

- Keep pen and paper by your bedside. As you wake up, try not to think of the day's routine. Focus on your dreams and their images and jot them down. Any distractions will cause the memory of your dream to fade. If you can't remember the dream, record the last thing you remember, or even fragments of the dream. It may not make sense right away, but eventually it may form a pattern that you'll understand.

- Don't try too hard to remember dreams. Sometimes, the harder you try to remember the easier it seems to be to forget. Be patient and persistent and stick with it for at least a few days before expecting results.

Using a dream diary

When you have written down your dream, read it through. This will help you to remember more details and make it easier to interpret.

Record as many details as you can. What was the mood of the dream? Think about how you felt in the dream, your actions, decisions, the location, the characters, symbols, colours or anything that stood out as distinctive.

Write down anything that has been causing you anxiety, stress or joy in your waking life. Compare these emotions with those felt during your dream. Sometimes the relevance of the dream is not immediately obvious. Ask yourself what your unconscious is telling you with the help of a dream dictionary and your own intuition.

Dream interpretation

The most important factor when learning to understand the messages in dreams is that they are your dreams and that it is up to you to unlock that message. Dream interpretation is very general, as the same dream can have a different message for each individual dreamer. It is best to use the dictionary of dreams as a guide only.

Ideally, break down the dream into symbols, archetypes, common elements and images first and then work out the more specific details. Follow your own instinct, relating the dream to your conscious life and, using all the information in this book, design your own individual guide to your dreams.

How to interpret a story dream

To interpret a dream that has a story-like structure with a beginning, middle and an end:

- Break down the dream into scenes, as you would with a movie. Write them down.

- Identify the main elements of each scene and pay attention to the characters. Are they authoritarian, passive, helpless or frightening? Is there a conflict or problem?

- Look for emotions, especially those that are easy to identify such as love and fear.

- Interpret the dream literally at first and try to make sense of its main purpose. How did the dream end? Was there a resolution?

- Link your dream to something that's happening in your waking life. Try to identify the characters from your dreams.

- Decide what you're going to do and how you're going to act on the dream's message.

Case study: A story dream about an icy adventure

The dreamer is a 40-year-old woman who is deciding whether or not to end her marriage.

I was on a large ship floating on ice. 'I wonder if the weight of the ship will break the ice?' I thought. I looked outside and saw no sign of life—just ice and icebergs. But then I saw something moving in the distance. There, all in a row, were tiny baby snow goslings. They were white and fluffy and had orange beaks with black edges. I called out to my brother excitedly, but he didn't believe me at first. Then, with time, he saw the goslings too. Soon someone sighted a whale circling the ship. Time slipped by and I was home again. My parents asked me where I'd been. I told them I'd been on a trip to a cold place far away, but I was now back.

There are a number of symbols in this dream:

Symbol Meanings

Ice | Frozen emotions; the dreamer's lack of warmth in the marriage; her present life.

Ship | The dreamer (a vessel); she questions whether she can hold out in the state she's in—that is, the marriage being like an inhospitable frozen sea, ready to break at any minute. Would the ship (dreamer) float (make it)?

Goslings | New beginnings; taking new chances.

Brother | Masculine side of the dreamer—the rational and logical; the voice of reason doubting the dreamer's instincts.

Whale | Large part of life—the future/the unknown waiting to embrace the dreamer.

Parents | Nurturing or conscious side of self.

Interpretation

The dream is reassuring the dreamer that there will be a new life for her despite her indecisiveness. The future is bright and she will be able to cope with whatever decision she makes. It is a positive dream, full of reassurance and hope.

CHAPTER TWO
Animals

Dreams about animals can represent the animalistic side of the dreamer; that is, the dreamer's instinctive rather than intellectual nature. Animals often symbolise parts of ourselves or our personalities that are present in our waking lives. Freud attached a sexual significance to animal dreams, but many dream interpreters give various meanings depending on the type of animal. Usually a domestic animal symbolises harmony and happiness, but a wild animal represents an enemy or an uncontrollable force.

Invertebrates

Insects

Generally, the insects in our dreams stand for the things that 'bug' us in our waking lives. Like insects themselves, these things may be small, but they can also be annoying and when there are large numbers of them, threatening or scary. You probably have your own list of the insects you avoid. Over the centuries, most common insects have also acquired broad cultural associations and these may be reflected in your dreams.

Ants

Traditionally, ants symbolise industry, hard work and discipline. However, they also have more sinister associations including lack of individuality, lack of imagination and militarism. Dreaming of ants may suggest pride in your work, but also your sense that you are overly regulated in your job or home life, or that you don't have enough opportunities for pleasure or self-expression.

Caterpillar

Caterpillars are symbols of change or metamorphosis into another state. The caterpillar that is destined to turn into a butterfly could be a symbol of those parts of yourself that also have potential and are waiting for the right moment to emerge from their cocoon or to discover their wings. As a result this dream may signal your desire for a change of activity or environment.

Butterfly

Because of their life cycle, butterflies are traditional symbols of rebirth and transformation. However, they also suggest a fragile, short-lived beauty or happiness. The butterfly's erratic, flitting progress could also be a warning to you that you need to settle down and stop 'flitting' from one person or situation to another.

Beetle

Like ants, beetles have several, different, popular associations. For example, they are associated with dirt (in which case they may suggest your disgust at your surroundings, whether at work or home) but also—because of their hard shells—with a desire to be protected. Another traditional association with the beetle is blindness. A dream with beetles in it could be suggesting that you are scurrying around in the dark, unable to see what's going on around you.

Cricket

The phrase 'merry as a cricket' conveys this insect's traditional associations with good times and a cheerful attitude to life. This dream could be a sign that you or someone close to you is feeling particularly 'chirpy' or happy. Alternatively, it could also function as a compensatory dream when you are feeling blue.

Grasshopper

Traditionally, the grasshopper was compared with the ant and regarded as a symbol of laziness. Dreaming of grasshoppers may suggest your guilt that you're whiling away your time while failing to be productive, or your sense that you should be saving more.

Flies

In Western culture, flies tend either to be a symbol of uncleanness, in which case they may stand for troubling emotions or thoughts we would rather brush off, or a sign of annoyance.

Fleas

These tiny, biting creatures tend to stand for the things that annoy us or make us uncomfortable. Because they are hard to see with the naked eye, they can also suggest those emotions or impulses that lurk at the edge of our consciousness and which, as a result, we find hard to identify so that we can deal with them.

Lice/Parasites

These creatures probably represent those things or people that you feel fasten onto you, drain your energy and prevent you from making the progress you desire. If the lice are in your hair, they could be a symbol of some force—such as a rival or a dependant—which you fear is making you less sexually attractive or desirable.

Cross-reference

For Lice/Parasites, see Hair p.113, Parasites p.125

37

Invertebrates

Leech

Leeches are regarded both as medical wonders and as a way of describing people who 'suck you dry' with their requests and demands. The interpretation that applies to your dream often depends on your view of these creatures. Medically, leeches have been used to cleanse wounds. Socially, however, being labelled a leech is not a desirable trait. Consider which of these two definitions best suits the circumstances of your dream.

Moth

In traditional European mythology, moths symbolise the soul or psyche. As a result, this dream may have spiritual connotations, or be associated with a person who is no longer alive, but with whom you still feel emotionally connected.

Mosquito

Their habit of attacking at night makes mosquitoes a symbol of persecution, perhaps by unseen enemies. Of course the mosquitoes in your dream could also represent your own tendency to attack others, or a propensity to undermine your own best interests.

Locusts

As the expression 'a plague of locusts' suggests, these insects are considered to be symbols of misfortune. Their appearance in a dream could be a sign that you feel your problems are reaching 'biblical' proportions.

Maggots

Because of their associations with death and waste, a dream of maggots may suggest your anxieties that you aren't living fully enough, or that there is something badly wrong with your home life. Alternatively, you may feel that others are using you or behaving in an inconsiderate way.

Spider

A dream of spiders can signal a desire to be productive and creative. Alternatively, it may suggest that you are feeling caught up in or smothered by the emotions and conflicts of those around you, especially in your home or family life. Traditionally, spiders were thought to symbolise powerful maternal or female figures. They are considered lucky in a number of Eastern cultures. The size of the spider in a dream will indicate the degree of luck.

Wasp

In traditional dream lore, these stinging insects were believed to be a sign that the dreamer had jealous enemies. In modern times, dreaming of wasps is an indication of your fear of being stung by another's 'waspish' tongue, or even your concern about the damage that you may do with your own.

Snail

The latest use for this word is 'snail mail', meaning postal mail, which is slow in comparison to e-mail. Therefore, if you dream of a snail, chances are that you associate it with some aspect of your life that is slow in moving along. On the positive side, the snail leaves a trail and you can follow its progress.

Worm

The metaphorical meaning of a 'worm' is of an insignificant or even contemptible person. Thus, this dream is likely to symbolise your feelings of unimportance or ineffectiveness, or your sense that others are treating you this way. A Freudian interpretation would see the worm as a symbol of the penis, in which case this dream could signal lack of sexual confidence. However, the expression 'even a worm will turn' is a reminder of our potential to change and to grow. Similarly, the worm is recognised today as a crucial part of a healthy garden and is associated with recycling and growth. Calling someone a 'bookworm' isn't necessarily an insult either, but it can indicate that they are studious.

Leech

Moth

Maggots

Mosquito

Spider

Locusts

Wasp

Worm

Snail

Cross-reference

For Leech, see Wound
p.126, Sucking
p.175
For Spider, see Web
p.60, Cobweb p.60
For Worm, see Garden
p.66

Bird breeds

Blackbird

These common birds signify domestic happiness and the protection of your home. Dreaming of one could mean that you want to settle down, or be a sign of anxiety about the well-being of your family.

Crow/Raven

Traditionally regarded as an omen of death, this bird is more likely to be interpreted nowadays as a symbol of change or renewal.

Dove

Dreaming of this bird can symbolise your desire for a peaceful resolution of a conflict. A dove is also a symbol of pure love.

Eagle

This majestic bird represents aspiration, vigilance and authority. Its appearance in a dream is a positive sign in business or romance.

Duck

The duck is a traditional symbol of good fortune in Chinese dream interpretation.

Quail

Traditionally, these small birds were regarded as a symbol of good luck. However, eating them was also thought to symbolise the risk of over-extravagance.

Vulture

This is a sign that you fear the evil nature in people.

Parrot

Parrots are associated with mimicry. For that reason they can represent anxieties about originality or self-expression. Do you feel as if you are required to 'parrot' somebody else's words or ideas rather than being allowed to develop your own? If so, this dream could be a message that you need to consider striking out on your own and trying to find your own voice.

Stork

This bird foretells change and is traditionally associated with the birth of a child.

Ostrich

Because ostriches are famous for burying their heads in the sand, their appearance in a dream is a sign that you are trying to avoid something by refusing to look at it. Your dream may also be telling you that this is not going to solve your problem. As the ostrich is a flightless bird, it can also indicate you are grounded by present circumstances and are unable to see a solution because you're not looking.

Peacock

Peacocks are traditional symbols of vanity, especially of the male variety. Are you trying to impress somebody with your exaggerated behaviour or fine clothes? This dream could signal anxiety about your need for approval and admiration.

Alternatively, the peacock in your dream could symbolise someone who is trying to make an impression on you. However, your dream may be a sign that you don't entirely trust them, or that you suspect them of too much vanity or self-love.

Blackbird

Crow/Raven

Dove

Eagle

Duck

Quail

Vulture

Stork

Parrot

Ostrich

Peacock

Cross-reference

For Duck, see Water pp.98–103
For Parrot, see Jungle p.96
For Ostrich, see Sand p.83

Birds, general

Birds of prey

Hawks, falcons, buzzards and other birds of prey represent our hunting instincts and our wish either to dominate or to be in control of our environment. These birds all have excellent vision and, together with their hunting skills, represent a formidable group of predators.

Feathers

There are many, different interpretations of feathers in a dream, just as there are many sayings in which feathers occur—'a feather in your cap'; 'birds of a feather flock together'; 'feather your nest'; and 'as light as a feather'. Generally, when we think of feathers, we think of softness and lightness. As a result the dream may be suggesting that using a softer or gentler approach to a situation may be a better method for achieving your ends.

Flock of birds

Flocks suggest that the dream is about your relationships with others.

Caged birds

These symbolise frustration, unhappiness and your desire for expansion and release.

Singing birds

These birds are symbols of happiness and contentment.

Flying birds

Birds in flight suggest a desire for freedom, expansion and independence. Perhaps the flying birds in your dream represent your desire to escape from a situation that is 'holding you down'. Birds in flight are also associated with sexual desire and freedom.

Birds of prey

Feathers

Flock of birds

Caged birds

Singing birds

Flying birds

Injured birds

Waterbirds

Injured birds

A bird that is injured or unable to fly suggests that some area of your life needs attending to before you will be able to move on.

Waterbirds

Waterbirds such as ibises and swans are a connection with our emotional and subconscious natures.

Cross-reference

For Caged birds, see Cage/Cell p.331, Captivity p.200
For Waterbirds, see Water pp.98–103

Mammals

Ape/Monkey

Dreaming of apes or monkeys is a warning that there are those among your friends or co-workers who are being mischievous and will try to get you into trouble. It may also mean that your childish nature may prevent you from achieving your goals and that you need to pay more attention to your work and less to 'monkeying around'.

Antelope

Antelopes are a sign of a financial gain or they can suggest that someone has sought your advice.

Badger

Badgers are traditionally associated with persistence, hence the phrase 'badgering away' at something. Dreaming of a badger indicates that your perseverance will pay off and that success may be close at hand.

Wolf

Hunting in packs is what we associate most with the wolf. The dream may suggest that you feel threatened on either an individual level or as part of a group.

Bear

In general, bears are often considered as representative of motherhood, whether it's the image of a possessive or a caring mother or someone who is overbearing. Fighting or killing a bear means that you will be successful in a present struggle. If you are attacked however, it means someone or something is after you with great ferocity.

Boar

Trouble is ahead when you dream of wild animals and the boar is both wild and dangerous. If you chase or run away from a wild boar, it means that you will be disappointed as you may be escaping from an issue that you should be facing head on. Freud saw the boar as a symbol of power and oppression. In biblical terms, the boar is a sign of impurity. Dreaming of killing a boar, however, means improved conditions in your life, particularly when dealing with authorities at work.

Elephant

It is said that an elephant never forgets so it is no surprise that dreaming of an elephant signifies memory as well as wisdom and patience. The Eastern belief is that the elephant is a symbol of luck and prosperity.

Bat

Bats spell trouble for you in financial matters or in personal relationships. As these nocturnal creatures have been regarded with fear for centuries, they are a symbol of misfortune or upset plans when you least expect them.

Zebra

According to traditional gypsy interpretation, the zebra was a symbol of ingratitude and misplaced trust in friends. Its stripes denote a more modern meaning about the need to balance the positive and negative in your life.

Ape/Monkey

Antelope

Badger

Wolf

Bear

Boar

Elephant

Bat

Zebra

Cross-reference

For Elephant, see
   Ivory p.60
For Bat, see Vampire
   p.309, Night p.441
See also Being chased
   p.197, Hunted
   p.194

Mammals

Deer/Reindeer

These animals are regarded as a symbol of hierarchy. The herd is organised with ranking in place and therefore the dream may suggest a questioning of your place in life—of where you fit into the scheme of things in general. Deer have also been depicted as innocent and as creatures able to move with grace and speed. Antlers are traditionally associated with masculine superiority. In some cultures, powdered antler was thought to give one the power of the animal or enhance sexual prowess. The dream could suggest the desire for control and power over a certain situation.

Fox

Dreaming of a fox signifies someone sly and cunning. It is a warning to watch out for this sort of person or behaviour in your life.

Hare

Hares are nimble and very resourceful animals. If you dream of a hare coming towards you, it may suggest that you will be experiencing a new venture in your life.

Hyena

Hyenas are scavengers by nature, so to dream of one or more of these animals denotes deviousness.

Jackal

For the ancient Egyptians, the jackal was a symbol of judgement and watchfulness. Over time, however, dreaming of jackals has become linked with death and their watchful place—the graveyard. Be mindful to watch those who are trying to discredit you in some way or who are trying to bring about the 'death' of your reputation.

Kangaroo

Since a kangaroo is a wild animal, dreaming of one or more may mean unexpected and exciting travel. It may also represent a subconscious need to unleash the wild side of your nature.

Leopard

These animals usually represent aggression and tyranny. They are also a symbol of rivalry, so if you dream of one you should be aware of dangers and difficulties ahead.

Hedgehog

The hedgehog is a symbol of prickly defensiveness. If you dream of this animal, it could be a warning that you need to consider how effective your current strategy is for dealing with threatening people or difficult situations.

Instead of 'rolling into a ball' as a hedgehog would, it may be necessary to engage more actively with a problem or issue. A hedgehog may also represent your need to be more protective of yourself in your waking life.

Cross-reference

For Deer/Reindeer, see Horn p.60
For Kangaroo, see Jumping p.254

Mammals

Cat

These animals are considered to be independent and refined, yet powerful as predators. This duality in their nature often makes people wary of cats and reluctant to trust them. They have often been linked to the sensuous side of human nature—especially the feminine side. The dream is telling you to be aware of the cat's qualities that you may not be making use of, such as independence or intuition. To dream of a black cat has been traditionally associated with treachery and evil, but this may have been a result of cultural superstitions.

Lynx

The lynx is famous for its excellent and keen eyesight. Are you being watched carefully by someone or do you need to keep a careful eye on a situation or person?

Rat

Rats are unpopular because of their association with spreading diseases. To call someone 'a rat' is to cast aspersions on their character, as rats are regarded as untrustworthy or devious. The dream could be a warning of impending disloyalty from someone around you.

Mouse

Mice are an indication of trouble with family and friends. This stems from the fact that as rodents they scavenge and fight each other for their food. The mouse is also known for its shyness and unobtrusive personality, so the dream may be about your lack of individuality.

Mole

Moles are usually associated with darkness and blindness. Make sure that you go about your business with your eyes kept wide open.

Rabbit

Rabbits are recognised as symbols of fertility and the start of new life.

Dog

Dogs are considered loyal, faithful and devoted companions. However, if they appear in your dreams as vicious, they may represent aggression. If they are friendly dogs, they may indicate either that you are faithful in friendship, or be representing someone in your life with these qualities. Expressions such as 'top dog' or 'underdog' can also express themselves in dreams. Jung and Freud classify dreams of being bitten by animals as erotic or sexual dreams.

Weasel

Weasels warn us of our devious nature or that of someone in our lives. This may have a negative impact on our present situation.

Lion

The lion is a symbol of power, strength and courage. If you dream of fighting with a lion and win without being either hurt or killed, it means you will be successful in your present struggle. A lion is also known as 'the king of the jungle' and, as such, stands for the ego. The dream needs to be interpreted in the light of its outcome.

Squirrel

In a dream squirrels indicate that you will get by in life if you work hard. They can, however, also suggest an element of possessiveness in your personality.

Tiger

This is an obstacle dream. The image of a tiger is that of a powerful and dignified predator. It has the power to create and destroy, and to get away from one in your dream means that escape from a destructive element in your life is on the horizon.

Cat

Mouse

Lynx

Mole

Dog

Rat

Rabbit

Weasel

Lion

Squirrel

Tiger

Cross-reference

For Mouse/Rat, see
Pesterer p.304
For Dog, see Dog lead
p.61, Kennel p.63
See also Pet p.62

Reptiles & amphibians

Reptiles

Generally reptiles are seen as a symbol of our basic instincts—for example, reproduction, the need for food, flight or fight—all of which are necessary for survival. We connect with the reptile in our dreams through our survival instincts stemming from some ancient parts of our brain. As cold-blooded creatures, reptiles are also associated with emotional coldness. In this respect, the reptile in your dream could represent someone around you who is acting in a cold or calculating way. Alternatively, it could represent these qualities within yourself.

Snake

Since the biblical story of the Garden of Eden, snakes have been associated with deceit and trickery, as well as temptation. In modern interpretation, the snake represents our suppressed sexual urges and uncontrollable passion. Freud regarded it as a phallic symbol. A snake coiled around you means that you are enslaved to sexual passions. A snake in the grass, however, is telling you that there is disloyalty and trickery around you. Because snakes are sometimes poisonous, most people fear them and usually associate them with death. On the other hand, a snake coiled around a stick is considered a symbol of wisdom.

Lizard

In dreams lizards indicate qualities such as single-mindedness and quick instinct in a person.

Crocodile/Alligator

These animals symbolise a cunning enemy or obstacle to your progress. Being attacked by one means that you are insecure and have a fear of an impeding situation or people. If there are more than one of these reptiles in your dream, beware of new ventures or business dealings.

Frog

Frogs are seen as a symbol of transformation, usually from something insignificant to something of value (the frog turning into a prince).

Tadpole

A tadpole denotes new life, and the appearance of one in a dream indicates that a new phase is beginning in your life. This may be a new project, attitude, relationship or lifestyle that has not yet taken shape but is still forming in your mind.

Tortoise/Turtle

Take note of this dream, as in Aesop's fable 'The Hare and the Tortoise', slow and steady wins the race. It may be telling you that if you slow down, success will eventually be yours.

Dinosaur

These exaggeratedly large animals tend to represent our most primitive fears. But because they are extinct, they may also stand for emotions or problems that belong in our past, or that we have outgrown. In this case, they can be our mind's way of telling us that we don't need to worry about these things any longer.

Reptiles

Snake

Lizard

Crocodile/
Alligator

Frog

Tadpole

Tortoise/Turtle

Dinosaur

Cross-reference

See also Swamp/
Marsh p.96

Water creatures

Eel

When we say that someone is as 'slippery as an eel' it usually means that the person is not trustworthy. If you dream that you are trying to hold onto a slippery eel, it may be pointing to a situation in which you risk losing a grip on something (an issue or emotion) or suggesting that something is slipping away from you.

Crab

Because they wear their skeletons on the outside, these creatures suggest a defensive attitude to life. Their pincers also denote the need to exercise caution when attempting to explore the emotions or go to the heart of a matter. The crab is also a symbol of the zodiac sign Cancer, and so it is possible that the crab in your dream could represent a person born under this sign.

Octopus

An octopus symbolises freedom of movement and adaptability. But if the octopus is threatening you, its eight arms may suggest that you are feeling 'strangled' or under attack from a number of different sources.

Shark

When we talk of someone being a shark, we mean that they are unscrupulous. Sharks are also perfect predators in the sense that they have no natural enemies of their own. Dreaming of a shark may suggest that you feel unprotected and vulnerable around people or in situations that are out of your league.

Otter

Otters work well as a team and thrive in complicated environments. Dreaming of an otter could indicate that you might be working in an environment that involves interacting and solving complex problems.

Eel

Crab

Octopus

Shark

Otter

Fish

Fish

The fish symbol was adopted by the early Christians to represent Christ and the Church. In a more general sense, when we dream of fish, we are getting in touch with our deeper selves and our search for a higher self or spirituality. For the Chinese, fish are a symbol of financial gain, while the image of two fish going in the opposite direction represents the astrological sign of Pisces. Or, you may be feeling as if you are living in a fish bowl, open to criticism for all to see. Perhaps you are 'a big fish in a small pond' and you need to expand your horizons.

Cross-reference

For Fish, see Fishing
    p.193, Zodiac
    pp.144–5
For Crab, see Shell
    p.88
See also Water
    pp.98–103

Water creatures

Whale

The primary association of these sea mammals is with size. In this respect, dreaming of a whale may indicate a concern about your weight, or how you appear to others. More positively, the expression 'a whale of a time' indicates a social event or other situation in which those involved are having a lot of fun. In today's society, however, whales are also thought of as an endangered but valuable species so their appearance in a dream may indicate your desire to protect something of value.

Jellyfish

Jellyfish lying on a beach indicate that you are feeling surrounded by dangers that are hard to see and therefore to avoid. These may come from people or situations that don't seem openly confrontational, but are nonetheless a potential source of danger.

Lobster

A lobster is a mini armoured tank—a symbol of aggressive masculinity. You may want to be more like the lobster—protected in your impenetrable armour and able to defend yourself against your enemies. If you are lacking confidence and feeling victimised, this dream may be pointing out the need to take on these qualities to help you get through this difficult emotional period.

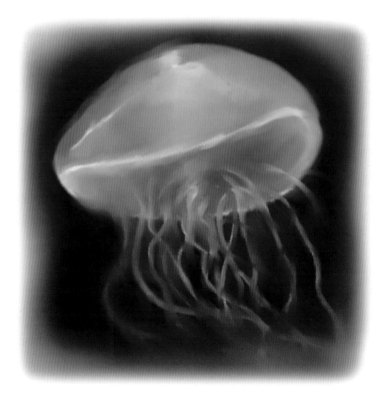

Seal

Dreaming of a seal symbolises our ability to be in touch with the elements around us, while not straying too far from our safety zone. Like seals, we need rocks (stability) to rest, form relationships and for recreation. This dream may suggest that you feel ambivalent about a new situation that requires you to venture into new waters.

Whale

Jellyfish

Lobster

Seal

Oyster

Walrus

Oyster

The oyster's tough shell is associated with things that are difficult to reach or have valuables inside. This aspect of the oyster represents something you greatly value or desire, but that is surrounded by obstacles so that it can be protected against intruders. More positively, the phrase 'the world's your oyster' suggests a more optimistic attitude towards getting what you want from life.

Walrus

The walrus is most famous for its large size. For this reason dreaming of one is likely to signal anxieties about weight. Perhaps you feel like a walrus, or someone else has made you self-conscious about your size.

Cross-reference

For Whale, see Size
    p.442
For Jellyfish, see
    Beach p.96
See also Water
    pp.98–103

Farm & working animals

Bull

To dream of a bull suggests negative and destructive emotions the dreamer may be experiencing in real life ('like a bull in a china shop'). Anger, aggression and impulsiveness ('like a bull at a gate'), as well as sexual passion, are all associated with the image of the bull.

Camel

Camels are known as the 'ships of the desert' because of their stamina in hostile environments. They are a symbol of patience and perseverance. They are also submissive animals so the dream may indicate that you are no longer willing to 'endure' your present situation and submit to others.

Chicken/Hen

As symbols of family life, chickens are possibly a sign that the dreamer wants to be a 'mother hen'. If in the dream you are having trouble keeping the chickens together, it could indicate anxiety about your children.

Cow/Cattle

A nurturer and a mother figure, the cow represents warmth and nourishment. Dreaming of a cow may suggest that you are in need of either emotional or physical sustenance. Cattle are a sign of prosperity and plenty. In biblical terms, cattle are regarded as a symbol of success.

Goat

The goat is the symbol of perseverance. If you see one perched on a high cliff, it indicates that, with patience, you will overcome problems.

Pig

The qualities associated with pigs are usually negative—greed, selfishness and filth. However, the fattened pig may stand for a healthy bank balance or satisfied home life ('as happy as a pig in mud').

Horse

It is generally a good sign to see a horse in your dreams. It usually represents your vitality ('as strong as a horse') and independence. As the horse was traditionally a mode of transport in the past, dreams of horses also relate to travel. The colour of the horse is important to interpreting the dream. A white horse is a symbol of your spiritual awareness; a brown one highlights the practical or earthy side of your personality; and a black horse is a sign of your 'dark' nature or the uncontrollable part of yourself. Traditionally, dreaming of a black horse was a bad omen. If a woman is the dreamer and is kicked by a horse, it may reflect her relationship with a man.

Bull

Camel

Chicken/Hen

Cow/Cattle

Goat

Pig

Horse

Cross-reference

For Camel, see Desert p.95
For Horse, see Horse-shoe p.60, Riding and Saddle p.188
See also Farm/Farmyard p.182

Farm & working animals

Sheep

Sheep are known for their innocence, lack of intelligence and flock instinct. In a dream these qualities need to be explored further before you can decide whether they apply to you or a situation.

Rooster

A rooster represents both virility and self-confidence (cockiness). You may have 'something to crow about' as you tell everyone about your achievement by 'crowing' loudly. The dream may also be suggesting that you are in need of a 'wake-up call'. Take care of your health or listen to any warning that people pass on to you.

Lamb

A lamb is a symbol of innocence, dependency and the vulnerable part of ourselves. Are you easily deceived, 'like a lamb to the slaughter', or are you 'as gentle as a lamb'? Depending on the outcome of the dream it may be communicating the need to either put these traits into use or to adopt a stronger approach.

Ram

Unlike sheep, rams are a symbol of masculine power and authority. The message may be that you need to stand up to authority.

Donkey/Ass

These possess the qualities of obstinacy and humility. They can also suggest hard work and the need to be more patient in your life.

Mythical animals

Dragon

A dragon is a very ancient symbol. In the Christian West, dragons tended to symbolise evil, as in the representation of Satan as a dragon. For the Chinese, however, the dragon is a symbol of wisdom and authority. Because dragons breathe fire, they can represent heightened emotions such as anger or passion. The emotions in the dream will help explain what the personal significance is.

Sheep

Rooster

Lamb

Ram

Donkey/Ass

Dragon

Unicorn

Werewolf

Unicorn

The unicorn is an ancient symbol of purity and innocence. It suggests your desire to escape from the practical and indulge in the realm of fantasy. This isn't always realistic, of course, and you need to make sure your life is balanced to include both the innocent and the savvy aspects of yourself. Unicorns are also magical creatures, which are associated with good luck. In a dream they may suggest that you are wishing for a change of luck or some magic in your life.

Werewolf

These imaginary animals were once believed to be able to transform themselves from human to beast-like form. Dreaming of one may indicate your fears about your more primitive or 'animal' instincts getting the upper hand. On the other hand the werewolf's transformation was meant to take place on the full moon, so this dream may be referring to a monthly cycle, such as menstruation.

Cross-reference

For Sheep, see Fleece
  p.63, Wool p.425
For Mythical animals,
  see Mythical beings
  pp.308–9

Animals, general

Horn

The horns of animals such as deer are a traditional symbol of masculinity and potency. For this reason they may stand for the part of you that is most 'animal' or aggressive. Musical horns, on the other hand, suggest a summons or call of some kind—whether spiritual, or from another person.

Horseshoe

A traditional symbol of good luck, the image of the horseshoe is also strongly associated with weddings. This association may help to determine what the significance of this dream is in your life.

Ivory

In traditional gypsy lore, a dream of ivory was said to foretell prosperity and success. Today ivory is more likely to symbolise something of great value that we feel needs protection or conservation. For example, the ivory in your dream could stand for a person whom you admire for his or her beauty or pure soul. It could also represent your own internal qualities or attributes. An ivory tower continues this theme of soul searching, but is also indicative of feelings of isolation and an absence of close communication.

Web

As in spider webs, the web in your dream can suggest entrapment or getting caught in a 'sticky situation'. The complexity of a web also symbolises the complexity of your life, where everything is interrelated, and damage to a small part can ruin the whole. The expression 'a web of lies', on the other hand, suggests our potential to become trapped in the complicated deceits that we ourselves weave when we fear being honest. The larger the web, the more complex and large is the situation in your life that you need to untangle.

Cobweb

A sign that something from your past is preventing you from moving forward. You will be able to overcome it, but the process may require you to confront something that is either unpleasant or that you have tried to brush out of sight. On a positive note, the cobweb is an intricate trap effective in catching prey. Perhaps you need to try a new strategy to get what you want.

Dog lead

Dreaming of a dog on a lead or leash indicates the need to balance the animalistic nature in us with our better selves. If you are wearing the dog lead, then you may be feeling controlled and restricted emotionally and creatively.

Tail

Dreaming of a tail, either on a person, animal or yourself, implies a concern with the things that you carry with you from your past experiences. You may be at the 'tail end' of a stage in your life. Think about the general meaning a tail has for you and apply this meaning to your dream.

Tame wild animal

To dream of taming a wild animal symbolises the need for more restraint in our lives. Our animal self can get out of hand, craving excitement and recklessness. Sometimes self-discipline and self-control are better in the long run, even if they do appear to be dull and predictable. However, if a negative feeling accompanies this dream, it may mean that the dreamer needs to break loose a little.

Horn

Horseshoe

Ivory

Web

Cobweb

Dog lead

Tail

Tame wild animal

Cross-reference

For Horseshoe, see
    Wedding p.210
For Web, see Spider
    p.38
For Cobweb, see
    Spider p.38
For Dog lead, see Dog
    p.48

Animals, general

Zoo

This dream symbolises your attitudes toward the more natural or instinctive parts of your own personality. Dreaming that you are in a zoo may signal your desire to understand your natural urges or instincts as they relate to issues such as sexuality, family relationships or social interactions. This dream may also suggest the need to integrate these basic needs into your present life and activities. If you feel trapped or imprisoned in a zoo, it may be that you are not coping well with your artificial environment and need a more open and natural space for your well-being.

Pet

Dreams of adopting or looking after a pet symbolise the dreamer's desire to give and to receive love. If a pet is following you around trying to get your attention, it could be a reflection of your awareness that someone around you is vulnerable and needs care. The way you feel about the pet in your dream will reflect your attitude to this person and his or her demands. The pet could also stand for your own vulnerable aspects, in which case it suggests your need to be protected and loved.

Kennel

A kennel in a dream may suggest 'doggedness' on your part or another's. Or, it may be a sign that you feel yourself to be excluded or treated as if you were inferior. In this case the dog that has been sent off to its kennel, or is howling outside it, may be an attempt to draw attention to your unsatisfied needs.

Baby animals

These suggest a need to be nurtured. Baby animals could also represent new ideas or the immaturity of the dreamer.

Fleece

When we think of fleece, we tend to think of woolly sheep, security, comfort and warmth. These are creature comforts we crave for and hold in high regard. Are these comforts being met in your waking life? On the negative side, this dream may be a sign that you are worried that you are being 'fleeced' or cheated.

Fur

Animals have fur to protect them against the elements. If your dream has fur in it, consider what you are trying to protect yourself from. If you dream of wearing a luxurious fur coat worthy of a movie star, pay attention to the emotion in the dream. Is the fur coat a symbol of fame and stardom and is it wishful thinking on your part?

Zoo

Pet

Kennel

Baby animals

Fleece

Fur

Cross-reference

For Kennel, see Dog
    p.48
For Fleece, see Sheep
    p.58
For Fur, see Clothing
    p.166, p.364

CHAPTER THREE
The natural

The natural world encompasses a wide variety of subjects including plants and flowers and trees, as well as the weather and other natural phenoemena such as electricity, eclipses and meteor showers. Water dreams are covered in detail as they occur often and are interesting to interpret, because they nearly always reflect your emotions.

world

Plants & flowers

Garden

A garden is a symbol of the dreamer's inner self. Ideas and values are cultivated, or 'grow' and expand throughout a lifetime. It's important to note the condition of the garden. If it is a tidy garden, it indicates that you have an organised and conservative mind. An untidy or overgrown garden, on the other hand, reflects your lack of order and direction. It could be pointing to past disappointments and a fear of new setbacks. A beautiful garden is a sign of happiness and prosperity, while an overgrown one is a warning to be more focused on your goals. It may be time to 'weed out' the unpleasant aspects of your nature.

Herbs

Determining whether this dream is positive or negative depends on the kind of herb you dream about. If it is fragrant and wholesome, it is likely to signal good health and a positive mental attitude. Poisonous herbs such as rue or hemlock, however, suggest a negative influence in your life that requires an antidote.

Flowers

Flowers represent beauty and pleasure. To be given a bouquet is to feel rewarded and appreciated. It is also a token of love and tenderness, as well as having sexual significance—the genitals resembling the shape of specific flowers. In Christian symbolism, living flowers are a representation of immortality, whereas cut flowers are associated with death. Traditionally, each individual flower had a special significance in dreams. Some of these meanings are still associated with specific flowers, depending on the dreamer's cultural, spiritual and geographical background.

Plants

In general, plants are symbols of life and growth. The plants in your dream may represent emerging aspects of yourself such as talents or enthusiasm. If you dream of withered or dying plants, it suggests either a lack of emotional nourishment, low energy levels or perhaps the neglect of a relationship.

Ivy

Ivy is linked with vigorous growth and tenacity, but these positive qualities can also turn into dependency and a tendency to cling or smother. In Christian tradition, ivy is a symbol of immortality or eternal life and this religious meaning, which is most commonly associated with Christmas, may also be reflected in your dream.

Garden

Herbs

Flowers

Plants

Ivy

Thorns

Weeds

Thorns

A thorn indicates some form of physical suffering. Christ was made to wear a crown of thorns, making thorns the symbol of the Passion. If someone is 'a thorn in your side', it suggests that they are causing you some grief or discomfort. Pricking your finger on a thorny plant, such as a rosebush, means you are vulnerable and that your defences can be penetrated.

Weeds

In our dreams, as in our gardens, weeds represent the unplanned, unwelcome or obstructive elements in our lives. A dream in which you are digging up weeds suggests the desire to 'weed' out or get rid of your negative emotional baggage. A garden that is overgrown with weeds suggests that these thoughts or elements may be choking the more positive aspects of your life, to the point of hindering your growth.

Cross-reference

For Herbs, see Poison p.146
For Ivy, see Entwining p.162
For Garden, see Gardener p.293

Plants & flowers

Seed

This dream is most likely to be about potential, or how the 'seed' of an idea can grow and become a reality. At a basic level, seeds are a symbol of human reproduction, referring to the sperm and the egg. Are you hatching a project or idea?

Grass

If in your dream the grass is greener on the other side of the fence, consider how this term reflects your emotions. Do you feel that others are better off than you are? Perhaps you ought to reflect that the grass is not always greener there. Green grass is a symbol of success and growth, while dry or burned grass generally means failure and misery. Dreaming of the latter may mean that it is time to move on to greener pastures. Planting a lawn and helping it grow suggests that you will overcome financial difficulties through your own efforts and hard work.

Daisy

Dreaming of daisies signals emotional openness or simplicity. This dream can also be associated with a young or naïve person—'as fresh as a daisy'.

Nettle

When nettles appear in a dream, beware of being stung. You may feel stung by someone's remarks. It is best to avoid certain situations where you know this is likely to happen.

Cactus

To dream of a cactus suggests that the dreamer is a real survivor and will flourish despite the barren and arid circumstances in his or her life. If the cactus is in a desert, it is a sign that you or someone close to you is struggling to stay on track in an inhospitable environment. If the cactus is in a pot, it may symbolise your attempt to nourish a relationship with somebody who is prickly or defensive. How you react to this plant in your dream may tell you whether or not the relationship is worth persevering with.

Lily

Lilies are a symbol of chastity and innocence. Water lilies grow from mud, through water and then reach for the light. This makes them a symbol of our regeneration and purification.

Rose

Roses traditionally represent love and femininity.

Bluebell

These flowers suggest that arguments might be erupting in your household.

Marigolds

These are happy flowers once thought to break the power of enchantment.

Iris

Irises are an indication that good news is to come.

Myrtle

Myrtle is a flower of happiness and tranquillity.

Seed

Grass

Daisy

Nettle

Cactus

Lily

Rose

Bluebell

Marigolds

Iris

Myrtle

Cross-reference

For Cactus, see
Desert p.95
For Lily, see Pond/
Pool p.103
For Bluebell, see
Forest p.73

Plants & flowers

Buttercup

Buttercups are about taking stock of your financial affairs. They are rich, golden flowers that are often associated with childhood and plenty.

Forget-me-not

This forget-me-not is just the opposite of its name. It means that your partner cannot fulfil your emotional needs.

Mistletoe

This is a romantic plant and reminds you to be attentive to your lover.

Clover

This is a fortunate omen if it has four leaves, but if there are three it means that someone will ask you for money.

Carnation

Carnations are flowers of passion and were once traditional buttonhole flowers for men.

Daffodil

Daffodils are flowers you give someone to mend a friendship. These flowers suggest plenty, optimism and emotional well-being. Because of their associations with spring, they can also be a symbol of new beginnings or a fresh start in life.

Vine

The vine is a traditional symbol of fruitfulness and abundance. Dreaming of a vine reflects the family ties that bind you. It also points to your own growth. A clinging vine, on the other hand, is one who finds it difficult to 'let go' of things.

Chrysanthemum

White chrysanthemums are associated with loss. This could be because, in the northern hemisphere, these autumn flowers come out around All Souls' Day in November, a time when people visit their departed loved ones in cemeteries.

Peony

Peonies are about the dangers of self-restraint. Let yourself go.

Primrose

Primroses are a symbol of new friendship.

Poppy

This is the flower that symbolises memories of war; its bright red colour reminding us of the futility of bloodshed.

Lotus

Lotus flowers represent new life and immortality. The ancient Egyptians copied this flower profusely in paintings and held it in high regard for its healing properties.

Buttercup

Forget-me-not

Mistletoe

Clover

Carnation

Daffodil

Vine

Chrysanthemum

Peony

Primrose

Poppy

Lotus

Cross-reference

For Mistletoe, see Christmas tree p.77
For Vine, see Entwining p.162

71

Trees

Tree

The tree symbolises all aspects of our life. It represents our growth throughout our lives, both emotionally and physically. When we speak of roots, we refer to connections with people and the environment as well as our 'family tree'. The branches of a tree represent different sides of our personalities—the wider they are, the more gregarious and generous you will be. 'Branching out' is another term that describes growth and direction. Buds, leaves and fruits on the tree are symbols of stages of life—from bud to flower to leaf to falling leaves and bare branches. Usually, these are positive images as they give the dreamer faith in his or her future by pointing out that aspirations, hopes and achievements will come to fruition, after which a new stage will come along.

Falling leaves denote the things that we leave behind because we no longer need them. If you dream of bark, the dream may be showing you your protective attributes. However, you may need to shed these a little if you are to absorb new energy and allow people into your life. A dead tree symbolises something that was once alive but is no longer with you. This may be of an emotional, spiritual or personal nature. It could also represent a person who once featured in your life but has now moved on. A tree that is in full flower represents fertility and the feminine aspects of ourselves, which we may have been ignoring. Dreaming of a tree that is about to fall suggests that you are feeling a deep loss over something. The bigger the tree, the greater the loss you are feeling.

Cypress

These trees are traditionally associated with mourning and graveyards, particularly if you are from the northern hemisphere. Dreaming of them suggests your anxiety about a loved one.

Branch

If branches are blocking your progress in your dream, then you need to take a look at the obstacles in your waking life. Perhaps you've lost the ability 'to see the wood for the trees'. Branches that snap off in your hand suggest incompleteness, or frustration at work or in your relationships. They may suggest that you're having trouble finishing something that you've started. If the branches are swaying in the wind, get ready for change to come your way.

Forest

In fairytales, there is always a fear of the hero or heroine being lost in the forest. As a result, the image of the forest as a place of hiding, of loss and of dangerous encounters is probably imprinted on our memories from childhood. In the forest also live witches, ogres, trolls, fairies, elves and other woodland people: in other words, the positive and negative forces in our lives.

In psychological terms, a forest is a symbol of testing and of coming to terms with our own true natures. The trees may obscure our way ('can't see the wood/forest for the trees'); that is, represent narrow-mindedness or old patterns of thought. On the other hand, the trees are an intrinsic part of the nature that makes up the forest and each of us must learn how to come to terms with his or her nature. If the forest is covered in dead leaves, it may mean that a situation or a relationship has come to a final conclusion.

Tree

Cypress

Branch

Forest

Cross-reference

For Forest, see Wood p.382

Trees

Palm tree

Palm trees are associated with tropical climates, beaches and holiday resorts. This dream could be an indication of your desire to relax and take time out. But if you are trying to climb a palm tree or pick its fruit, the dream suggests that you are striving for something that may be out of reach.

Blossom

Blossom signifies new growth, change and renewal. It may suggest that you're about to embark on a new activity or phase. In general, it suggests hopefulness about the future. Things are going to get easier, or you will begin to reap the rewards for previous actions.

Chestnut

To dream of these rich, brown nuts may be a reminder to you to appreciate something valuable in your life that you have been taking for granted or that you are in danger of throwing away.

Apple tree

In biblical imagery, the apple is the tree of life. To see one in bloom or thriving is therefore a good omen. A dead apple tree is indicating troubled times ahead.

Acorn

An acorn dream is one that foretells good health, wealth and happiness. It signifies there are many pleasant things ahead and that you can expect good luck. The saying that the great oak tree grows from a small acorn is symbolic. You can expect huge growth in your personal life but patience is needed for the process to become complete. In Europe, where anything related to nature's goodwill is a favourable dream, acorns are regarded as a symbol of well-being. Planting an acorn and seeing it grow is symbolic of a wonderful life ahead.

Yew

Traditionally, these trees were planted in graveyards and were symbols of mourning, a meaning that may be reflected in your dream. The dream may express your worries about the health of someone close to you, or it may commemorate the death of a friend or family member. However, because 'yew' sounds like 'you', the presence of these trees may also be an indication that the object of concern in your dream is yourself.

Nut

If you refer to someone as a 'hard nut to crack' it usually suggests that the person has a tough exterior, but that if you do crack that shell, he or she is quite different and may hold excellent qualities. That is why it's important to find the kernel in the nut. Consider whether this image is referring to yourself or to someone else in your life that you haven't yet been able to fully understand.

Palm tree

Blossom

Chestnut

Apple tree

Acorn

Yew

Nut

Cross-reference

For Palm tree, see
    Beach p.96
For Apple tree, see
    Apples p.348
For Nut, see Fruit,
    nuts & grains
    pp.348–51

Trees

Leaf/Leaves

Leaves indicate our natural cycle: from blossoms (embryo) to green leaves (young/fertile) and finally to withered leaves (old age). Leaves can also indicate the state of your emotions. In this case, green leaves represent hope and new opportunities, while dry leaves can suggest a period of no activity, of sadness or of giving up on some aspect of your life. The dream may be suggesting to you that you should view leaves as cyclical, that the tree regenerates and a new season will change the colour and texture of the leaves. In other words, your current situation is transient and will change in time.

Olive branch

An olive branch is a traditional peace offering, the symbolism of which may be reflected in your dream. Perhaps you have decided subconsciously that it is time to resolve a conflict or extend 'an olive branch'. Similarly, the olive's status as a source of valuable oil may make it a symbol of your desire to 'pour oil on troubled waters'. Olives are also associated with a healthy lifestyle. The message within the dream depends on what olives mean to you.

Maple

The maple is the national emblem of Canada. Dreaming of a national emblem suggests the desire to get in touch with all that is good and worthwhile. Maples are also a symbol of fall (autumn) or of the change of season from warm to cool. In this respect dreaming of them may be an indication of your current emotional state.

Oak

The oak tree is associated with strength, long life and tradition. Its wood was traditionally used for building ships and houses as well as furniture. If an oak tree appears in your dream, or you dream of furniture made of oak, the dream may be telling you that some aspect of your life, such as your living situation or relationships, has strongly built foundations and is likely to endure.

Orchard

An orchard is usually a happy place in dreams, which may convey associations with childhood pleasures, fertility or plenty. Perhaps you are longing to enjoy the 'fruits of your labours'. Alternatively, this dream may be a sign of your desire to leave an urban environment and enjoy a life that is closer to the earth and to natural rhythms and pleasures. More symbolically, the fertility of the orchard may reflect a concern with your own fertility: perhaps you or someone close to you may be thinking of or about to conceive or give birth.

Christmas tree

This festive tree denotes the need to exercise special generosity or care in your dealings with significant persons in your life.

Pine cone

In gypsy lore, dreaming of a pine cone foretold good health. This was probably because the pine cone, with its many seeds, is a traditional symbol of life and abundance.

Leaf/Leaves

Olive branch

Maple

Oak

Orchard

Christmas tree

Pine cone

Cross-reference

For Orchard, see Apples p.348
For Christmas tree, see Celebrations pp.202–4

Natural phenomena

Eclipse

Dreaming of an eclipse of the sun indicates a loss of some type. It may be a loss of success or confidence in your own abilities. It may also be a loss of health due to excesses in your life. An eclipse of the moon suggests not being able to attain your goals or that someone else overshadows you. We are told to 'reach for the moon' but 'the moon' is not attainable if it is eclipsed.

Air/Sky

A dream about the open air may be interpreted in various ways, depending on the details. Clean air and blue skies is an indication that life is positive and optimistic for you. Cold air or a draught suggests that plans may not go the way you'd hoped and that emotions need to be kept in check. Beware of anyone giving you the 'cold shoulder' or an 'icy look'—all these idioms can alert you to why you're dreaming of the image. If the air is foggy or misty, trouble may be lurking and it's best to postpone any plans or changes. Stormy or cloudy air in your dream could be warning you that an illness or an unforeseen event is on the horizon.

We associate the sky with peace (heaven) and limitless expanse. We also see it as a reflection of our moods. If the sky is dark, it indicates our own anxiety, whereas if it's blue and clear, it reflects our sunny disposition. On a psychological level, the sky represents the mind and our potential ('the sky's the limit') and our tendency to dream or fantasise ('a pie in the sky'). A dream in which you are floating in the sky suggests that you are escaping into daydreaming in an attempt to avoid reality.

Comet

Traditionally regarded as a sign of approaching disaster, a comet in your dream is more likely to signal the need for an important change to take place in your life.

Eclipse

Air/Sky

Comet

Earthquake

Draught

Echo

Earthquake

Just as the earth is firm and solid, an earthquake is a total disruption of this. You may be experiencing an upheaval in your life—as a result of which your emotions and sense of security are no longer stable. This may also be a positive dream; an eruption of emotion or feelings can indicate a major change occurring in your life, such as an important transition from which you can grow.

Draught

Being aware of a draught in your dream suggests your uneasiness or feelings of discomfort and/or insecurity. It is generally a sign that you feel unprotected in a relationship or work situation.

Echo

Dreaming of an echo could be a message that you have to keep repeating yourself before someone takes you seriously. Perhaps you are lacking in confidence and need to convince yourself and others of your talents.

Cross-reference

For Air/Sky, see Clouds p.92
For Earthquake, see Disaster p.200
For Eclipse, see Sun p.85

Natural phenomena

Ice/Icebergs

Dreams involving water often relate to our emotions, so dreaming of ice is likely to suggest a hardening of your feelings about somebody. If ice is a sign of emotional coolness, or even a loss of libido, a dream of thawing ice symbolises the thawing of a hostile relationship or the end of a period in which you have been forced to keep your feelings 'on ice'. If you are skating on thin ice, the dream suggests your sense of insecurity at home or at work. Icebergs symbolise a distant emotional threat.

Icicles

Icicles can be a symbol either of male impotence, or the inability on the part of a man to make emotional connections. If the icicles are melting, the dream suggests that this coldness may also be about to disappear.

Electricity

Electricity is a powerful force that can energise, produce light and even cause death. It is also instant and quick. Consider the idiom 'blowing a fuse'. Are you burning up with anger? Perhaps you have been called a 'live wire' if you have excessive energy. Generally an electric shock or electrocution may suggest that you are in for a surprise: a big shock, or a wake-up call about something. It may be a good idea to protect yourself from injury and become more aware of what is around you. A switch could indicate your need for control.

Gas

Gas is a natural resource that provides us with energy. However, if it is misused it can cause injury and death. Dreaming of wearing a gas mask could indicate that you are prepared for possible dangers ahead of you. A gas leak represents a fault that, if not repaired, will be dangerous. This may have something to do with your relationships. If you are unable to light a gas appliance, it suggests that there is energy lacking in some area of your life. You should also consider taking this dream literally, as your subconscious can sometimes take note of things that your conscious mind overlooks. Have your appliances and connections checked. Other idioms to note are 'full of gas' (empty words) and 'step on the gas' (accelerate).

Fire

Fire is associated with life and passion and is one of the four elements of the twelve horoscope signs (air, water and earth being the other three). Fire is a good friend when it warms us, but if we get too close we get burnt. It's a symbol of regeneration, so dreaming of fire may indicate that you are entering a period of renewal and painful reflection. More negatively, fire can suggest anger, resentment and destruction. 'Burning with desire' and other such idioms refer to the effect of fire on our desires and sexuality. The dream may suggest that you need more vitality and passion in your life.

To dream of being burnt alive may express frustration at not being able to handle a new stage in life or new circumstances ('too hot to handle'). 'Baptism by fire' means coming to a new awareness of ourselves. If you dream of fighting a fire, you may want to cool or put out fiery passions. A fireplace symbolises contentment in the home but any fire that is out of control indicates extreme, uncontrollable passions that are potentially destructive and overwhelming. Seeing a fire engine or being a fireman in your dream is a sign that you are in control of some explosive emotions.

Lava

Lava represents a situation in which deep-seated emotions erupt and come to the surface. This dream suggests that the dreamer has been covering up emotions for too long, with the result that an 'eruption' is likely. Lava can also be a symbol of sexuality or may indicate a medical illness such as high fever.

Smoke

If you agree that where there's smoke there's fire, this dream is a warning of danger ahead. Smoke is also a camouflage (smoke screen). Is there a situation in your life that is not as clear as it should be? If you dream that you are smoking, it indicates that you are feeling anxious.

Ice/Icebergs

Electricity

Gas

Icicles

Fire

Lava

Smoke

Cross-reference

For Ice/Icebergs, see
  Snow p.91, Igloo
  p.318
For Lava, see Volcano
  p.97

Natural phenomena

Quicksand

Sinking in quicksand is a typical anxiety dream. The terror we feel when the ground beneath our feet no longer supports us but instead sucks us into its depths, symbolises our fear that the foundations of our life may be similarly overturned, with threatening or painful results. The quicksand may also represent your own self-doubts. Can you remain firm or grounded in the face of your insecurities? If, on the other hand, you feel no fear during this dream, it may be telling you that you have come to terms with your insecurity, and that you can accept the need for change.

Dust

To dream that something is covered in dust suggests that you have been neglectful in your social or emotional life. The dream may be warning you that it's time to make some changes, or to get out more and shake the dust out of your life.

Rainbow

A rainbow is a sign of good things to come—usually a change that you've been hoping for. The dream is also reminding you of the beauty and value of life, despite the difficulties and conflicts.

Evaporation

Water transforms in its evaporative state and, just like water, we may transform ourselves or change state but remain basically the same. Investigate what it is about yourself or some situation that you wish would evaporate or go away, and deal with it. Evaporation can also mean a transformation in your ideas or emotions usually to a higher state. Evaporation is part of the water cycle and thus represents the cycle of life.

Mud

The mud we see in a dream denotes emotions that cause us to feel 'bogged down'. When something is 'muddy' it means that it is not clear, so this dream is a warning not to go ahead with any plans until the muddiness turns clear. If you are sinking in mud, it means that you are feeling helpless. Dreaming of mud and feeling repulsed by it, represents your feelings—do you feel guilty about some issue? Are you mud slinging or is your name mud?

Quicksand

Dust

Rainbow

Evaporation

Mud

Sand

Sand dunes

Sand

Sand is shifting and therefore unstable. Dreaming of sand in this context tends to refer to a lack of security ('a house built on sand'). Are your emotional or financial foundations unstable and liable to shift? Sand in an hourglass represents the passage of time, an image that may be highlighting your need to be more actively involved in shaping your life. Don't 'bury your head in the sand'. Try and live your life more fully while you can.

Sand dunes

Sand dunes represent your longing for protection and shelter from the elements. Try to work out what you need protection from and how you can feel secure.

Cross-reference

For Sand, see Desert p.95
For Sand dunes, see Beach p.96

Space & the planets

The Earth

Earth is usually a symbol of nurturing (Mother Earth) and of the feminine. It reminds us of our 'roots': our family and our social background. The ground, like the earth, supports us (terra firma), and holds all our experiences. If you dream of being buried underneath the earth, your unconscious needs, habits or drives are no longer sustaining you and it's time for a change of attitude or more flexibility.

Moon

The moon has symbolised the feminine since early times. Traditionally, it represents the unconscious or mysterious sides of ourselves, and has also long been associated with love and romance. That is why so many romantic novels and movies have a moonlit setting (slightly obscure, unlike the glare of the sun, with an air of unreality cast by the shadows of the surroundings). To 'reach for the moon' is to be unable to attain your desires while being 'over the moon' is to be emotionally ecstatic. The moon can also represent intuition, particularly in relation to unforeseen doom and gloom. It often indicates that you are concentrating too much on the uncertainty of situations, particularly the emotional aspects.

Stars

We associate the stars with ambition ('starry-eyed') and destiny ('it's written in the stars'). To 'look up at the stars' is to indulge in wishful thinking. It is no wonder therefore that movie idols and celebrities are referred to as 'stars'. They are so far removed from reality that they appear to be out of our reach. This dream encourages you to focus on what you are wishing for. Your aspirations may not simply be wishful thinking, but a wish that can come true. Such a dream may indicate that you are not aiming high enough in real life. Why aim for the moon when you can have the stars? If your goals and ambitions are realistic perhaps you should aim a little higher.

Sun

Traditionally, to dream of the sun was associated with achieving success. Today we tend to interpret the sun as representing our intellect and awareness of what is going on around us. It is also an image of vitality, warmth and creative energy. Being in the sunlight arouses feelings of well-being and relaxation.

Meteor

If you witness a meteor landing on earth in your dream, you may be expecting some sort of clash with someone from outside your comfort zone. This could be because you have an obstinate view of a situation and you are aware that your ideas will not change, despite the opposing force you will face as a consequence.

The Earth

Moon

Stars

Sun

Meteor

Cross-reference

For Moon, see Night
     p.441
For Stars, see Night
     p.441
For Sun, see Sunrise/
     Dawn and Sunset
     pp.440–1

Minerals, gems & stones

Quartz

Dreaming of quartz suggests that a new idea or project may be about to 'crystallise' in your life. More generally, the crystalline structure of quartz may suggest a desire to see through a difficult matter, or to achieve some form of clarity on a matter. The association of quartz with crystals may also indicate that the dream relates to healing.

Rock

The rock evokes many images. It conjures up the qualities of strength and reliability (solid as a rock). Are we looking for a more solid foundation in our lives? The dream may be highlighting a need to see the rock within yourself and all the qualities it embodies such as rigidity and coldness, as well as dependability. Are you somebody's 'rock'? Perhaps you need a break from this role.

Diamonds

Diamonds are associated with permanence, hardness, clarity and great value. In a dream they may symbolise a long-term relationship or marriage or, if you are single, some other precious or enduring aspect of your life. If you lose diamonds in a dream, it is a warning that you need to take better care of your relationships or possessions.

Crystal

Crystal in a dream signifies purity or something of great value. It may also signal a desire to protect something fragile from clumsiness or destruction—whether it's your own clumsiness, or that of those around you. Crystals are also credited with balancing and healing powers, so a dream in which crystals appear may provide a clue to something that is missing from your emotional or physical health.

Snow

Being 'snowed under' means that you are overwhelmed by your present circumstances. Emotionally, snow indicates coldness and in this context the dream may be pointing out the need for you to thaw a little. Snow is also associated with purity, beauty and a soft texture, while its presence can give a new perspective to something ordinary. Take note of the other symbols in this dream when seeking its significance. Sometimes snow can be linked with romance, so it is important to find the right meaning.

Storm

Storms represent outbursts of emotion, particularly anger. When someone is in a 'stormy relationship' it means that his or her relationship is filled with negative emotional energies. Violent storms suggest violent passions, while the way in which we 'weather the storm' reflects our ability to cope with life's hardships. Storms also clear the air and can give the dreamer a feeling of release after the storm (or argument) has cleared. Generally, a storm is symbolic of any type of conflict, whether it takes place on a personal or emotional level, or in the public arena. The conflict will usually cause emotional stress but once it is released the dreamer will feel calmer as a result.

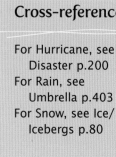

Weather

Gale

Thunder

Hurricane

Rain

Hail

Snow

Storm

Cross-reference

For Hurricane, see
    Disaster p.200
For Rain, see
    Umbrella p.403
For Snow, see Ice/
    Icebergs p.80

Weather

Tornado/Cyclone

To dream of being caught in a tornado indicates that you are struggling against an emotional issue you feel helpless to solve. Just like a tornado, the issue has swept you up and flung you where you don't want to be. This dream can also mean that communications with others in waking life have become unproductive and that the dreamer, instead of really resolving issues, is simply going around in circles.

Wind

Wind is related to breath, the vital force that sustains us. It is also associated with turbulent weather conditions, and in this respect may suggest that you are going through 'stormy' emotional times. The phrase 'long-winded' is used to describe people who talk too much and in this context the dream may express your impatience with someone who seems to be all talk and no action. The wind often changes direction, and therefore it may be symbolic of the dreamer's feelings of restlessness or need for change.

Fog

When we speak of being 'in a fog', the saying indicates that we are confused and unable to see the real issues that are affecting us. If you dream of walking in a fog, it is best not to take action at this time, but to wait until you are feeling more confident. At times your ideas can be clouded by others' judgement. Wait until the feeling of 'not having the foggiest idea' has lifted before making a decision on any issue.

Frost

'Icy frost' and 'frozen in time' are phrases that suggest a lack of movement and life. Are you unable to move forward? Are your feelings frozen? Is there a decision that you need to make but are unable to do so? This dream may also be indicative of how you are treating others in waking life—in other words it could be time to 'defrost' and show some warmth.

Clouds

To see clouds in a dream is a sign that you are not paying enough attention to practical details, that is, you 'have your head in the clouds'. The expression 'to cast a cloud over' is to be sad about something, whereas 'to hang over someone like a cloud' is the same as a menacing presence. Dark clouds usually indicate tough times ahead, but if your 'cloud has a silver lining' things will work out for the best.

Drought

To dream of drought signals your fear of emotional or financial loss. However, this dream also suggests that the problem is temporary, and that if you can weather the situation, then better times will lie ahead.

Thaw

To dream of a thaw is to be aware that our feelings and responses to a situation or person have changed. When our emotions thaw we become warmer and more loving. This dream indicates a desire to 'thaw' some emotional coldness that has been with us for a while. If you have this dream you should work out what it is that you want to 'melt away'. You may also need to consider whether there is someone you wish to forgive.

Lightning

Seeing lightning in your dream denotes unexpected changes, which come about suddenly (in a flash). It is also a destructive force that represents the knocking down of your comfort zone and the need to rebuild a new lifestyle. The enormous electrical charge released by lightning can lead to your discharging the old outmoded ideas and values in your life to make room for new ones. If you dream of being struck by lightning it is a sign that life changes are occurring at lightning speed in your life. If you dream of a tree being hit by lightning, it represents an ending, or a death of some issue that has been holding you for a long time.

Tornado/Cyclone

Wind

Fog

Frost

Clouds

Drought

Thaw

Lightning

Cross-reference

For Tornado, see
   Storm p.91
For Frost, see Ice/
   Icebergs p.80
For Clouds, see Sky
   p.78

Landscape

Cliff/Chasm

If you are walking on the edge of a cliff in your dream, it is a sign that you are engaged in a risky situation that demands all your attention and care. If you jump off the edge of a cliff, note whether you land softly or wake up instead. You may be taking a leap of faith or attempting to get away from your responsibilities.

Hills

Hills nearly always symbolise 'hills to climb'. Climbing a hill suggests our desire to surmount difficulties, or to gain a clear perspective on our situation. Being on the top of a hill looking down signals our achievement of a spiritual insight or awareness.

Not being able to reach the top of the hill, on the other hand, suggests the sense that some hard slog still lies ahead of us. Going downhill can either be a symbol of relief, or a sign that circumstances are preventing us from achieving our goals.

Countryside

Beautiful countryside in a dream is a symbol of happiness and emotional security. If you are in the middle of this beautiful landscape it indicates that you are close to achieving your goals. If you are viewing it from somewhere more distant, like a rocky cliff, the dream may be suggesting that you are currently involved in difficulties, but that there is a chance of happiness ahead.

Island

Islands are symbols of both escape and isolation. They can also represent the self in its most solitary or independent state. For this reason, to interpret the meaning of this dream you need to decide whether your dream island symbolises freedom and self-expansion, or rejection and low self-esteem. For example, if you dream of being cast up on a desert island, the dream is probably representing your fears of loneliness. If you feel relaxed and fulfilled on your dream island, or it resembles a paradise, the dream is highlighting your wish to escape from a crowded schedule and spend more time by yourself.

Desert

Generally, the desert is a symbol of barrenness or some kind of emotional or material lack. More positively, the desert can also represent a space in which material things and distractions are removed so that a person can focus on achieving spiritual insight.

Hedges

A green and flourishing hedge suggests contentment, prosperity and protection, while a hedge full of thorns can symbolise the obstacles that lie between you and your goal. If you get lost or scratched while trying to get through a hedge, it is a sign of frustration in your work or emotional life.

Park

A dream that suggests your desire to escape some confining situation, to explore the wide open spaces or to enjoy more play in your life.

Cliff/Chasm

Hills

Countryside

Island

Desert

Hedges

Park

Cross-reference

For Cliff/Chasm, see Typical dreams pp.22–5

Landscape

Beach

If you dream that you are on a beach, the chances are that you are overdue for a holiday and need to get away from it all. Dreaming of being on a beach can also signal that romance is headed your way. But if the beach is empty or threatening, then it can be a sign that you may feel rejected or lonely and want people to pay you the attention you deserve.

Marsh/Swamp

To dream of marshy or swampy ground signals that there is something that is making you feel bogged down or held. Losing ground, being stuck and lack of control are all issues that relate to difficulty in our emotional lives. If you want to move forward but can't, it could be that you are ready to move on to a new emotional level but that you either don't have the emotional support you need or lack self-confidence to do so. If this is a recurring dream, focus on the ways you can solve this issue in your life.

Mountain

To dream of a mountain represents the obstacles in your path that you need to overcome and any larger-than-life hazards that may be ahead. To reach the summit is to achieve your goals, but how you go about doing this will be different for everyone. Being afraid of being at the top of the mountain indicates your fear of success or that you fear failure, as you stand alone above the rest. Work through this symbol, taking into account all other aspects of the dream and discover what the dream is asking you to overcome and how to do it.

Jungle

The jungle is a primitive symbol of danger and the struggle to overcome obstacles. More specifically, it may suggest 'entanglements', whether in your romantic, family or professional life. If things are a little wild and unpredictable in your life, proceed with caution.

Valley

A dream in which a lush green valley surrounds us represents the nurturing and protective parts of our personalities. If you are safe yet lost in the valley, it may mean that changes around you are occurring that will take you to a more peaceful emotional state. A valley which is barren or marshy points to the parts of your life that need a feminine touch if they are to be brought back to life and made sustainable. In the Bible the valley of darkness is a symbol of death and the valley of tears represents grief about death. You may want to delve deeper into the meaning that holds the most significance for you.

Volcano

A volcanic eruption in a dream tells us that we have lost control of our emotions or a particular situation in our life. This violent release can be a healing experience for the dreamer after the build-up that comes from keeping feelings of hurt or anger inside. The lava flow and the damage it causes are a result of this emotional build-up. The more lava there is in your dream, the deeper the feelings that have 'erupted'. If, however, the lava has cooled off, so too have your anger and passion.

Beach

Marsh/Swamp

Mountain

Jungle

Valley

Volcano

Cross-reference

For Marsh/Swamp, see Quagmire p.206

Water

Water

In general, water, which is capable of flowing in many directions and taking many forms, symbolises our emotional lives and energies. The meaning of a dream containing water is likely to depend on the form that water takes. For example, deep water tends to suggest either danger (the risk of 'drowning' in our emotions) or a desire to explore the 'depths' of some feeling or emotional situation, while a dream of entering water may symbolise the beginning of a new relationship or life situation. Flowing water tends to suggest change and movement in our emotional lives, while calm or stagnant water can imply that we have become 'bogged down'.

Steam

Getting steamed up refers to extreme emotions that are held under pressure. What is making you feel this way and can you see a way to solve this problem? On the positive side, steam is also associated with steam rooms, spas and saunas. In this context the dream may be suggesting that you need to relax.

Puddles

Puddles can symbolise the obstacles that force us to take more roundabout routes towards our goals. Their watery content suggests that these issues are of an emotional nature, and our desire to avoid them can also suggest that we are afraid of involvement. If you are afraid of getting your feet wet, you may be forcing yourself to take a detour so that you won't have to directly face up to or 'wade' into a troubling problem or situation. The muddier the puddle in your dream, the more confused you feel about a certain issue in your waking life.

Whirlpool

A dream that indicates danger and confusion. If you see a whirlpool in your dream it may be prompting you to think about a situation in which you risk being dragged down or held under. The dreamer might feel that he or she is in a downhill spiral in waking life. There is a definite need for the dreamer to empower himself or herself.

Deluge

Because water is associated with our emotions, dreaming of a deluge or flood suggests that you fear being 'flooded' by powerful feelings. If you survive the deluge, however, this dream is a positive sign of your ability to cope with heightened levels of emotion.

Tap

Dreaming of a tap has connotations of turning our emotions on and off. How we do this usually depends on whether our needs are being met. An inability to turn off a tap indicates that we lack control over the things we take for granted as belonging to us. 'Tapping into' something suggests that you are gaining a new understanding, while tapping on a door means that you need to pay attention to some aspect of your life.

Tide

The tide in our dreams stands for our need to embrace the 'ebb and flow' of life. In other words the dreamer has to let go of things that cannot be controlled. If you're a control freak, the dream is telling you 'go with the flow'.

Water

Steam

Puddles

Whirlpool

Deluge

Tap

Tide

Cross-reference

For Tide, see Ocean p.102, Water pp.98–103
For Deluge, see Flood p.101

Water

Water tank

A water tank in a dream is a symbol of the dreamer's desire to get in touch with his or her emotional self. If the tank is full it indicates good times ahead. If on the other hand it is empty or leaking, you can expect to experience loss or to need help from outside sources.

Wading

We usually wade in water—a symbol of the emotions. But wading, like baptism, also suggests the desire for cleansing or symbolic rebirth in a purified state. Wading through water often suggests that the dreamer, though in touch with his or her emotions, is not really coming to grips with them.

Wading in muddy water is a result of not facing up to emotional issues. To interpret this dream you should pay attention to whether the water in your dream is clear or muddy, and take note of whether you are going with the flow or at risk of getting 'bogged down'.

Well

A well is a deep space, traditionally a source of water, so the well in your

dream may represent your own inner 'depths' of emotion and personality. This dream may signal your desire to access knowledge located in those depths. However, the double meaning of 'well' can also give this dream a meaning that is to do with health or healing. If the well in your dream is a wishing well, it may be a sign that you have been indulging in 'wishful thinking'.

Dam

Dreaming of a dam is a sign of your tendency to repress or 'dam' your emotions or your energy. If you are building a dam in your dream, it suggests that you have been erecting defences around your feelings. If the dam is in danger of bursting, take heed: it is probably a warning that you may not be able to hold these emotions back much longer.

Fountain

Dreaming of a flowing fountain is a sign of life, health and our ability to express our emotions fluently. Alternatively, a dried up or clogged fountain indicates problems in our emotional lives and the need to release negative or unproductive feelings.

Flood

Like fire, flood is an uncontrollable force of nature that can be frightening and overwhelming. Feeling inundated brings about anxiety and an inability to cope and sometimes this can suggest depression for the dreamer. We talk about a 'flood of tears' or a 'flood of memories', both of which indicate a release of bottled-up feelings as well as relief.

River

The river in our dreams represents the emotions that flow through us. We can 'go with the flow' of the river, which means that we are at ease with ourselves and confident about where life is taking us, or we can 'drown' in it—that is, drown in despair and a sense of being overwhelmed. Think about whether you are just floating along in your life journey, being tossed about or are taking control.

Water tank

Wading

Well

Dam

Fountain

Flood

River

Cross-reference

For Flood, see
    Deluge p.99
For River, see
    Water pp.98–103

Water

Lagoon/Lake

Dreaming of a lake or lagoon is the dreamer's connection to the unconscious. It represents the inner world of an individual's fantasies, emotions and feelings—usually not known or revealed to others. If you dream of looking into a lagoon, it may be that you are looking into yourself. Clear water indicates self-confidence and optimism while murky water indicates that you may be experiencing depression or a state of uncertainty.

Afloat

If you are floating on calm and clear water and are very relaxed, it indicates trouble-free times ahead. If the water is rough, on the other hand, be ready for a bumpy ride to wherever you are heading in your waking life. It may also mean that you cannot simply 'float' in life, particularly when it comes to emotional issues, and must make some responsible and concrete decisions. A dreamer feeling afraid of being afloat can suggest feeling cut off and isolated from part of him or herself or from others.

Ocean

The ocean is a traditional symbol of both life and the emotions. Watching or swimming in a stormy sea can denote an awareness of the powerful forces of spirituality or emotion within you. If the sea is calm and tranquil, it suggests that you have come to terms with an issue or feeling, and can expect easier times ahead. If you are underwater in your dream, it may be a sign of your desire to delve deeply into your emotions on a particular subject.

Immersion

Like most dreams involving water, dreaming of immersion has significance in terms of our emotional lives. This dream may suggest that you feel as if you are 'drowning' in your emotions, to the extent of finding it hard to breathe.

It also indicates that the dreamer is out of their depth emotionally in real life. Take note of this dream, as it may be a subconscious message to find a comfortable level of emotional expression.

Oasis

An oasis stands for any place of comfort and refreshment in a world that can sometimes feel desert-like. Dreaming of such a place suggests your desire to take time out, to be invigorated and nourished, and to stop struggling with your difficulties. You may long for your problems to disappear, or turn into a distant 'mirage' on the horizon. If, on the other hand, you dream that you are trying to reach an oasis but can't find it, it is likely that you are having trouble imagining an end to your current labours.

Pond/Pool

Ponds tend to symbolise our own need to reflect on or consider our emotional life in a state of tranquillity or calm. However, if the pond is stagnant or filled with weeds, our own emotional lives may also have become bogged down in some way. If this is the case, we need to introduce some new element into our lives or find a new emotional outlet that will allow things to flow more freely again.

Leak

A leak represents waste and loss. Consider whether you are wasting your energy in some way or being careless or reckless. If something 'leaks out' it means that it is revealed without authorisation. Be aware of your responsibilities and take action only when it's necessary. A leak could also be telling you that you are feeling 'drained'. Take care of your health.

Lagoon/Lake

Afloat

Ocean

Immersion

Oasis

Pond/Pool

Leak

Cross-reference

For Lagoon/Lake, see Water pp.98–103
For Afloat, see Floating p.256, Water pp.98–103
For Ocean, see Water pp.98–103

CHAPTER FOUR

The body &

In this chapter a wide variety of fascinating dreams about the body is explored. Interpretations of dreams about specific body parts and internal organs, or illnesses and medical procedures, as well as dreams about looking after the body and feeling good are included. Some of these dreams can reflect real illness or discomfort felt in waking hours; in other cases they represent emotional anxieties and desires. Some can even be prophetic. Most, however, act as important indicators of our physical or emotional well-being.

health

The body

Body

The human body is made up of many different parts, and one or more of these may figure strongly in a dream. If a particular aspect of your or another's body features strongly in a dream, the following interpretations will help you make sense of the message the dream is sending you.

Ankles

The ankle is both a support or foundation for the body, and a possible source of weakness. If you dream of ankles, chances are that these associations will be present in the dream. For example, if the dream is anxious, it could be signalling that the foundations of a certain matter aren't sufficiently strongly laid. But if you feel strong and happy in the dream, it is more likely to be a positive message about your strength and confidence.

Feet

We're familiar with the term 'getting cold feet', meaning that we are afraid of the action we are about to take. Reluctance to go through with something in a dream could relate to an issue in your life. Feet are also about movement—both negative and positive. 'Putting your foot in it' signifies that you have spoken out of turn whereas 'putting your best foot forward' is good advice on how to conduct yourself. Having 'itchy feet' indicates restlessness while 'getting back on' your feet signals victory over difficult times. The interpretation of this dream depends on what action takes place and what emotions are experienced by the dreamer. Feet are also the simplest form of transport and can suggest that the dreamer is, or will soon be, travelling over new ground. The feelings that are associated with the dream will indicate whether or not this is a wise decision.

Bones

To see bones in a dream is a sign that you haven't gone deep enough towards the heart of a matter.

Buttocks

Usually a sensuous dream; they can be a sign either of erotic satisfaction, or financial prosperity. Buttocks are also associated with redecorating, especially furnishings.

Arms

To dream of arms suggests an emphasis on striving if the context is business or adventure, and nurturing, if the context is romance or family life. If you dream that your arm is cut off, it suggests that you are anxious about losing someone close to you. A broken arm signals a fear of difficulties ahead.

Back

Back problems are a common injury, so a dream about a bad back could simply be warning you about your health. But if your dream is of people turning their backs on you, it is a sign that you fear the jealousy or disapproval of those around you. In general, the backbone is seen as symbolising strength of character and firmness.

Hands

Hands are associated with our creative powers and general ability to make things happen. Hands that are gesturing or using sign language indicate frustrated communication.

Fingers

A finger usually occurs in dreams as a symbol of our fear of losing something.

Cross-reference

For Bones, see X-rays p.129, Skeleton p.108

107

The body

Knees

Traditionally, gypsies interpreted dreams of falling on your knees as a sign of the dreamer's need for help.

Wrists

Like the ankle the wrist is both strong and delicate. It indicates a need for balance or coordination of opposites. It is also a symbol of connection or joining.

Skeleton

The idea of a skeleton occurs in many idioms. Thus, this dream may indicate the 'bare bones' of an idea or project. A 'skeleton in the closet', on the other hand, represents something about ourselves that we wish to hide—perhaps a secret of some sort. The skeleton also provides us with an image of death. Is there a part of you that has been worn away? Perhaps you've 'killed' off feelings or aspirations that were once your driving force?

Blood

Because blood is a precious life substance, it is sometimes taken as a symbol of the life force itself. If in a dream you are losing blood, it may suggest that you fear weakness or being disempowered. Because of its bright red colour it is also associated with passionate feelings, such as love or anger towards another. Dreaming of blood may also indicate that you feel called upon to make a sacrifice.

Navel

Our umbilical cord is a connection to the womb. As a result, dreaming of a navel suggests either our dependency on our mother, or the way we connect to the outside world. The dream may be indicating that we need to be more independent and not rely on things or others around us to get us through life.

Neck

The neck is the connection between the body and the head. Dreaming of it could indicate that you are facing a struggle between the two. The neck is also associated with risk—as in the expressions 'break one's neck', 'risk one's neck'. The neck is also associated with gracefulness or elegance, which may be traits the dreamer desires. Alternatively, someone close to the dreamer may be acting like 'a pain in the neck'.

Breasts

Because female breasts have both erotic and nurturing associations, they tend to symbolise contentment, plenty and gratification. They could also be drawing attention to the dreamer's relationship with his or her mother, or with the person from whom he or she expects nourishment and understanding. If a woman dreams that her breasts can be seen through her clothes, it may signal her sense that she is admired by someone.

Fat

Symbolically, dreaming of a fat person or animal suggests prosperity. We speak of a 'fat wallet', 'living off the fat of the land', 'jolly fat man' and other such idioms which associate fat with ideas of good health and prosperity. This dream depends on how we think of our bodies in real life. If we see ourselves getting fat and are uncomfortable about this state, the dream may be communicating our sense of inadequacy. Many people hide behind their weight when covering up insecurities and fear. Alternatively, this dream may be a warning that the dreamer is overindulging—not necessarily in food. If there is excess in your life the message here is of the need for balance.

Legs

Legs represent our support and 'drive'—that is, what motivates us. Legs carry us forward and support our whole movement. If you are dreaming that your legs are weak or paralysed, consider whether you have lost your confidence in some aspect of your life, or whether your motivation is not as strong as you wish it to be.

Change of body size

To dream that your body shape and size changes radically tends to indicate your difficulty in accepting a major change in your circumstances or personality.

Knees

Skeleton

Wrists

Blood

Navel

Neck

Breasts

Fat

Legs

Change of body size

Cross-reference

For Blood, see Haemorrhage p.122, Menstruation p.118
For Skeleton, see X-rays p.129, Bones p.106

Life cycles

Egg

Generally, dreaming of eggs is regarded as a good omen among people of all cultures. An egg is a symbol of potential of the individual that is yet to be realised. If you dream of eggs in a nest, money and financial security is on its way (a nest egg). If the eggs are cracked or damaged then expect some kind of disappointment or loss.

Embryo

An embryo is the beginning of creation and as such it's very vulnerable. To dream of an embryo may suggest that your vulnerability is being exposed. It may be a new project, new beginnings of a relationship, a move or a job—whatever it may be, it needs nurturing and care so that it can develop to the next stage.

Pregnancy

A dream in which you are pregnant can reflect either your desire for a child or your fear of falling pregnant. If you are actually expecting a child at the time of having the dream, it is probably the way your subconscious expresses and relieves the feelings of anxiety that are often associated with birth and looking after a baby. More symbolically, a dream of pregnancy may symbolise any new project or area of your life that is opening to change or growth. For example, it may suggest that you are about to give birth to a creative project or idea.

Birth

Giving birth in a dream is generally a positive image, suggesting new beginnings or the start of a project, in which you feel 'reborn'. If the birth is very difficult, it may reflect your fear of difficulties to be overcome.

Mourning

The process of mourning after a loss or an ending of an important facet of your life is one that is not easily practised in waking life. We put on a brave face and try to keep busy, however sad we feel inside. Mourning in your dreams, therefore, is a sign of your subconscious releasing the grief and of keeping the body healthy at the same time so that emotions aren't bottled up. Through dreams we can privately mourn and find ways to begin anew.

Age

To worry about your own age could mean that you are burdened and feeling older than you actually are. It is wise to consider seeking medical help or using relaxation methods to give you an energy boost and prevent you from getting ill. Seeing old people in your dreams suggests wisdom and it's a good sign. It may mean that you have achieved some sort of enlightenment or that through hard work you will achieve your goal.

Death

This dream is less likely to be about an actual death than a symbolic representation of loss, change, or transition. Often it is a positive dream, signalling that some form of burden or anxiety is about to be lifted from you, enabling you to move forward in your life. In this sense, death is actually a dream of new birth, that is, releasing the old and embracing the new. Dreams of death often accompany or forecast important life transitions, and signal the dreamer's consciousness of his or her need to take on a different role or a new challenge.

Egg

Embryo

Pregnancy

Birth

Mourning

Age

Death

Cross-reference

For Pregnancy, see
   Baby p.295
For Birth, see Baby
   p.295
For Age, see The
   elderly p.280
See also Death
   pp.208–9

Face & head

Head

The head usually symbolises the whole person, including personality, hopes and fears. A disembodied head signifies imbalance in your life.

Mouth

This part of the body symbolises our most basic needs, and tells us whether or not they are being fulfilled.

Face

Your own face seen in a mirror provides a clue to your current state of mind. If it's happy and smiling, things may be better than you think. If mournful or worried, it is a sign that you need to explore an issue that is giving you problems.

Eyes

As organs of vision, our eyes symbolise our qualities of perception and intuition. To dream of being blind suggests a disorder in these faculties, while dreaming of the eyes of another signals a fear of being observed or 'found out'.

Nose

The nose is associated with breath, and therefore with the dreamer's soul or essential qualities. To dream of a blocked nose can be an indication of spiritual or emotional problems. If your nose is a source of embarrassment, the dream implies your self-consciousness about a current aspect of your personality or your situation.

Lips

Lips are a sensual part of our bodies and are used to express love by kissing. Dreaming of lips may be an indication that you wish for this experience or may need more intimacy in your life. 'Giving lip' and 'lip service' on the other hand, suggest backchatting and insincerity. When someone's 'lips are sealed', it means that they will not divulge a secret. Take note of all the surrounding symbolism to make a more accurate interpretation.

Wrinkles

A dream in which you are conscious of wrinkles reflects your anxieties about age and the passage of time. However, the wrinkles in your dream can also signal the wisdom that comes with age and experience. If you see your face with premature wrinkles it may suggest that you are overburdened and feeling 'old'. In this case, take some time off to relax.

Teeth

Dreaming of teeth is a very common dream. Teeth represent our 'bite' or our aggressive nature. When we can't get our teeth into something, it suggests that we have little control. If you dream of losing your teeth, it has to do with 'loss' in general such as loss of youth and all things associated with our anxiety of getting older. A rotten tooth is a symbol of our painful feelings that keep 'aching' until we find relief. Could it be that your relationship or bond with someone is hurting? Perhaps you've said hurtful words that you now regret? Bleeding gums indicate a loss of blood (loss of life force) through lack of support from those around you. False teeth clearly indicate a fear of losing one's sense of true self; that is, of honesty and integrity. Look at all the images in the dream, such as grinding teeth or teething troubles, to determine the correct meaning.

Hair

Hair is a symbol of virility and also of our attractiveness to others. Dreaming of losing your hair symbolises anxiety about these matters. If you dream of long, luxuriant hair, it could be a sign of sexual fulfilment or the start of a new affair. If you're trying to untangle your hair, it is a sign of your need to pay attention to a 'knotty' problem or difficulty in your waking life.

Skull

Dreaming of a skull was once interpreted as a sign of the need for repentance. It was also the Christian symbol of life after death. If you dream of speaking with a skull, you may need to contact people you haven't seen for a while. If a skull is talking to you, it may be the part of yourself that you have 'killed off' or ignored and that is now showing up again.

Head

Face

Eyes

Mouth

Nose

Lips

Wrinkles

Teeth

Hair

Skull

Cross-reference

For Teeth, see Dentist
    p.286
For Hair, see
    Hairdresser p.286
For Wrinkles, see The
    elderly p.280

Body organs

Genitals

Traditionally associated with reproduction, genitals represent the sexual identity of the dreamer. It is not uncommon to dream of having genitals of the opposite gender. It usually refers to the feminine or masculine side of ourselves that we wish to connect with. If you dream that you are mutilated or injured in the genital area, consider what it is that is hurting your sense of sexual identity. It may have to do with past sexual or emotional abuse or a lack of confidence in your sexuality.

Castration

A classic male anxiety dream. Like dreams of losing one's teeth, a castration dream indicates a fear of impotence and loss of authority. Perhaps it is a sign that you feel threatened, whether by someone around you or by an attitude or person from the past, such as your parents' refusal to take you seriously as a child.

Penis

If you are a woman and dream of having a penis, the dream probably suggests your desire to behave more assertively or have more authority or confidence, qualities that are considered to be masculine. This dream could also be a result of the subconscious's desire to freely explore or imagine other roles and identities. For men, this dream is most likely to take the form of a threat or anxiety about castration, in which case it indicates lack of confidence or a fear of punishment by an authority figure.

Stomach

The stomach is connected to your 'gut' reactions and instincts. Dreaming of the stomach could be a sign of the need to examine a matter or emotion that you have been avoiding.

Bladder

If you are conscious of your bladder while dreaming it's probably just your unconscious registering an actual pressure on this part of the body. Symbolically, however, it may suggest 'pressure' on your general health or well-being.

Kidneys

These symbolise a need for cleansing and renewal.

Vagina

The vagina is associated with the dreamer's femaleness and sexuality. It may represent the confidence and self-image of womanhood, and the desire to create—either socially, reproductively or artistically. In a man's dream, it may suggest his desire for sexual expression.

Heart

To go to the heart of a matter is to explore its very core. To dream of your heart is therefore a positive sign of self-knowledge.

Womb

The womb in your dream represents your desire for protection, nurturing, and being free of adult responsibilities. This dream can be a response to a stressful situation, which makes you long to return to the dependency and protected state of infancy. But if the space is stifling or claustrophobic it suggests that you desire more independence or freedom.

Guts/Intestines

'Having guts' or being a 'gutsy' person means you are unafraid to do something. To dream of 'guts' may, therefore, be a sign that you wish you were 'gutsy'. 'Gut' reactions and instincts are also linked to your stomach.

Genitals

Castration

Penis

Stomach

Bladder

Kidneys

Vagina

Heart

Womb

Guts/Intestines

Cross-reference

For Intestines, see Pain in the abdomen p.127
See also Sexual behaviour pp.164–7

Bodily functions & actions

Defecating/Excrement

This dream suggests your desire to 'relieve' yourself of some burden or matter. It can stand for emotions that are blocking your ability to progress in your life. If you are having trouble finding somewhere to relieve yourself, it is a sign that your current circumstances are making it hard for you to unburden yourself.

Blushing

If you are blushing in your dream, it is probably an indication that you feel self-conscious, embarrassed, or uncomfortable about some situation or person. It might be a sign that you feel unfairly accused, or put in a humiliating situation by others, or that you fear that they will see through your defences. Blushing can also be a sign of sexual passion. Perhaps your blushing tells you that you are romantically interested in somebody, but afraid of embarrassment if your feelings became known.

Pulse

Our pulse is a vital sign and symbol of life. For this reason, being aware of your pulse in a dream is likely to reflect an anxiety about death or sickness. If you dream of taking someone else's pulse, it could be a sign that you are worried about losing them.

116

Perspiring

A dream in which you are perspiring could have a physical cause—indicating that you are too hot in bed. More symbolically it can suggest that something in your waking life is causing you to perspire—whether it's fear, anxiety or some other form of tension.

Defecating/
Excrement

Blushing

Pulse

Perspiring

Swallowing

Swallowing

In the context of a dream, swallowing suggests the holding back of emotions. We refer to 'swallowing our pride' or finding something 'difficult to swallow'. As swallowing is a natural function such as breathing, for it to be highlighted in your dream normally suggests some sort of blockage. What is it that you can't swallow?

Cross-reference

For Defecating/
Excrement, see
Toilet p.373,
Constipation p.135
For Swallowing, see
Eating and Drinking
p.358

Bodily functions & actions

Dreaming

It's not uncommon to dream that you are dreaming. This is often a sign that the content of your dream is particularly difficult or disturbing, and reflects your subconscious desire to keep it at a safe distance from the 'real' or waking world. To dream that you are dreaming is also the first step towards lucid dreaming, that is, the ability to recognise the difference between the conscious world and the subconscious world.

Menstruation

A woman who dreams of menstruating but has ceased to menstruate may be grieving for the loss of youth and fertility, or unable to accept her new stage of life. If a man dreams of menstruating, it represents his urge for more creative pursuits in his life.

Choking

This dream reflects any doubts you may have concerning your ability to successfully complete an enterprise or undertaking.

118

Urine/Urinating

Urination represents the control we have over our bodies and emotions. We may choose to hold our urine in or to release it. Therefore, to urinate is to release tension—particularly sexual tension. A common dream involves trying to go to the toilet, but finding that each one is either locked, blocked or in full view. This dream can be an indication that you actually need to urinate during the night. More symbolically, it may be indicating that whenever you try to express or release your emotions you keep finding there are obstacles in your way. As a result you are being prevented from releasing whatever it is that you've been 'holding in'.

Dreaming

Menstruation

Choking

Urine/Urinating

Yawning

Yawning

Yawning is an involuntary act, and so our subconscious is trying to get our attention. But yawning also signals boredom or tiredness, so a dream in which you are conscious of yawning may symbolise either your desire for more interest in your life, or it may suggest a sense of being overworked.

Cross-reference

For Urine/Urinating,
  see Toilet p.373
For Menstruation, see
  Blood p.108

119

Disease & illness

Sickness

To be sick highlights that all is not right with you. On a physical level, this dream may suggest that you need to watch your health. On an emotional one, it may signal that you are 'sick and tired' of something or someone in your life. It may be time to let go and be rid of whatever it is that makes you feel this way.

To dream of a particular illness may be an early indication that some aspect of your physical health needs attention. More symbolically, illness in a dream can also stand for an emotional problem, in which case the nature of the illness may help you to 'diagnose' the feeling that is concerning you. If you dream that someone else is ill, the dream may be a reflection of your concerns about either that person, or your feeling that all is not well in your relationship with them.

Health

To dream of your health denotes the need to slow down and take a more considered approach to a hectic lifestyle. More symbolically, this dream can be a sign that something is out of balance in your emotional life.

Abscess

A dream about an abscess is a dream of contrary meanings. If you are presently ill, dreaming of illness actually signifies that you will enjoy good fortune, health or a speedy recovery. These dreams can also reflect illnesses in various other parts of the body, in which case suggesting that your system is in need of attention or cleansing of impurities that will enable it to heal more quickly. On a symbolic level, dreaming of an abscess indicates the need to rid oneself of bad influences, particularly friends.

Affliction

If something is bothering you, or isn't quite right with you, it would be a good idea to pay attention to the details. Any health issue should be heeded. Traditionally, dreaming of affliction suggested that success was approaching and change for the better was assured.

Blindness

Being unable to see can be a frightening dream experience, signalling the dreamer's sense of helplessness or inability to know or perceive something. Perhaps you are 'in the dark' about a matter affecting you. You may even be deliberately closing your eyes to an aspect of a situation or person which you find it difficult to acknowledge. However, blindness can also make us more aware of the information we obtain through our other senses. In classical mythology blindness is a characteristic of those gifted with the powers of inner vision and prophecy.

Cancer

Unless you are actually ill, a dream in which you have cancer is unlikely to reflect a genuine illness. Rather, it suggests that you have not sufficiently come to terms with a major source of anxiety or insecurity, and that this is eating away at you from within. If it is someone else in your dream who has cancer, the dream represents your concern for either his or her well-being.

Deafness

Dreaming of deafness can be your subconscious's way of telling you that there is something or somebody you are refusing to hear. This dream can also represent your fear of being cut off from your surroundings or other people. In general, this dream is a sign that you need to work on new ways to listen to your own needs or to communicate with others.

Deformity

To dream of a deformity in one part of the body is often a sign that one part of your life has a problem or is out of balance with the rest. Use the interpretations of the different body parts to work out which part of your lifestyle or personality the deformed limb may actually represent.

Sickness

Health

Abscess

Affliction

Blindness

Cancer

Deafness

Deformity

Cross-reference

For Blindness, see
    Eyes p.112
For Sickness, see
    Nausea and
    Vomiting p.133
See also Doctor p.286

Disease & illness

Haemorrhage

Do you feel drained or emptied in some way? Blood is a significant dream symbol of our energies and life force. Similarly, its rich red colour suggests strong emotions or passions. Therefore, a dream in which you are unable to control a sudden flow of blood tends to suggest loss of strength or potency, whether in your emotional, spiritual or physical life. Alternatively, it may suggest the sudden release of pent-up emotion. Consider whether something or someone is 'bleeding you dry'.

Gangrene

To dream of having gangrene or that someone else has this infection indicates decay and loss of some part of your life. It can also suggest that you are holding onto an aspect of your life that is physically or emotionally toxic.

Disfigurement

To dream that you are disfigured can suggest your guilt over an action you have recently undertaken. If another person in the dream is disfigured, the dream implies a doubt about the motives of someone close to you. Generally, any sort of disfigurement is associated with negative aspects of the dreamer coming to the surface. It represents not just guilt, but jealousy, intolerance and other negative emotions that are usually hidden.

Infection

Like dreams of sickness, dreams of infections usually have an emotional meaning. For example, the infection in your dream may symbolise negative attitudes you have internalised from those around you: attitudes or emotions that are 'festering' within your mind, or threatening to invade your waking thoughts. This dream may be warning you to re-examine the negative influences on your life, and consider the ways in which they might be overcome.

Lameness

Dreaming of lameness is an indication of our awareness of the imperfections and weaknesses in our personalities. Or, you may be experiencing a lack of confidence and motivation (what is your 'lame' excuse?).

The left side of our bodies represents the creative and intuitive parts of ourselves, whereas the right side is the active and rational part. Work out whether it is your left or right leg that is lame. To dream of someone else being lame indicates that your plans are not solid and they will not be attained at this stage.

To walk with a crutch in a dream symbolises fear of failure. It can also denote too much dependency on others. Think about whether you are a crutch for others to lean on or vice versa.

Injury

Injuries in dreams represent the harm that we feel others have done to us. If this is a persistent or very troubling dream, it may be a sign that the dreamer is in need of inner healing, perhaps to recover from the emotional damage inflicted in childhood, or at some other vulnerable period of life. However, we all feel 'wounded' by others from time to time, and this dream may be no more than a dramatic way of expressing this sense of hurt.

Jaundice

If you dream of suffering from jaundice, it is most likely a sign that you lack energy or are overworked. If may also suggest that you have anxieties about diet and nutrition.

Haemorrhage

Gangrene

Disfigurement

Infection

Lameness

Injury

Jaundice

Cross-reference

For Haemorrhage, see Blood p.108
For Lameness, see Legs p.109

123

Disease & illness

Insanity

To dream that you or another is insane suggests your fear of emotions that are out of control. This dream could be warning you to avoid a particular person or situation in case you get caught in negative emotional currents. Alternatively, it could be a sign that you haven't been expressing or exploring your emotions enough. As a result, they may have built up to the point where they demand release, or could even be threatening your stability. Whatever it is, you need to get it off your chest.

Mutation

To see something that is not quite right indicates that you are not taking things at face value. If you see morphing, that is, a situation in which one thing flows into and becomes another, it may be a warning that a person or a situation is not what it seems.

Miscarriage

A miscarriage represents a loss—one that is untimely and unexpected. It could indicate the loss of some aspect of ourselves that has disappeared through

no intention of our own and that we now grieve for. It could also stand for the loss of work, a relationship or a new scheme that you never got the chance to see through. A 'miscarriage of justice' is an unfair result. If the dreamer is a woman and she has suffered a miscarriage, it is an indication that she has not given herself enough time to grieve in order for her to be healed completely.

Paralysis

Paralysis in a dream is likely to symbolise some situation in our waking lives in which we feel helpless and unable to act. What circumstances in your life are preventing you from functioning as you would like? This dream can also indicate that your vital functions have been blocked or 'paralysed' by emotions such as fear or guilt. Examining the source of these emotions may help you to make them less paralysing.

Scar

If you see a scar on yourself or on another person in a dream, it denotes past hurts and injuries. Whatever has happened in the past still pains you today and perhaps this permanent memory has 'scarred you for life'. Try to deal with this emotional hurt so that you can heal and move on.

Insanity

Mutation

Miscarriage

Paralysis

Scar

Parasites

Pus

Parasites

Parasites in dreams represent the way we feel about people or things that cling to our emotional lives, drain our energy or confuse us. If, in the course of your dream, the parasite leaves your body, it may be a sign that you are ready to leave these negative emotions behind you. The dream is telling you that if you have people around you who are behaving like parasites, it's time to leave them behind.

Pus

This bodily substance is associated with wounds and indicates that infection is present. Therefore, it can symbolise the presence of the negative emotions—such as envy or unhappiness or self-doubt—that infect our thoughts and undermine our self-esteem. However, pus is also associated with healing, so its presence may signal your desire to resist these negative emotions or to recover from a hurt or wound.

Cross-reference

For Mutation, see
    Deformity p.121
For Insanity, see
    Maniac p.304
For Miscarriage, see
    Pregnancy p.110

125

Disease & illness

Wound

The physical wound in your dream is probably a graphic representation of the more invisible 'wound' or hurt caused to your feelings. The other symbols in the dream will help you to interpret the source of this hurt. However, a wound doesn't always have to be interpreted negatively. As an opening in your body it can also symbolise your openness to an outside influence or emotion such as love or friendship.

Ulcer

An ulcer is an erosion of tissue that has caused bacteria to come to the surface. Like a boil, the purpose of this eruption is to clear the system. As with all dreams about health, it may be worth making an appointment with your doctor. However, this type of dream usually points us towards the need to heal emotional ruptures or hurts. A mouth ulcer suggests issues to do with communication while a stomach ulcer has more of an emotional significance. Ask yourself if you are going through a stressful time of change in which you need to make decisions that affect your lifestyle. If you are feeling agitated the ulcer could be a symptom of this dilemma and of your high levels of stress.

Hurt

The physical hurt we imagine in a dream usually stands for an emotional pain. The nature of the hurt, and where it is located, will help you to locate the source of this pain so that you can begin to find ways of healing it.

Plague

Dreaming of plague suggests that some force or emotion is out of control in your life and threatens to render you helpless. It may also suggest that you feel threatened by some misfortune or by the ill intentions of another. Often a plague suggests that there are negative people or circumstances around you, which are beyond your control. Don't try to change things—just protect yourself.

Madness

If you dream of acting in a mad or irrational manner, it may represent your fears of being confronted by what is irrational to you. You may be confronting the part of you that is uncontrollable and has not been allowed to merge with the rest of your unconscious. Dreaming of madness, whether in yourself or others, is often a sign you are experiencing intense emotional situations in waking life. If this is the case then the dream is indicative of your sense of being out of control. Seeing a mad dog or a mad person can symbolise the parts of ourselves that are unable to come to terms with a new situation in our lives.

Pain in the abdomen

If you dream of pain in this area, it's a good idea to have it checked out by your doctor. Sometimes our conscious minds may be concerned about parts of our bodies and this anxiety may come out in our dreams. It may also be a sign to trust your 'gut' instincts about people around you. Feeling the naked abdomen indicates a recovery of money according to traditional beliefs.

Wound

Ulcer

Hurt

Plague

Madness

Pain in the abdomen

Cross-reference

For Pain in the abdomen, see Intestines p.115
For Madness, see Maniac p.304
For Hurt, see Ache p.132

127

Medical procedures

Drugs

Obtaining or using drugs in a dream often suggests your desire to improve your health or well-being, perhaps through the use of a supplement or a better diet. However, if in your dream you are using or smuggling illegal drugs, it is more likely to be a sign that you are concerned about the legitimacy of some activity you are involved in or contemplating, or that you fear that others disapprove of your lifestyle.

Medicine

Dreaming of taking medicine represents the need to undergo unpleasant experiences in order to achieve a positive outcome. It is a symbol of healing through unpleasant or unpalatable means that is ultimately good for us. 'Taking one's medicine' or experiencing a 'taste of your own medicine' are terms used to describe the need to accept your fate in order to learn a valuable lesson. If you choose to take the dream literally, have a health check.

Ointment

An ointment is a substance you rub on a wound to heal it, protect yourself or make a problem go away. If you are using ointment in your dream, it pays to ask yourself what problem or emotion you are trying to solve. (A word that sounds rather like 'salve', another traditional name for ointment.) The rubbing action involved in applying ointment also suggests the desire to smooth or rub a problem until it disappears.

Taking a pill

In general, taking a pill is something we associate with duty rather than pleasure. For this reason it tends to stand for something we do because we know it will be good for us, rather than from inclination. This dream may suggest your need to take some action—perhaps suggested or 'prescribed' to you by another person—to prevent a situation from becoming worse. The phrase 'a bitter pill to swallow' associates the act of taking a pill with coming to terms with an unwelcome realisation. Traditionally, the word 'pill' was also used to describe a worthy, but boring or unimaginative person. Perhaps someone around you is behaving in this way?

Abortion

As the action suggests, abortion dreams are about the release and termination of anything that is not working or is no longer wanted in your life. It also represents feelings of rejection, guilt, sensitivity and anxiety associated with starting new ventures. It should be viewed as a sign to overcome troublesome events in your life and get rid of those things that are hindering your progress.

Amputation

To dream of a limb being amputated is a dream of personal loss. It may be the loss of someone close, a friend, a family member or even finding yourself retrenched and having your livelihood taken away from you. There are many sayings related to amputation which refer to cost ('to cost an arm and a leg') and value ('I'd give my right arm for that'). Therefore, beware of giving away something valuable as it may cut you off from your sense of individuality.

X-rays

Because X-rays are invisible, they tend to stand for the things that influence us without our being conscious of it. This dream could be pompting you to try and bring these influences into the light. But because X-rays are also associated with sickness and healing this dream can also represent your anxieties about your health, possibly even fear of some illness that has not yet become visible or whose effects have not reached your full awareness. In addition, an X-ray can represent something that is not available through normal vision, so the dreamer may wish to see what is not exposed to everyone in his or her waking life.

Drugs

Medicine

Ointment

Taking a pill

Abortion

Amputation

X-rays

Cross-reference

For Drugs, see
  Chemist p.291
For Amputation, see
  Legs p.109
For X-rays, see Bones
  p.106, Skeleton
  p.108

129

Medical procedures

Contraception

A dream about contraception may simply reflect your anxieties about falling pregnant, or, if you are a man, about your partner conceiving. More symbolically, it may suggest that you fear the consequences of an activity or project, or are not yet ready to make a new start.

Anaesthetics

To be anaesthetised is to feel nothing. This dream may be telling you that you are avoiding painful situations because of your fear of the outcome. Avoidance is not going to resolve the issue. Facing the consequences is a better option in the long run.

Heart surgery

If you dream of having heart surgery it is a sign that you need to pay more attention to your emotions. This dream tends to refer either to the desire to get rid of an emotional blockage, or to free yourself from a negative emotion altogether. The dreamer might feel that someone is manipulating or playing with their emotions in waking life.

Surgery

Dreaming of undergoing surgery suggests that you feel as if some aspect of your individuality—whether it's your way of life, values or ideals—is being interfered with. If you are due for surgery, this dream may be an anxiety dream that reflects your fears of the procedure. If not, you should still take note of what part of the body the surgery was performed on and the subsequent result. Generally, if the surgery was associated with the heart, it's an emotional issue that is troubling you, whereas if the surgery was on a limb it may indicate your inability for flexible movement. As with all dreams relating to health, consider getting a medical check-up. Your dream may be prophetic or a reflection of something that the subconscious has picked up on but that your consciousness hasn't yet acknowledged.

Injection

A dream in which you are having an injection suggests feelings of vulnerability or invasion. The dreamer's inner space has been 'punctured' or penetrated, perhaps with painful or fearful consequences. But such a dream is not always negative. After all, injections are also associated with healing or inoculation. Therefore, to dream of an injection may signal your desire to recover from an injury,

or to develop the strength and skills needed to ward off future emotional harm.

Operation

It is common to dream of an operation before going into hospital. In this situation the dream is allowing us to express our anxiety about an upcoming event. But if there is nothing physical to explain the dream, it probably has a symbolic or emotional meaning. Perhaps there is something wrong with your life or your character that you would like to 'cut out' or have removed? Alternatively, it could be that you or someone around you is persisting in damaging behaviour, and needs to 'cut it out'.

Quarantine

A dream in which you are forced to put a pet into quarantine probably suggests your fear that you are unable to take proper care of something or someone in your life. This could be a dependant, such as a child or partner, or a vulnerable part of yourself. Another meaning of quarantine is isolation. Either you feel unable to stay in touch with others, or you fear that they may have reason to avoid you.

Contraception

Anaesthetics

Heart surgery

Surgery

Injection

Operation

Quarantine

Cross-reference

For Heart Surgery, see Heart p.115

Minor ailments

Indigestion

Often a dream of indigestion will have a physical cause. However, if there is no direct physical reason for this dream, a symbolic meaning is more likely. Generally this dream suggests either that you have 'bitten off more than you can chew' (or digest) and need more time to think it over, or that there is something in your life that isn't agreeing with you. Ask yourself what's making your stomach churn. This dream could be a sign that you need to do something differently, or tackle problems in more bite-sized pieces.

Insomnia

A dream in which you are unable to sleep may appear very contradictory indeed! In general, this dream probably signals anxiety, not necessarily about sleeplessness, but about the problems or issues in your life that are most likely to keep you awake. This type of dream is one step away from lucid dreaming (see p.viii, Introduction). If the dreamer can recognise he or she is asleep during the dream, the dreamer can take control of the dreamscape.

Ache

Depending on the particular circumstances, a non-threatening ache can be attributed to some physical experience and a sign of ill health. If the ache is intense, it suggests that an upcoming important event will be very beneficial to you personally. This is likely to be a reference to the saying, 'no pain, no gain'. Aches in specific body areas, such as the back, suggest a lack of support or a feeling of being 'exposed'; a headache relates to the unsettling of the mind and heartache denotes some kind of emotional distress.

Vomiting

Vomiting is a release of that which is indigestible to us. How many times have we said that something made us 'sick to the stomach' or made us 'want to vomit'? Dreaming of vomiting is your way of getting rid of (throwing up) what is unacceptable, unethical or poisonous to you. There is a common phobia associated with vomit, and when others are vomiting in a dream it can be associated with this fear, particularly if the dreamer has a strongly negative response to the person vomiting in the dream.

Indigestion

Insomnia

Ache

Vomiting

Itch

Nausea

Itch

An itch prompts you to scratch, and itchiness in a dream may be telling you that you need to seek relief from something that is bothering you. This dream may also signal your sense that someone around you is causing you irritation. Expressions like 'the seven year itch' suggest an additional, more sexual meaning for this dream.

Nausea

You need to expel whatever is making you feel sick—either physically or emotionally. Think of a person who is making you feel this way in your life and deal with the problem—either by removal or confrontation. On a physical level, this dream could be warning you of a potential health problem.

Cross-reference

For Nausea, see
  Sickness p.120
For Vomiting, see
  Sickness p.120
For Ache, see Hurt
  p.126

Minor ailments

Stiffness

Feeling uneasy and being inflexible are both causes of stiffness. Therefore, to dream of being stiff highlights your feelings of anxiety or tension. It also suggests that these feelings are mainly due to your rigid attitudes and lack of flexibility. You may not be able to move forward unless you start tp adopt a more relaxed approach.

Splinter

A splinter is a minor irritation that causes discomfort until it is removed. Words can also be hurtful and cause negativity and pain. Dreaming of having a splinter suggests that you are hurt and irritated by someone's opinion of you. However, if you are labelled as belonging to a splinter group, the dream is showing you that it is fine to break away from the mainstream if that makes you happy.

Fainting

If you faint in a dream, it may suggest that you need to take better care of yourself, and not overdo strenuous physical activities, in order to avoid a 'collapse'. The dream could also be telling you that you are overworked and that your body needs a rest.

Pimple

If you are self-conscious about a pimple in a dream, it's probably a sign that you are worried about others noticing the 'blemishes' in your personality. As a result this dream tends to symbolise issues with self-esteem and your concern about the way you appear to those people around you. The pimple may also represent some issue or aspect of your personality that has swelled completely out of proportion and is therefore threatening to mar your social life. Squeezing a pimple in a dream (something we're all told not to do) may suggest you have a desire to get rid of some negative emotion or feeling.

Warts

Like pimples and other blemishes, warts suggest a concern with self-image; especially with the things that we fear will mar or spoil our physical appearance. More symbolically, a wart can also be a negative emotion that we can't seem to get rid of.

Constipation

This is a symbol of the dreamer's inability to let go of attachments or certain forms of behaviour that are no longer relevant.

Stiffness

Splinter

Fainting

Pimple

Warts

Constipation

Cross-reference

For Constipation, see Defecating/ Excrement p.116

Personal grooming

Washing

A dream in which washing occurs suggests a desire for purification, whether it is spiritual or emotional. This dream could indicate your desire to cleanse your life of unwelcome or negative attitudes and emotions. It may also suggest that you wish to start some situation over again with a clean slate. The object or body part being washed will help you interpret the aspect of your life the dream applies to. For example, washing your hands implies that you want to get rid of guilty feelings concerning an action you are responsible for, while washing your genitals indicates the desire to get rid of negative sexual feelings, or even to end a relationship that you feel is no longer working. The expression 'washed out' is about tiredness, while 'washing your hands of something' denotes your wish not to take responsibility for the consequences of an action. The biblical reference to this is obvious, as Pontius Pilate washed his hands of the execution of Christ.

Soap

An obvious interpretation for soap is the need for cleansing or freshening up. 'Cleaning up one's act' or 'coming clean' are phrases we use to describe changing our negative habits and actions. Your dream may be highlighting the need for this cleansing process to occur.

Comb

A dream in which you are combing your hair denotes a desire for order and, possibly, for relaxation. However, if your hair comes out as you are combing it the dream denotes an anxiety about your inability to control certain aspects of your life.

Shower

Dreaming of being 'showered with compliments' denotes your desire for praise. A shower is also hygienic and cleansing, washing away what is not wanted (grime and dirt). You may wish to be cleansed of (to get rid of) something that is no longer a part of you or your beliefs.

Shampoo

Dreaming of shampooing your hair is an indication that you need to clear your head in order to make a decision or take decisive action.

Shave

Shaving is an unmasking of our true selves—usually by removing an unwanted veneer or façade. Men do this by daily facial shaves and women by shaving other parts of their bodies. If you dream of having 'a close shave', be careful not to take too many risks.

Tan

If you dream of acquiring a stunning tan despite your natural colour, it may be a sign that you are changing yourself in obedience to fashion trends. This implies a degree of vanity as well as a need for approval from others. Focus on why image is so important to you and why you need to 'show' your eagerness to be accepted through your skin colour.

Nail file

A metal file or a nail file could be an indication that you are being abrasive and that you need to take a softer approach with those around you. A dream in which you are filing something down to shape it to your specifications suggests that patience and perseverance are going to be needed to help you to achieve your goals.

Tattoo

A tattoo represents identity, individuality, adornment or the desire to make a statement through artistic expression. If you can see the tattoo in the dream, regardless of whether it is on your body or someone else's, it probably holds a special significance for you. Initials, shapes, words, patterns or animals all represent things that you may want in your life. As a tattoo is permanent, it may be a reminder of a past experience, memory or relationship which may have been painful to the dreamer.

Cross-reference

For Nail File, see Finger p.137

For Comb, see Hair p.113

For Shampoo, see Hair p.113

CHAPTER FIVE

The spiritual

This chapter covers dreams of a religious or spiritual nature. These dreams, however, can be interpreted on many different levels. As well as revealing your spiritual feelings or needs, they can symbolise problems on an emotional level and even on a more earthly physical level. For example, the signs of the zodiac, as well as being linked with personality traits, are each associated with a different part of the body so dreaming of one of these could signify ilness or disease in that area.

& mystical

The spiritual & supernatural

Ouija board

This device used to be employed by mediums to try and channel messages from the spirit world. As a result dreaming of one symbolises your desire to access your 'other side' or unconscious, and to bring back a message of value. It suggests that you are looking for answers or advice on some issue in your life. If feelings are negative in such a dream, it's a warning that you're messing with something you know nothing about and you're apprehensive about the consequences in waking life.

Séance

To dream of conducting or being part of a séance indicates our need to get in touch either with our intuition or our spiritual side.

Oracle

An oracle tells the future, but often in a mysterious way or in a riddle that can be hard to interpret. A dream with an oracle in it suggests your desire to see what lies ahead of you, or to obtain information about the outcome of an action. But it is also a reminder that because we and others around us are responsible for making our futures, such information is difficult to obtain. Sometimes such a dream is basically telling the dreamer to focus on the present, not the future, in order to achieve present goals.

Magic

When we dream of magic, we are attempting to connect with the deepest powers within us. It may well be that we wish to accomplish great deeds or be in charge of situations that are beyond our human control. This is a positive dream, highlighting our subconscious wishes to gain more control over our present situation.

Occult

Dreaming of the occult suggests your desire to solve some mystery in your own life or to explore emotions that you usually keep hidden below the surface. If you have a negative association with the occult, you are actually frightened of exploring those feelings that are just under the surface, or of trying to solve the mystery.

Horoscope

In general, dreaming of a horoscope symbolises either your desire to know the future, or to explore your own identity. If you dream of a particular sign of the zodiac, it may be a clue that the dream is about a person close to you who has that particular birth sign.

Spirits

Spirits in your dream reflect your fears and anxiety about death. If you see spirits of dead people, you are searching for reassurance. If they are kindly spirits, you will feel more positive about your life or sense that you are being 'looked after'. Spirits are also associated with messages from the 'other side' or with the gaining of an insight. This is a common interpretation in practically all cultures. If the dreamer is looking for an answer to some problem in waking life, the message from the spirit world may provide the answer to his or her question.

Séance

Ouija board

Oracle

Magic

Occult

Horoscope

Spirits

Cross-reference

For Horoscope, see Zodiac p.144

141

The spiritual & supernatural

Talisman/Charm

A lucky charm is a less serious version of a talisman, yet is used to achieve the same result—protection of the wearer against bad luck. A dream involving a charm or talisman points to a lack of self-confidence in the dreamer and his or her need for external assurance. If you have this dream think about what may be making you feel inadequate and try to take more control over your life.

Ghost

When we dream of being haunted by a ghost, we are not actually being haunted by a spirit, but by our own feelings of guilt, memories and unfulfilled ambitions. The 'could have beens' and 'should haves' are the ghosts that haunt most of us. Such a dream can be indicative of unresolved issues that are associated with the person who is haunting us. In this case the answers that the subconscious mind is trying to find to these issues may be present in other symbols within the dream. If the dream recurs, it is a sign that the issue remains unresolved.

Wand

Wands are strongly associated with magic and fairytales so dreaming of one suggests your desire for some kind of 'magical' transformation in your life. Alternatively, this dream may signal your sense that someone close to you wields too much power or influence over your actions. It may be that you are too dependent on the opinions of others whom you consider to be more 'qualified'.

Invisibility

Something in your dream that is invisible, but is affecting you, is likely to be a sign of some force in your life, such as a parent or other authority figure, who is continuing to play a role in your life. If you yourself are invisible, the dream suggests either that you feel unable to make the impact on others that you would like, or that there is something in your past that you would rather forget. Generally, if you feel as if you are constantly put on public display in real life then such a dream is playing out an internal waking desire.

Wizard

Wizards are magical figures in myths and fairytales, who stand for both wisdom and power. Dreaming of a wizard could relate to someone in your life, such as a teacher or a mentor. Alternatively, it could be drawing your attention to your own untapped skills or powers.

Transformation

If you've ever dreamed of being able to transform yourself, others or things around you by some magical means, you would have experienced feelings of confusion. This is because you are coping with major changes in your life in which your actions can make an impact on a current situation. You may be entering into a new physical, emotional or psychological state that is making you feel confused about this unfamiliar territory or uncertain about that which has been transformed. The dream is telling you not to be concerned with this change, as it is a natural progression. It suggests that once you accept this as true, you will feel more in control.

Witch

The witch is an archetypal figure for the negative aspects of feminine power and the female personality. For that reason, traditional dream interpretation tends to associate the witch with the dreamer's more negative feelings about his or her mother. The witch can also stand for a part of yourself you feel ambivalent about or have trouble accepting, such as your feelings of jealousy or rage. If there is a positive association with this type of dream, the dreamer may be curious about the power of feminine energy and how it relates to natural forces.

Talisman/Charm

Ghost

Invisibility

Wand

Wizard

Transformation

Witch

Cross-reference

For Invisiblity, see Transparency p.310

The zodiac

Zodiac

The zodiac was devised by the ancient Babylonians who, through observation of the stars and planets, sought to explain the influence of these heavenly bodies on the personalities and lives of those born under particular constellations. Because the animals or figures of signs and their meanings are still so widely known today, it is possible that they may appear in your dreams as symbols either of your own or others' personality traits. For example, if you dream of a lion, it may represent someone in your life born under the sign of Leo, or the parts of yourself that are courageous or exhibitionist (two of the traits said to be characteristic of this zodiac sign). If the lion is interacting with a goat, the dream may signal the need to be courageous in pursuing your ambitions (represented by the sign of Capricorn or the goat). The different zodiac signs are also traditionally believed to govern or relate to different parts of the body, and these associations may also appear in your dreams. The twelve zodiac signs and the parts of the body with which they are associated are as follows:

Aries

Aries, or the ram, is associated with the head.

Taurus

Taurus, or the bull, is associated with the throat.

Gemini

Gemini, or the twins, is associated with the shoulders, arms and hands.

Cancer

Cancer, or the crab, is associated with the stomach and digestive organs.

Leo

The sign of Leo, or the lion, is associated with the heart, lungs and liver.

Virgo

Virgo, or the virgin, is associated with the abdomen and intestines.

Libra

Libra, or the scales, is associated with the lumbar region, kidneys and skin.

Scorpio

Scorpio, or the scorpion, is associated with the genitals.

Sagittarius

Sagittarius, or the archer, is associated with the hips, thighs and nervous system.

Capricorn

Capricorn, or the goat, is associated with the knees.

Aquarius

Aquarius, or the water-bearer, is associated with the circulation and ankles.

Pisces

The sign of Pisces, or the fish, is associated with the feet and toes.

Cross-reference

For Zodiac, see
    Horoscope p.141

145

Religion

Halo

Dreaming of someone with a halo suggests feelings of serenity, protection and purity. If on the other hand you are wearing a halo in your dream, it could indicate that you feel pressured into a role that isn't allowing you self-expression.

Cross/Crucifix

Dreaming of a cross or crucifix suggests that you feel burdened by other people's problems. It can also be a symbol of protection and hence a need to protect yourself from others.

Hymn

To hear or sing hymns in a dream may suggest a desire for spiritual growth. It can also be a sign of our own desire or need to be praised or appreciated.

Heaven

A dream of heaven is often compensatory in nature; in other words, it serves to console us at a time when our actual lives may be filled with a range of difficulties. It can be particularly reassuring when the health or well-being of ourselves or of someone who is close to us is in question. In this situation, the dream suggests the need to accept our absence of control over the inevitable processes of life and death. Less positively, this dream can also be regarded as a temporary wish to retreat from the realities of life. In other words, it can be a wish dream, a desire for a little heaven on earth.

A dream of paradise is likely to be compensatory, offering us pleasure and consolation when our waking lives are less than perfect. As an ideal image of harmony and plenitude this dream can be a reminder of the goals we are striving for, and a message to not give up on our attempt to achieve them.

Holy communion

To dream of this solemn ritual suggests a desire for transformation to occur in some area of your life. It can also symbolise your sadness at the absence of a friend or a relationship.

Hell

This dream suggests your feeling that things in your life can't get much worse. Chances are that if you experience this dream, you have already hit rock bottom and your life could be about to take a change for the better. It is worth remembering that we can make our own hell, and this may be a warning for us to take a more positive attitude.

Halo

Hymn

Cross/Crucifix

Heaven

Holy communion

Hell

Cross-reference

For Hell, see Devil p.304
For Hymn, see Singing p.251, Choir p.250

Religion

Prayer

A dream in which you are praying has several possible meanings. It may signal your desire to overcome uncertainty and find definite answers to a problem. It may also represent your need for guidance on an issue that you are concerned about or a desire for approval from those who are in positions of authority.

Altar

An altar can represent a dedication to some cause that is important to you. In olden times, sacrifices were carried out on altars and therefore may represent your craving to be acknowledged. To see someone getting married at the altar may be a 'giving up' of the individual to become a 'whole' new entity.

Bible

The earliest examples of dream interpretation come from the Bible. The most famous biblical dream is Pharaoh's dream about the seven fat and thin cattle and the seven fat and thin ears of corn, which Joseph interpreted as a prophecy of seven years of abundance and seven years of famine. Joseph's interpretation had a huge impact not only on Egypt but also on the future of dream analysis.

Religious buildings

Abbey

To dream of an abbey or church environment means peace of mind, comfort for the soul and freedom from anxiety and stress. This building symbolises a place of sanctuary where guidance and direction can be sought and a peaceful and positive resolution to your problems can be achieved.

Church/Temple

These sacred or religious buildings help us either to reflect on the things that are most 'sacred' to us, or to assess the state of the spiritual aspects of our lives. Churches also carry traditional associations of refuge or sanctuary from problems or issues that may be pursuing us.

Prayer

Altar

Bible

Abbey

Church/Temple

Convent

Convent

The convent is traditionally a symbol of seclusion, of retirement from the world and from the conflicts of sexuality and the emotions. If this dream is a happy one, it is likely to symbolise your desire for rest and recuperation, for time out from emotional striving or conflict. But if the dream is anxious and unhappy, it is more likely to signal your fear that life and pleasure are passing you by, possibly because you are too focused on your job or 'vocation'.

Cross-reference

For Abbey, see Abbot p.151
For Covent, see Nun p.152
For Church/Temple, see Steeple p.323

Religious figures

God

Dreaming of God or a god-like figure is a symbol that we acknowledge the divine—that there is a power greater than ours. God may also represent an authority figure—a mighty father figure who is able to take charge and protect us, which can be a comforting image. Think about what is burdening you and try to come to terms with the idea that although the 'buck stops with you' in some situations, there is always a higher force that takes care of you. Alternatively, this dream may be suggesting that you have to learn to be responsible for your actions.

Christi

To dream of Christ signals your fear that you will be called upon to perform a superhuman task or to make a sacrifice. Christ is also the ultimate symbol of unconditional love, and maybe this is what's missing in your life.

Adam & Eve

It is considered a good omen if you see the first biblical parents, Adam and Eve. The creation story may be telling you that you'd like to be 'first' at some achievement and seeing Adam and Eve will make those plans come to fruition. It can also be symbolic of the balance between feminine and masculine aspects of the inner self—the coming together of the dark and light side of personality, which again represents balance.

Angel

Throughout history, angels have been described as 'messengers' from a divine source. They represent goodness, protection and divine grace. To dream of angels is a good omen, forewarning you of some change in your situation. Their appearance could be a warning of things to come and to keep faith during trying times ahead.

Abbot

This dream may be warning you of negative vibes around you, particularly those of judgement and criticism. Be aware of smooth talking and flattery and do not be taken in by it. To dream of becoming an abbot or monk suggests you are longing for peace and time out to reflect on your present lifestyle.

God

Christ

Adam & Eve

Angel

Abbot

Cross-reference

For Abbot, see Abbey p.149
See also Martyr p.300

Religious figures

Nun

A nun symbolises sexual restraint and morality. If you dream of becoming a nun, the dream may be expressing a wish to connect with the more idealistic side of yourself. However, depending on the mood of the dream, it may also represent feelings of restriction or frustration.

Apostle

If an apostle speaks to you in your dream, it will contain a spiritual message. Pay attention to the details in the dream, as it may be trying to communicate to you that some area of your spiritual life needs to be attended to. Dreaming of an apostle indicates the dreamer's need for meaning in life, for something to believe in and a need for spiritual guidance.

Vicar

Sometimes considered a more approachable authority figure than a priest, a vicar in your dreams represents your spiritual quest or progress

Holy person

The holy person in your dream may represent someone you have a deep respect for. There will usually be some aspect of the dream figure that will help you to identify them with a person or persons in your waking life. Interpreting this dream requires you to pay attention to the way you feel about the person in your dream. Alternatively, this dream may represent your own aspirations to a more spiritual or 'perfect' life.

Archbishop

As head of many Christian denominations, the archbishop is an important authority and spiritual figure. To be in the company of an archbishop could mean that you are holding onto religious beliefs of your childhood years. Your personal attitude and how the role of the archbishop was presented to you in your early years will determine the meaning of the dream. Are you struggling with a moral dilemma or a crisis of faith?

Judas

The figure of Judas is one of the most basic symbols of betrayal. But Judas can also be a sympathetic character, who expresses our sense of being placed in a morally difficult situation in which we are pressured to betray our principles or tempted to do something we suspect is wrong. This dream could be inviting you to think carefully about your own actions or motivations in relation to those around you.

Nun

Apostle

Vicar

Holy person

Archbishop

Judas

Cross-reference

For Nun, see Covent p.149

CHAPTER SIX

Behaviour &

Dreams in which strong emotions are revealed are very common. While these dreams may often be of negative emotions and leave you feeling anxious or alarmed, often the interpretation is more positive. For example, dreaming of despair or distress is seen as symbolic of healing and moving on. Alternatively, the dream can be giving you a message about how to deal with difficult feelings in a more constructive way. This section also explores dreams about sexual behaviour, which can reveal much about your needs for intimacy as well as allowing you to play out fantasies that would be difficult in your waking life.

feelings

Emotion

Passion

A dream in which you are experiencing intense passion probably points to a lack of it in your waking life. Perhaps you tend to be emotionally inhibited, or your situation isn't giving you many chances to experience passion. This dream could be a sign of your desire for a new relationship, or of the need to renew an existing one. Alternatively, it could reflect the fact that you feel stale and uninspired in a job or project.

Love

The love you feel in a dream is a genuine emotion. You may be actually experiencing it in your waking life or it may be a wish-fulfilment dream (a reflection of something you desire but which you have not yet attained). There are times when we feel unlovable, or love has not shown itself in our lives, and we dream of love in some form. This dream is compensation for not receiving that love.

Anger

Anger in a dream can be a release of hostility you actually have towards someone. At times we cannot express anger openly in our waking lives because we're afraid to hurt someone or they may be in a position of authority at work or in our personal lives. In sleep, anger emerges because it can no longer be contained. It is worth paying attention to this emotion as it may indicate your true feelings towards someone or some situation.

Calmness

If your dream radiates calmness and reassurance, it may be telling you that the foundations of a particular matter are firmer and more positive than you think. This dream may also be encouraging you to relax, slow down and learn to appreciate some peace and quiet in your life.

Laughter

Laughter is the best medicine and laughing or hearing laughter represents a sense of joy and a release of tension which makes us feel light-hearted. The dream may be telling you to 'lighten up' and not take life so seriously.

If you are on the receiving end of the laughter, it may be more a case of it's 'no laughing matter' or 'a laughing stock'. We may feel embarrassed at being ridiculed as a result of saying or doing something that is not appropriate for the occasion or the audience.

Pity

If you feel pity in a dream, it may be yourself rather than someone else who is the object of the emotion. This dream should prompt you to ask why you feel you are in need of sympathy.

Admiration

Being admired in a dream suggests that you have made useful friendships and that you crave approval from your peers. To admire others means that you are looking for guidance in some area of your life.

Passion

Love

Anger

Calmness

Laughter

Pity

Admiration

Cross-reference

For Anger, see
    Conflict pp.178–9
For Love, see Heart
    p.115

157

Emotion

Despair

Experiencing despair in a dream can be a sign that the dreamer has moved on from a particular situation or emotion. In this case the dream represents the emotion you have left behind, rather than that which lies in the future. Despair in a dream is definitely a sign of healing and moving on.

Dislike

A dream in which you feel or express a strong dislike for something is often a positive sign, suggesting that you know your own mind and are not prepared to be overly influenced or pushed around by others.

Distress

Rather than forecasting unhappiness, a dream in which you experience distress is often a reference to an influence in the past that once caused you unhappiness, but which is passing out of your life. Psychologically this type of dream represents healing from past distress or hurt.

Envy

Although envy is listed as one of the seven deadly sins, it is said that it's only when you envy someone that you come to terms with what you really want. Pay attention to envy in dreams—it is pointing you to where you want to be or what you want to possess. If someone is envying you, there is a good chance that you have achieved a significant goal in life.

Hate

To dream of experiencing such a strong emotion is an indication of the presence of powerful negative feelings in your life that should not be ignored. This dream is positive if it prompts you to consider what aspects of your relationships with others are causing you unhappiness.

Gall

Gall is a symbol of bitterness and irritability. Do you recognise this feeling? See what you can do to express it in a positive way.

Guilt

To analyse this emotion, you need to look at the other symbols in the dream. Maybe you are feeling guilty because of something that is going on in your life. Alternatively, the dream may be telling you that you should feel guilt for some deed.

Despair

Dislike

Distress

Envy

Hate

Gall

Guilt

Cross-reference

For Hate, see Enemy and Adversary p.299
For Guilt, see Confession p.236

Emotion

Crying/Weeping

If someone else is crying, the dream may be telling you that you are neglecting another's needs. If you are the one crying, it suggests that your own needs are not being answered. In waking life weeping is a sign of grief, so a dream in which weeping occurs symbolises your need to express such an emotion. This dream may be reminding you of feelings or sadness or loss that you have kept 'bottled up'. Sometimes this motif is displaced onto a related object, such as a 'weeping willow'.

Waking in tears

Have you ever woken up from a dream in tears? If you have, it suggests that some hurt has been brought to the conscious level while you've been asleep. For this to happen, the hurt or strong emotion must have been quite intense. Often we cry in dreams because of our tendency to cover up our real feelings in our daily life.

Obsession

A dream in which you are obsessed points to a source of anxiety in your life that needs to be worked through before it will stop bothering you. This dream could also be trying to draw your attention to some repeated activity or emotional situation in your life. Either way the dream calls for action in waking life.

Fear

This dream can be interpreted in many different ways, depending on the type of fear you suffer from and the form in which it is manifested in the dream. Fear is usually expressed as an obstacle dream. If you dream that you overcome the fear by some means—being rescued, running away, outwitting the enemy or saving yourself—it suggests that you will overcome whatever is hindering your progress. If you remain a victim in your dream, and feel helpless, then you need to reassess the steps that you are taking to address your fear.

Hysteria

A dream in which you or someone around you is hysterical suggests your anxiety about emotions that are out of control. It may also be a representation of your fears that a situation or relationship is no longer working, or is about to take a turn for the worse.

Crying/Weeping

Waking in tears

Obsession

Fear

Hysteria

Cross-reference

For Fear, see specific fears such as Flying p.255, Drowning p.198, Chased p.197
For Crying/Weeping, see Wailing p.239

161

Affection

Caress

This dream is a symptom of our need for basic reassurance and affection. If you dream of being caressed, the dream may be reflecting your desire for being nurtured and simple physical affection. If you can't find this kind of affection from humans around you, domestic pets such as cats and dogs make a suitable alternative.

Kissing

This dream tends to symbolise a desire for intimacy, whether erotic or domestic in nature. More symbolically it can also be a sign that you have accepted or come to terms with something or somebody. For example, if you are kissing a friend goodbye, it could be a sign that you have accepted the need to change something, or to move on to another stage of your life.

Entwining

Depending on what is restraining you, dreaming of entwining is usually a sign of your need to extricate or untangle yourself from some emotional bind—whether that of a parent, spouse, partner or job. If you feel that the entwining chokes you, it is time for you to cut ties to whatever it is that you are allowing to restrain you. Perhaps you should be reclaiming your individuality.

Devotion

To dream of caring for another suggests that you have become too emotionally detached from the people around you. If someone in your dream is expressing devotion towards you, it is a sign either that you feel constricted by your close personal relationships, or that you are thinking too much about your own emotions and needs. Dreaming that you are being looked after by your mother suggests that you are experiencing some level of emotional insecurity in your waking life.

Touch

Touch is a means of communication. In the physical arena touch communicates love, tenderness, intimacy or simply contact. This dream may indicate that you are searching for more physical contact. Alternatively, it may be encouraging you to acknowledge that you need others around you to offer support, particularly at times when you feel alienated.

Caress

Kissing

Entwining

Devotion

Touch

Cross-reference

For Entwining, see
   Tangle p.207
For Touch, see Fingers
   and Hands p.107
For Kissing, see Lips
   p.112

Sexual behaviour

Sex

Dreams of a sexual nature serve to make us aware of our basic life force and the need to accept our sexual urges and fears. Take note of the setting in which the sexual encounter takes place, as this can indicate your sense of sexual identity. We often play out sexual fantasies in our dreams. These dreams allow us to explore various possibilities and 'what ifs'. If we dream about homosexual activities it doesn't necessarily mean we have these tendencies but it may indicate that we perceive the qualities within such relationships to be either more intimate or sexually arousing than our own. If we dream about having sex with someone famous or even our next-door neighbour, it is often some quality in them that we desire rather than actual sex or intimacy with that person.

Explore the nature of the feelings you experience within the dream. If, while dreaming, you feel disturbed or threatened by the events occurring within it, such as rape or sadism, it suggests that you may be feeling exploited, dominated or abused in some sense in your waking life. If this is the case, then the message of the dream is that you need to take control of your life and try to move away from the negative influences that are affecting you.

A whole range of sexual behaviours and identities can be explored in dreams about sex. The key to interpreting such dreams lies in examining your own personal attitude towards sex and intimacy.

Masturbation

This relates to the need to be comforted and to release sexual tension.

Intercourse

Dreams of intercourse are a reflection of our need to communicate on a deeper and more intimate level with someone.

Incest

Incest may represent our need to express love (rather than sexuality) more openly with family members.

Sex

Masturbation

Intercourse

Incest

Fetish

Sadism

Fetish

Dreaming of fetishes is an indication that you have a fear of being intimate.

Sadism

This is an escapist dream. If you are put down or are fairly submissive in your waking life, you may find yourself playing out your frustrations in a dream in which you have the power that is missing from your life.

Cross-reference

See also Body organs pp.114–15
See also Harem p.281

165

Sexual behaviour

Orgy

An orgy is an occasion for the release of pent-up energy, especially of a sexual nature. This dream could be compensating for an excess of self-control in your waking life. But it can also be about the way you relate to people in a group, especially where issues of inhibition or self-expression are concerned.

Rape

Rape in a dream can reflect the dreamer's feelings of being 'violated' whether sexually or not. Most rape dreams are about the balance of power between men and women and the ways in which it is abused.

Clothing

Clothing worn during sex suggests that the dreamer feels guilty about indulging in a sexual encounter.

Homosexuality

This often occurs in dreams that highlight the need to find someone who is similar to ourselves, not necessarily in terms of gender, but in other ways as well.

Bisexuality

This dream is about balancing the feminine and masculine aspects of our sexual selves. It may indicate an acceptance of both of these aspects in your sexual nature.

Adultery/Affair

Dreaming of an affair can indicate your need for excitement and stimulation. To dream of your partner committing adultery brings out your own feelings of sexual inadequacy or insecurity with emotional commitment. It may also be making you aware of temptation in some area of your life where 'cheating' or some other dishonest method can be employed to make your life more exciting. The dream in this case is warning you to resist this temptation and not to stray. An affair with a famous or powerful person signifies that it's fame or power that you crave in your life.

Orgy

Rape

Clothing

Homosexuality

Bisexuality

Adultery/Affair

Cross-reference

For Adultery/Affair, see Dishonesty p.178

167

Situations &

This chapter examines both positive and negative actions that commonly occur in dreams. Positive actions or situations can give an insight into your creative or productive side such as being a painter, playing sport, music and entertainment, or celebrating a happy event. Negative actions or situations include the 'horror' type of dreams that most people have experienced at one time or another such as being hunted, being lost or left behind, drowning or being punished. Most of these reflect our inner insecurities, which if interpreted carefully can be used to increase our confidence in daily life.

actions

Actions

Defending

If you are forced to defend yourself in a dream, it is a sign that you feel under attack in some aspect of your waking life, and that you need to stand up for yourself. If you manage to defend yourself successfully, the dream is a sign that you will overcome your obstacles.

Devouring

Devouring something can be a symbol of the removal of some negative force or influence. This dream also carries the meaning of a return to our more basic, primitive emotions.

Calling

If you dream that someone is calling you by name, it may be a sign that a friend or someone close to you needs your help. This dream may also be reminding you to take care of a matter you have been trying to ignore or put off. If the person calling your name comes from your past, the dream is a sign that your emotions are still too engaged with this person, and that it's time to move on.

Cheering

If people are cheering for you in your dream, it can mean that you feel you don't get enough encouragement and support from your friends or work colleagues.

Digging

In general, a dream of digging implies your need to explore the more deeply hidden aspects of yourself. This is a dream in which the object of your search may also represent an experience or person that you may have tried to 'bury'.

Defending

Devouring

Calling

Cheering

Digging/
Excavation

Cutting

Plunging

Cutting

If you are cutting something in your dream, it is a sign that you will soon be required to make a difficult decision. It may be connected to 'cutting away', 'cutting out' or 'cutting up'.

Plunging

The expression 'about to take the plunge' associates this action with the start of a new project. It also suggests this enterprise or activity (whether it's taking on a new job or asking somebody out on a date) is one that requires courage, and may involve the risk of failure or getting hurt. This dream may be preparing you to take a decisive step towards something new.

Cross-reference

For Calling, see Name
   p.310
For Digging, see
   Shovel p.410
For Cutting, see Knife
   p.393, Scissors
   p.412

Actions

Holding

If you are conscious in your dream of holding something, the object probably represents something that you're trying to protect or are afraid of losing. In general, holding suggests a desire for control, ownership, intimacy or, more indirectly, for knowledge or awareness (as when, for example, we feel we have finally 'grasped' a concept or idea). If what you are holding is struggling to get away from you, however, the dream may be telling you to reconsider a possessive attitude, or to let go of something that is no longer serving a valid purpose. Holding yourself in a dream symbolises an overwhelming desire for intimacy and protection.

Pointing

If you or someone else is pointing to something in your dream, your subconscious is trying to draw your attention to something you have been ignoring. Expressions such as 'getting to the point' suggest the need to arrive at some meaning or decision. A 'pointed remark' is an insight that can hurt, but that also contains a revealing truth.

Kneeling

Kneeling in a dream can have several meanings. It may suggest your sense that others require you to take a lower or secondary role. Alternatively, it may also indicate that you want something so badly you are prepared to beg for it. The emotions that accompany the dream should help you to interpret its meaning. The dream is indicative of a need for submission, particularly in those who find it difficult to take a supporting role.

Shrinking

If you dream of shrinking in size, you are obviously reverting back to a former state—that of childhood. This dream may not be so much about childhood itself as the fears, anxieties and emotions that go hand in hand with that period of your life. You may be feeling insignificant and helpless in a situation. When other things shrink around you on the other hand, it indicates that parts of your life have become less threatening or perhaps less important to you.

Selling

If you dream of selling, it suggests that you are trying to use convincing arguments to win your point. What idea or point of view are you trying to 'sell' someone in real life?

Shopping

Retail therapy is another term for shopping. Looking at shops or purchasing goods represents our desires and needs. These may be for love, sexual fulfilment, wealth or a career. Pay close attention to what type of store you see in the dream. A clothing store has to do with image, whereas gifts are symbolic of talent and potential. A fun or game store could indicate your need to be more laid back and young at heart.

Waiting

Failing

Rescuing

Shrinking

Selling

Shopping

Cross-reference

For Failing, see Exams p.245
For Shopping, see Marketplace p.335

177

Conflict

Disputes

The dispute or argument in your dream may represent not only potential disagreements with friends or colleagues, but also a conflict between different aspects of yourself or your contrary desires. Paying attention to the nature of the dispute and the position you are taking in it will help you to interpret this dream.

Quarrel

The quarrel in your dream probably symbolises a conflict within yourself. Perhaps your emotions are pulling you in different directions, or you are having trouble reconciling your head and your heart.

Dishonesty

To act dishonestly in a dream can actually suggest the opposite, in other words, that you are overly concerned with making sure that your behaviour is above board. If others are behaving dishonestly towards you, it is a sign that you fear being cheated by those around you.

Aggression/Obscenity

If you have a dream that shocks you, you should not be too alarmed. Dreaming is an activity in which the censors that operate in our waking life are often absent. Your dream may be representing aggressive urges or sexual fantasies that you don't allow into your waking life, and it could be a way of releasing tension. This is healthy, as dreams enable fantasies to be explored without them being confrontational or harmful. Dreams also often represent our attempt to process images and ideas that we encounter in our waking lives—in films, books or news broadcasts for example. If you repeatedly have dreams that shock you, however, it may be an indication that you have an overly controlling attitude to your sexual or aggressive urges.

Pushing

This dream symbolises the pressures that surround you. If you dream that someone pushes you, be alert to the circumstances in your waking life in which you feel prodded into action. If you feel resentful towards the person in your dream, it may be a sign that you are reluctant to accept change, or are taking an action unwillingly. If, on the other hand, someone is pushing past you in your dream, the dream may be more about your worries of being left behind.

Giving offence

A dream in which you are offending someone suggests either that you need to pay more attention to other people's feelings, or that you are oversensitive to their opinions. Use the other elements within the dream, combined with your knowledge of your own actions, to interpret which meaning is the most applicable to you.

Disputes

Quarrel

Dishonesty

Aggression/ Obscenity

Pushing

Giving offence

Cross-reference

See also Enemy and Adversary p.299
See also War, fighting & violence pp.230–3
See also Anger p.156
See also Hate p.159

Domestic activities

Ironing

A dream in which you are ironing may symbolise your desire to look your best for a particular occasion. It may also suggest your intention to 'iron' out a problem, or solve a particular issue. Iron is a traditional symbol of strength and stamina. However, it can also represent inflexibility or a lack of emotion. If the iron is rusted, it suggests a fear of losing something precious as a result of the effects of time or neglect.

Sewing

Sewing a garment represents the creation of a new idea, theory or set of values. Mending a tear in clothing is symbolic of healing a relationship or situation.

Sweeping

When we dream of sweeping, it suggests that we are clearing away attitudes and ideas that we no longer hold to. Consider these idioms— 'making a clean sweep', 'sweep someone off their feet' and 'sweeping something under the carpet'. Which of these sayings best reflects your present situation?

Darning

If you are darning in your dream, it may be a sign that you need to take the time and trouble to repair a relationship with a friend, family member or lover.

Knitting

Knitting suggests the desire to make something grow. It can symbolise domestic pleasures or any slow but rewarding activity. However, if the wool is tangled or you can't form the stitches properly (for example, if they keep falling off the needles)

then this dream represents your anxieties about not being able to make progress in your work or home life. If the garment being knitted has a complicated pattern, what is desired will take careful consideration as well as patience.

Weaving

Weaving can symbolise any attempt to make something, whether it's an object or a relationship. Weaving can also suggest 'the web of life', and in this respect the woven fabric can represent the patterns or design you are making as a result of your own actions.

Yarn

As the thread or wool we use in knitting, yarn symbolises our ability to make things. Whichever meaning is relevant to your dream, yarn represents your ability to fashion yourself out of the raw materials which you are given. In its meaning of tale or story, a yarn suggests our sense of continuity or place in family history.

Ironing

Sewing

Sweeping

Darning

Knitting

Weaving

Yarn

Cross-reference

For Sewing, see
  Needle p.408
For Darning, see
  Needle p.408
For Knitting, see Wool
  p.425

Farming

Grain

Grain is associated with success and harvest. A grain of wheat indicates the germ of an idea that is then harvested with success. It may mean that you have created opportunities for yourself over time and that now you can reap your reward. A wheat field also suggests personal growth from a seed to a field (from immaturity to experience). If the feelings in the dream are negative, you may need to change the type of grain you are sowing in order to bring about ultimate success.

Harvest

To dream of a harvest tends to symbolise your desire either for prosperity or for the completion of a project. If you're worried about whether the harvest can be brought in in time, it may be an indication that you feel rushed in a project. But if the harvest is going to plan, it is a positive sign that things are on schedule. To dream of a perfect harvest is associated with prosperity in a material as well as a spiritual sense.

Hay/Haymaking

Hay and hayfields suggest warmth, prosperity and friendship. They can be a symbol of good times or of an increase in productivity in your work or social life. They also carry childhood or family associations. The proverb 'making hay while the sun shines' signals the need to make the most of favourable circumstances while they last.

Farm/Farmyard

A farm signifies productivity and solid manual work. A well-kept farm is an indication of good health and prosperity. It also represents the down-to-earth side of the self. A run-down farm, however, is a sign of loss and emptiness. A farm is also symbolic of an idealistic or simple lifestyle, away from the fast pace of city life.

Ploughing

Because ploughing prepares the ground for sowing seed, it is a traditional symbol of sexual intercourse. However, this dream may also represent your desire to bring other things to fruition, like ideas or creative projects. In general, it symbolises the hard work that needs to be done if you are to make something in your life 'grow'.

Wheat/Wheatfield

A dream with wheat or wheat fields in it is likely to symbolise the things in your life that you need to grow or cultivate, whether a talent, relationship or career. Wheat also carries associations with harvest: the time of year when we reap the benefits of our experience or hard work.

Straw

Straw is traditionally associated with poverty. Humans are reduced to a minimal level of survival when they need to use straw for warmth and bedding. In modern times, straw implies that something lacks stability or permanence. You need to work out what is permanent in your life and make it work for you.

Corn/Cornfield

Traditionally, ripe corn is associated with plenty and well-being. Dreaming that you are in a cornfield indicates that you will have financial and social successes ahead of you.

Field

Dreaming of animals in a field suggests the dreamer's contact with his or her natural self. It may be telling you to get back to nature, or basics. Like a farm, a ploughed field indicates prosperity, while a barren one conveys the idea of stagnation. 'Playing the field' is an indication that we may desire freedom from social pressure or expectations. A field can also represent the 'field' of activity, study or expertise that you are involved in. In this context it may be communicating a need for you to renew or consider your satisfaction in your chosen field.

Grain

Harvest

Hay/Haymaking

Farm/Farmyard

Ploughing

Wheat/ Wheatfield

Field

Straw

Corn/Cornfield

Cross-reference

For Grain, see Fruit, nuts & grains pp.348–51
For Hay/Haymaking, see Pitchfork p.409
See also Farm & working animals pp.56–8

Hobbies

Photography

Taking a photograph may signal a desire to reach some insight or realisation about a current situation or emotion. If you are developing photographs in a dream, it is likely that you are trying to shift some perception from your subconscious over to your conscious mind. Looking at a photograph of yourself, or being photographed, is more likely to reflect your concerns with your self image. If you are developing photographs in a dream, it is likely that you are trying to shift some perception from your subconscious to your conscious mind.

Decorating

If you are decorating in your dream it suggests either that you desire more frivolity, fun or celebration in your life, or, perhaps, that you are being overly superficial.

Chess

To dream of playing this game of skill and strategy denotes the need for careful thought in a business or financial matter.

Lottery

Lottery is collective gambling, where large groups of people take a chance at winning their life-long dreams of riches and wealth. If you dream of having a lottery ticket, it is a symbol of your desires and dreams. If you dream you've won the lottery, it could indicate that you've achieved something but not as a result of your own efforts. Generally, dreaming of a lottery can be taken as encouragement to take a chance in the game of life—especially if you've been too cautious up until now. On the other hand, if you've been reckless in some undertaking, dreaming of playing the lottery or losing could be a suggestion that you will be disappointed in some way. Winning a lottery is usually a feel-good dream, particularly if the dreamer has financial problems. In this case, the dream is offering the dreamer psychological relief from his or her financial woes. While dreaming of lottery numbers hasn't unfortunately been proven to be successful, it probably wouldn't hurt to write them down as soon as you wake up.

Gambling

Dreaming of gambling symbolises a reckless code of behaviour and refusal to take life seriously. If you dream of winning, it usually means the opposite. The dream could be cautioning you to change your ways before you risk losing. Alternatively, the dreamer could be feeling as if he or she is taking a risk in their waking life. In this case the dream may be a warning from the subconscious to proceed with caution.

Poker

The card game of poker is associated with gambling in its aspects of both luck and skill. Perhaps you are about to take a chance on something, or you are thinking about the cards you have been dealt in life. A 'poker face', on the other hand, is one that doesn't give away what the player is thinking or feeling. In this context you should think about whom you are reluctant to share your feelings with.

Photography

Decorating

Lottery

Chess

Gambling

Poker

Games

Games

Dreams of playing games represent the way we cope with life. If we play well then our lives are on target and we are managing well. If we play badly, we need to consider upgrading our skills. Ball games are often team sports and, therefore, indicate the way in which we relate to people socially. They are also competitive games so consider how competitive you are in the game of life and whom it is you struggle against to reach your goals. Thinking games, such as chess, are more to do with ideas and how well you make your moves and reflect your successes in life. Card games and gambling are symbols of balancing calculated risks and recklessness.

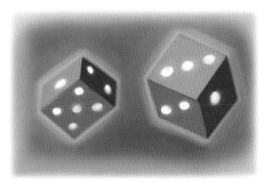

Cross-reference

For Photography, see Photographs p.418
For Gambling, see Wagering p.173
For Games, see Toys & games pp.398–401

Hobbies

Tapestry

A rich tapestry represents the tapestry of life—that is, our history and our experiences. To be weaving a tapestry is a symbol that you have control over your life's direction. If the tapestry is complex and full of detail it is indicative of the way in which the dreamer conducts his or her life. The message here is of the need to find balance in life and to take control of its direction (symbolised by the tapestry's pattern and the way it takes shape). Examine the tapestry in the dream carefully and try to interpret all the surrounding symbols in it so that you can gain a fuller understanding of the message of your dream.

Sculpture

Dreaming of a sculpture means that you are connecting with your artistic side. As a sculpture is permanent and can be viewed from all angles, the dream may be telling you to examine a work from every perspective before deciding how to evaluate it. If the dreamer is creating the sculpture, the dream may symbolise a desire for beauty and perfection.

Carving

This is a dream that denotes emergence and creativity. If you are carving something in your dream, this activity probably reflects your desire to give shape to your life and to bring order and focus to a particular event or circumstance. Paying attention to the shape that you are trying to carve, whether the surface is soft or hard, and the ease or difficulty with which it emerges, will help you to interpret the current state of your progress. Idioms such as 'carving a niche' highlight our need to make our lives fit in with our talents.

Varnishing

What are you covering up? Varnishing furniture either covers up imperfections or adds an external layer to restore and protect the wood. If you are varnishing, ask yourself if you are building layers of protective coating around you, so that the influences of others are unable to penetrate and get to you. If you see others varnishing, take care not to be deceived and be honest about your own intentions.

Painter/Painting

Dreams involving paintings can have several meanings. On the one hand, painting is associated with self-expression and creativity, so a dream in which you are painting or watching someone else paint may be a reflection of how successfully you express yourself.

A painting can also be a subconscious 'picture' of the way things are in your life. If you are painting a room or a house, as in decorating, the dream suggests a desire for change and renewal. The expression 'paint the town red' suggests the desire to celebrate. The colours of the painting in your dream may also be a reflection of your current mood or situation—is your picture predominantly dark, or rosy?

Reading

Reading involves a search for knowledge and information. This may be from an external source such as a book or on a computer screen, but it may also take the form of an internal scanning that can help us to understand ourselves better.

Beads

Beads suggest accumulation and order, and can symbolise material, spiritual or emotional wealth. If you are stringing beads in your dream, it may represent the need to be careful with something of value to you. If the beads are broken or spilled, it may signal your feeling that things are slipping out of your grasp.

Tapestry

Sculpture

Carving

Varnishing

Painter/Painting

Reading

Beads

Cross-reference

For Reading, see Novel p.396, Books p.240
For Tapestry, see Weaving p.181
For Varnishing, see Wood p.382

Sports

Race

If you dream of taking part in a race it suggests rivalry or competitiveness. It also points to how you feel about your 'position' in life, either socially or professionally. Ask yourself who you are competing with and why.

Marathon

Running a marathon represents our participation in life ('the rat race'). How we conduct ourselves in the race is an indication of how we truly participate in life. If you feel that life is a slog, you will be dragging your feet in the marathon—a race that requires a steady pace and which tests your endurance. If you see yourself enjoying the marathon and participating willingly, then you are ready for a challenge and able to take things in your stride. If you are a spectator or an official, note how these roles might be relevant in your life situation.

Riding

Riding has many connotations depending on the dreamer's use of this word. You may be feeling that you are in 'for a rough ride', or that you need to 'let something ride' for the time being. Search carefully for clues that will help you to understand this dream.

Swing/Swinging

The backwards and forwards motion of swinging reminds us of the cradle and the motions of the swings of childhood. Dreaming of swinging indicates a desire to go back to the carefree feelings of childhood when swinging allowed us to be playful and relaxed. 'Going with the swing' and 'getting into the swing of things' are sayings that highlight the need to let go of adult limitations. This dream may be showing you that the best way to be at ease is to adopt this childlike attitude.

Saddle

If you dream of being in a saddle, it suggests that you feel you are in control of your own life. However, if you are 'saddled down', it means that you feel burdened and pressured by someone or a situation. If you are thrown from a saddle, unexpected events will destabilise you and cause you to lose control. This dream is essentially about control and your own sense of authority.

Swimming

Swimming upstream with your head above water denotes success and confidence. Personal survival is important to you and swimming to your destination means that you will achieve your goals. Swimming against the tide indicates that you will meet with an opposing force or move against the general consensus. Swimming with others suggests that you have things in common with others—you are all swimming in the same pond. It indicates that you feel accepted at a social level. Swimming underwater suggests going deep within yourself over some issue, particularly an emotional one, in order to see the whole picture. Diving into water stands for 'taking a plunge' or a risk. Clear water indicates that you are feeling positive, while muddy water could be a reflection of your gloomy state of mind. If you are swimming underwater and feel as if it is a struggle or even scary, then you are not ready to face the deep emotional issues surrounding you. A swimming pool represents our innermost thoughts and feelings. These feelings are more contained than those in dreams of a lake or the sea.

Race

Marathon

Riding

Swing/Swinging

Saddle

Swimming

Trampoline

Trampoline

Jumping on a trampoline in a dream reflects anger (which is causing you to jump up and down) that you have experienced in your waking life. Possibly this anger has not been expressed outwardly, which is why it is resurfacing in your dreams. Images of bouncing and springing up may also suggest that you need to take more of an active role in a situation or relationship.

Cross-reference

For Swimming, see
   Water pp.98–103
For Riding, see Horse
   p.57
For Trampoline, see
   Jumping p.254

Sports

Football

Football is a competitive game of skill and teamwork, which represents how we identify with a group of people or connect with this group. If you dream of being in a football team, take note of your relationship with other players. Are you part of the team or are you a star? Perhaps you are sitting on the bench waiting to be called, or you are being 'kicked around'. Identifying your role will shed light on how you relate to people around you.

Goal

Scoring a goal suggests success, but missing a goal means that you need to work harder on your skills in order to score.

Karate

To dream of this martial art suggests that your aggressive impulses are well in control, and able to be expressed without hurting others.

Fishing

Consider why this dream appears at this stage in your life. Perhaps you are looking deeper—'fishing around'—for something? Catching a fish may indicate that you will achieve success—'a big catch'. Alternatively, you may be feeling as if you are living in a fish bowl, open to criticism for all to see. Perhaps you are 'a big fish in a small pond' and you need to expand your horizons. 'A cold fish' is unfeeling and something that 'smells fishy' suggests that not everything is as it seems. Pay attention to the fish in your dream and monitor your reactions to this symbol.

Diving

Often this dream suggests the need to take some radical action or make a new departure. It can be a way for your subconscious to prepare you to 'take the plunge' into something new.

Exercise

The purpose of exercise is to become fit, so if you are managing to do this easily in a dream, it suggests that you are keeping on top of things. However, if you are struggling and are too tired to complete your exercise routine, it may be time to slow down and reassess your priorities so that you overcome obstacles in yout way.

Football

Fishing/Fish

Goal

Diving

Karate

Diving

Exercise

Archery

Archery

A quiver has significance in archery, as the pouch in which arrows are stored. In this context it stands for our 'armoury' or the resources we have available to help us aim for our goals. If you dream of an archery quiver, take note of how full or empty it is. Quivering can also be a symptom of being cold, or a response to fear or excitement. In either case, it signals a state of physical or emotional vulnerability. Perhaps some situation in your waking life has left you 'a-quiver'. In this case the dream may be drawing your attention to your heightened emotions or, if these emotions are something you are trying to downplay in your waking life, encouraging you to adopt a more emotionally receptive state.

Cross-reference

For Football, see
    Toys & games
    pp.398–401, Ball
    p.398
For Fishing, see Fish
    p.53

Losing & looking

Loss/Losing

The loss of something in your dream could be a reflection of what you actually believe yourself to have lost in your waking life. It may be a loss of spark (such as a lack of vitality or motivation), loss of health or loss of a partner. To have suffered such a loss and dream of it may mean that you have also lost part of yourself and need to find a way to cope with the grief you are now suffering. To lose an object in your dream means that you are not in tune with what's going on and you've 'lost the plot'. The dream may be suggesting that you need to be more in touch with people around you and to communicate clearly. If you choose to take the dream literally, make sure that you label your possessions, especially if you are travelling.

Absence

Dreams in which something is 'absent' suggest that there is a 'missing' element from the picture that prevents it from being whole. For example, if you are placed in a room that has no door, this can signify that there is 'no way out' of a situation, whereas an absent window may indicate a need for more 'openness' in a situation. These types of dreams can also have contradictory meanings. For example, if you dream that an absent friend dies, it means that a wedding is imminent, while if you are happy over the absence of friends, it means that you will soon be rid of people who are causing the problems in your life.

Reflection

Seeing a reflection of ourselves represents our self-image. If you catch a glimpse of your reflection and it's not the way you usually see yourself, it could be your subconscious pointing out other ways to see yourself or how others see you.

Searching

Searching for something or someone in a dream is about being on a quest or mission. What is it that you need to find to give your life more meaning? This dream also indicates a loss of some type. Perhaps you are looking for a lost part of yourself, such as your childhood, or you may be mourning the loss of someone in your life.

Looking

To look at something in a dream is to give your full attention. Being looked at by someone else implies seeing oneself from another's point of view. Looking out from windows or high places suggests ambitions (unfulfilled at this stage). Looking down on a person suggests being judgemental, whereas looking down on or into something indicates reflection.

Loss/Losing

Absence

Reflection

Searching

Looking

Being left behind

Vanishing

Disappearing

Being left behind

Dreaming of being left behind is a sign that you feel rejected and inadequate in some way. If you leave something or someone behind, it may be referring to the past—leaving the past, people or situations behind as you move forward to a new stage in your life.

Vanishing

If you dream of something or someone vanishing in your dreams, you should consider what opportunities you may have lost or whether there are people in your life who are no longer there.

Disappearing

A dream in which people disappear before your eyes highlights your insecurities, in particular your fears that people or situations are at risk of disappearing from your life. This dream suggests there is a lack of confidence or self-esteem on the dreamer's part.

Cross-reference

For Reflection, see Mirror p.372
For Looking, see Windows p.324
For Vanishing, see Invisibility p.142

193

Losing & looking

Following/Being followed

If you dream of following someone it means that a habit or an attitude is leading you. Perhaps you are pursuing something that will give you a stronger sense of identity. This might be a worthy cause, an ideal or an organisation. This dream may also be questioning whether you prefer to be a 'follower' or to take a more of a leadership role, particularly at work. Following an animal suggests that your basic drives or instincts are leading you forward. If you dream of being followed, then you need to work out whether the dream is positive or negative. If it is a positive experience, the dream is assuring you that you have initiative and all you need to do is put it into practice. If the experience is negative and you feel 'stalked' in the dream rather than just followed, then you need to deal with past fears, memories or guilt that are still pursuing you. Try to put them 'behind you'.

Quest

The quest is one of the chief archetypal symbols of the life journey. While a dream quest can take many forms, they all tend to relate to the dreamer's need to progress. In this context the obstacles and difficulties facing you in your dream quest will help you to interpret the fears that hold you back in your waking life.

Hunting/Hunted

The figure of the hunter stands for our aggressive, go-getting tendencies, whether in romance (where it is likely to suggest that we are taking an active, pursuing role) or in our working life. This dream could be telling you that you need to take a more aggressive approach to getting what you want.

Hiding

It is common to dream either that you are hiding yourself or something else. If it is you, or the person that corresponds to you in the dream, who is trying to hide, the dream may be suggesting your desire to protect yourself from something or somebody. This could be a threatening situation or negative person, or even some aspect of your own personality you don't want to face up to. If in the dream you are hiding an object, the nature of this object will help you to interpret what it is you would rather not face up to, or what it is you wish to protect from others.

Finding

A dream of finding something can be telling you either that you have lost something in the first place or that you have 'discovered' or 'realised' something about yourself or your life that will change your perspective. It is a positive dream, because it helps you to become aware of some aspect of yourself that you hadn't acknowledged before and which can now be of use to you.

Watching

If you are conscious of watching something closely in a dream, it suggests that something in your life requires vigilance. Perhaps you are suspicious about the motives and goodwill of someone close to you. Alternatively, you may need to pay more attention to your own actions and motivations.

Following/Being followed

Hunting/Hunted

Quest

Hiding

Finding

Watching

Being lost

Being lost

Being lost means that you are feeling confusion, are lacking in direction and are unable to make clear decisions. If you are lost in an alien environment, it implies that you are feeling out of depth in a new situation in your life, whether it is work related or personal. If you are feeling lost in a familiar surrounding, it could be that you are suffering from a bout of insecurity and are feeling overwhelmed. Slow down and don't act until you get your bearings right. Pay attention to anyone who comes along and offers assistance. It may help you to get back on track.

Cross-reference

For Following/Being followed, see Chased p.197
For Quest, see Journey p.275

Danger

Accident

Interpretation of an accident dream varies according to the surroundings and circumstances of the dream. One interpretation views the dream as a premonition of an actual accident threatening the dreamer, so it may be a good idea to avoid any type of travel for a short while. Accident dreams in different settings such as at sea, on land or in a car suggest disappointments in your love affairs and concerns in your personal and business ventures. They also warn of unexpected circumstances that can be accompanied by deep feelings of anxiety and insecurity. Dreams about accidents may also be drawing attention to issues such as safety and the need to take extra care in your daily life.

Danger

The danger threatening you in your dream tends to represent, in an exaggerated or symbolic way, the problems you feel confronted by in your everyday life. In general, dreaming that you are in a dangerous situation suggests insecurity in some aspect of your waking life. Interpreting the danger symbolically rather than literally will help you to understand this dream. If the dreamer faces the danger, then problems in waking life will not be so confronting.

Buried alive

The dream of being buried alive is one of the most terrifying dreams we can experience. However, this dream can be positive if, by indicating that you feel trapped or that others are disregarding your needs, it prompts you to take action. If you are observing someone else's burial, the dream may indicate your relief that a worrying issue or matter has been successfully laid to rest.

Suffocating

Suffocating in a dream is an indication that we feel overwhelmed by external forces. As a result, this dream makes us aware of our lack of control in our environment. If someone is suffocating us, it suggests that we are being emotionally pressured by their demands, and this may include an overdose of love and possessiveness.

Because suffocating implies an absence of oxygen, this dream may also indicate that we feel restricted and unable to 'live' our own lives. If you are feeling pressured and life is no longer fun, think why you are experiencing this dream. You may also want to get your health checked, as the dream could be alerting you to a physical problem.

Accident

Buried alive

Danger

Suffocating

Chased

Betrayal

Chased

Dream chases are typically both vivid and frightening, making it a relief to wake up. If you have a dream of being chased, it may pay to think about what you are afraid of in your waking life. Pay attention to who or what was chasing you, whether you were caught, and how the dream ended. These details can help you to unlock the meaning of this dream. Don't forget that the 'pursuer' can be a part of your own psyche, and not just an external person or persons.

Betrayal

Dreams of betrayal suggest a fear of being disappointed by a thing or person. Perhaps you are worrying about a purchase or decision you have made. The dream may also be warning you that you have misgivings about a friend, associate or family member, or that you need to think about the advice others are giving you.

Cross-reference

For Buried alive, see Tomb p.342, Coffin and Funeral p.208
For Chased, see Following/Being followed p.194

197

Danger

Sinking

Sinking reflects the dreamer's feelings of desperation and loss of confidence. If you are sinking in water, it suggests that you feel overwhelmed by some emotional issue. You have to decide to 'sink or swim' in this situation. Sinking in sand is associated with feelings of insecurity (a lack of solid ground beneath). This dream could be warning you to beware of sinking funds into some project or scheme. Seeing someone else sink can make us aware of a problem that requires us to take action.

Drowning

This frightening dream usually symbolises your anxiety about being out of control in some aspect of your life. For example, it can represent your fear of being overwhelmed by powerful emotions that you have not yet managed to integrate into your waking life, or suggest that you feel inadequate to cope with a stressful social situation.

Abandonment

Being abandoned in a dream suggests that you are experiencing feelings of being unloved, unwanted and emotionally isolated to the point where you have difficulty focusing on any future success in your life. If you abandon others in a dream it indicates your anxiety about overcoming difficult conditions involving other people and situations. Trouble and quarrels, loss of money and loss of friends are all associated with abandonment dreams.

However, abandonment dreams can also be seen as expressing a need to 'let go' of people, tensions and conditions that have been causing you grief, or confining you to a negative perspective. It may be worth your while trying to view abandonment dreams as a sign of release and your need to move forward in a more positive manner.

Trapped

Being caught in a trap represents the inability to break free of old attitudes, habits and outside influences. We feel trapped because we are afraid to move on. It may be that we feel trapped at work because of a loss of opportunities or that we are trapped in an unhappy relationship. Whatever the situation, it is our fears that keep us in the trapped state. If you are having this dream regularly, you may need to seek outside help to get you out of your predicament. A trap door, on the other hand, often leads to a mysterious or secret place where we want to hide ourselves when we are faced with a perceived danger.

Sinking

Drowning

Abandonment

Trapped

Starving

Starving

If you dream of starvation it may be a sign that you are ignoring your needs or not taking care of yourself. The starvation in your dream stands for a lack of something that is vital for your life and suggests that your body is being denied necessary nourishment. In medical conditions such as anorexia, the mind prevents the body from feeding itself, by holding onto a distorted image of that body. If you dream of starving, think about what you may be denying yourself, and why. There may be other options than neglect and punishment, which would help you overcome your anxious state.

Cross-reference

For Trapped, see
    Cage/Cell p.331
For Drowning, see
    Water pp.98–103
For Starving, see
    Hunger p.359

199

Danger

Escape

As the word suggests, escape reflects our need for freedom and release and, depending on the context of the dream, it may be telling you that you are avoiding facing difficult issues/decisions and therefore 'escapism' here may be a better term. If something is threatening you or burdening you with responsibility, this may also result in a dream of escaping.

Disaster

Generally, the disasters in our dreams are exaggerated representations of everyday worries. Often the dreamer will be solving or overcoming problems in the dream to keep safe, which tells the dreamer they do have the strength and knowledge to overcome just about anything. Interpreting the disaster symbolically rather than literally can help you to come to terms with these anxieties and reduce them to their proper size.

Kidnap

Kidnapping symbolises loss of control and dependency. This dream, therefore, expresses insecurity, especially your fear that sudden changes may be about to occur in your life. The dream may also represent your fear that something precious to you is at risk of being lost or taken away from you, whether that thing is a relationship, a talent or an occupation.

Captivity

Not surprisingly, captivity dreams express our fears and feelings of being trapped. The nature of your prison in the dream will help you to interpret the matter or the circumstances that are holding you back. If you succeed in breaking out of your dream prison, it is a sign that these obstacles can be successfully overcome.

Being strangled

Dreaming of being strangled suggests that you feel stifled. Your emotions and self-expression are probably being suppressed or 'killed off'. Because we are generally conscious while being strangled in a dream, the dream is a wake-up call that is telling the more assertive part of ourselves not to let this activity go on for too long. Normally this dream makes us feel so uncomfortable that we push away our attacker or wake up.

Abduction

Dreaming of abduction can have different meanings depending on the position and circumstances of the events surrounding the dreamer. If you are the abductor, the dream suggests that you have a desire for control and power over a person or situation. If you dream that you are being abducted, this shows that you are not in control of circumstances surrounding your life and that you feel yourself being carried away by the enormity of it all. Dreaming of being abducted also reveals that you could be experiencing trouble and unrest in present relationships and situations in your life. It suggests that others are calling the shots and that this is leaving you vulnerable to their actions.

Escape

Disaster

Kidnap

Captivity

Being strangled

Abduction

Explosion

Explosion

When we say that we're about to explode, we really mean that we are overwhelmed by anger and that it needs to escape. An explosion in a dream is a release of energy or burst of emotion—usually reaching this stage because it has been bottled up and self-expression denied. It is also symbolic of pent-up sexual energy, resulting in orgasm.

Cross-reference

For Explosion, see
   Bomb p.375,
   Dynamite p.416
For Captivity, see
   Prison p.226,
   Chains p.206,
   Dungeon p.225

201

Events & celebrations

Party

A party in a dream is associated with our feelings about the ways that we relate socially to others. It also relates to how we are able to relax and enjoy ourselves. As in waking life, parties in dreams can be a source both of pleasure (if we are 'the life and soul of the party') and anxiety (if we feel uninvolved, ignored or nervous about our social skills). This dream could be helping you to assess the way you feel about being around large groups of people. It could also be enabling you to relieve any fears you have about demanding social situations.

Festival

A festival symbolises both celebration and tradition. Depending on the context of the dream and whether you are enjoying the feasting, it can be interpreted as giving you permission to enjoy life more, join in with a wider social group, or share good spirits and fun.

Invitation

An invitation in a dream may symbolise a new opportunity in your waking life. How you respond to the dream invitation may help you to interpret your feelings about taking up an offer, or beginning a new project. Alternatively, dreaming of an invitation may signal your desire for a social or work opportunity to become available to you.

Mardi Gras

Dreaming of being in a Mardi Gras parade or watching one represents celebration, fun and exhibitionism. Are these qualities lacking in some areas of your life or personality? Traditionally, Mardi Gras is also an exaggeration of the unusual or a celebration of the grotesque or abnormal. In a dream it can suggest there is some part of the dreamer's personality that he or she would like to expose but is frightened to do so, for fear that it will be considered abnormal or deviant.

Parade

If you dream that you are 'on parade', it could be a sign that you feel anxious about having to present yourself in your best light or take on a public role. It could also suggest that you have been 'parading about': overexposing or boasting about yourself to others. If you are watching a parade from the sidelines, it is possible that you feel shunted to the side or that you are not allowed a big enough role in a current activity or relationship.

Party

Festival

Invitation

Mardi Gras

Parade

Cross-reference

For Party, see Friends p.281

203

Events & celebrations

Fireworks

Because fireworks are associated with festivities and celebrations, they suggest that the dreamer will soon be celebrating some good fortune. The explosive nature of the fireworks, as well as their dazzling display, indicates that whatever we are about to celebrate in our lives will be a little overwhelming and spectacular. The success may belong to someone you know, in which case you will share in the excitement by being a spectator.

Birthday

Dreaming about a birthday is likely to suggest pleasure, shared celebration and a sense that you feel appreciated. If the dream is anxious, however, it may be a sign that you worry about ageing and the passage of time. If you are being given gifts in a dream, your response to the gift may provide clues to how you feel about your friends. Dreaming of someone else's birthday could be a sign that you feel undervalued or forced to give your attention to others.

Rituals

Baptism

Baptism suggests that you want the blessing of someone around you on a new project or activity. It may also suggest your desire for a new beginning or that you want recognition from your superiors of some special talent or property that you possess. In general, this is a positive dream that suggests you should move forward with confidence. It can also represent a cleansing or rebirth, being relieved of past transgressions, unhindered by the past.

Canopy

This ancient form of covering suggests mystery, formality and power. Perhaps a sign that, for better or worse, you are currently surrounded or protected by traditional, ritual forms of behaviour. Usually a canopy is part of a celebratory ritual. Therefore, it is a good sign that there will be something to celebrate or that the dreamer will overcome current problems.

Fireworks

Birthday

Baptism

Canopy

Cross-reference

For Birthday, see Gifts
    & giving p.394
For Baptism, see
    Religion p.148,
    Baby p.295

Restrictions

Chains

Like cages or prisons, these are symbols of the forces that prevent us from making the progress we aspire to.

Quagmire

If you dream of a quagmire it is more than likely that you feel seriously 'bogged down'. Perhaps you are stuck in a rut, and need an injection of energy or new ideas to get yourself moving again. This dream could apply to a relationship, an activity or a business.

Hanging

If you are hanging from something in a dream, it may be a sign that some issue in your life is suspended or lacking a conclusion. If in your dream you are trying to hang something up, however, you may be reflecting your wish to put order into your life by trying to keep things in their place. If you are hanging the object high up, it could be sign of your insecurity about keeping something you possess that you believe others want. If you are hanging something upside down though you may be longing for a complete change in your life.

Obstacle

Obstacles in dreams take many forms, all of which represent our anxieties and the things that prevent us making as much progress in life as we would like to. Paying attention to the nature of the obstacle in your dream, and the way you are overcoming it, can help you to diagnose the obstacles in your waking life and assess how well you are coping with them.

Barriers

Dream barriers tend to symbolise our frustrations or the obstacles in the way of our progress, whether these come mainly from others, or ourselves. If you are struggling to cross a barrier in your dream, it suggests that your current situation requires effort and struggle. It may also suggest that you need to stop what you are doing and consider taking a different route towards your goals.

Tangle

Being tangled in a dream indicates confusion. Possibly one object is tangled with another and you need to untangle it before you can make use of it. Take note of how you eventually get the object untangled, as this will show you how well you will succeed in undoing a difficult situation in real life. Tangled hair is a symbol of the image you portray to others. If ties are being tangled in your dream, the dream is about relationship ties and the difficulties you may be facing in this area of your life.

Chains
Quagmire
Hanging
Obstacle
Barriers
Tangle

Cross-reference

For Chains, see Prison p.226, Captivity p.200
For Quagmire, see Marsh/Swamp p.96
For Tangle, see Entwining p.162

207

Death

Coffin

An empty coffin can signify grief at the loss of a friendship, whether through death or some other cause. If sadness and anxiety accompany this dream, it suggests the need for you to work hard if you want to preserve a relationship that is on the verge of 'dying'. If your feelings are more detached or positive, it is a sign that you are ready to lay a matter or relationship to rest. This type of dream also denotes fear of failure.

Funeral

Because a funeral is an acknowledgement of death, dreaming of attending one is a sign of our need to accept death or an ending of some kind. It may be a loss of part of your life, your beliefs, or your relationship that you need to come to terms with in order to move on. A funeral allows mourning to take place, and this is a healthy response to a painful loss. If you dream of the funeral of a parent, it may suggest that you are cutting the umbilical cord and becoming independent. Dreaming of your own funeral is a common dream that symbolises a feeling of 'deadness' in your life and a wish to make the most of life while you still have it. It also indicates leaving the old self behind. Dreaming of someone else's funeral may be a sign that you wish that they were dead—a reflection of a fantasy that you engage with during your waking hours.

The Grim Reaper

If you hold to the belief that you 'reap what you sow', this dream is indicating that you need to work hard to get the results you want. On a more negative side, the 'grim reaper' is the image of death that is pictured with a scythe ready to reap in the dead. Don't take it literally. Death in this instance is symbolic of the things in your life that you no longer need but which you still are holding onto.

Coffin

Funeral

The Grim Reaper

Wake

Obituary

Wake

A wake is the part of a funeral that allows the mourners to release their emotions. This dream is likely to occur at a period of transition in your life, when you are being forced to give up something in order to move forward. Like a real wake, a dream wake emphasises the need to let go and to accept change.

Obituary

If you dream of reading someone else's obituary it is a sign that you are concerned about your relationship with them. If you are reading your own, the dream suggests your need to reflect on your life and achievements to date. Think about what you'd like others to say about you in your obituary. It may give you a better idea about the direction that you wish to take in life.

Cross-reference

See also Wreath p.220
See also Murder
    p.222, Killing
    p.230
See also Tomb p.342,
    Cemetery p.343

Marriage

Marriage/Wedding

Couples sometimes refer to each other as their 'better' or 'other half'. This indicates a union that brings about a wholeness or completeness. Dreaming of a marriage or wedding can represent the two aspects of yourself—such as the practical and spiritual, rational and emotional—and suggest how uniting these aspects would bring into existence new abilities and insights. Dreaming of a wedding dress suggests how you are feeling about your own marriage or relationship. If you are feeling negative or anxious about the relationship, your emotions in the dream sequence will indicate confusion, anxiety or illness.

Engagement

An engagement is a promise that you intend to honour—whether it is a business engagement or a relationship. Dreaming of an engagement—either broken or kept—most likely suggests that you have doubts about fully committing and are looking for some signs of reassurance.

Confetti

A symbol of celebration and, therefore, of happiness, confetti can also suggest awareness of short-lived pleasures and the fear or risk of being discarded.

Bridesmaid

If you dream of being a bridesmaid, it may suggest that you're jealous of someone who's getting more attention than you are. But if you feel comfortable in the dream, it could be a sign that you're happy to take a supporting or background role in some activity or venture.

Bride/Bridegroom

In general, dreaming of a bride or bridegroom suggests your desire for harmony and union in some aspect of your life. If you are a woman and your dream contains a bridegroom, it may suggest that you need to listen to the 'masculine' side of your personality, and vice versa. If your current partner is the bride or bridegroom, and in the dream he or she is walking down the aisle with somebody else, then it's a sign that you have a real or imaginary rival, or that you don't trust your partner. Either way, the dream could be telling you to take a look at your relationship, and that you need to come to grips with your feelings of jealousy and insecurity.

Marriage/
Wedding

Engagement

Confetti

Bridesmaid

Bride/Bridegroom

Cross-reference

For Engagement, see Ring p.403

Marriage

Honeymoon

Because we often use the term 'honeymoon' or 'honeymoon stage' to refer to an initial period of infatuation or a stage at which things are going well, this dream tends to symbolise new beginnings, optimism or the desire to undertake a new and exciting project. It may also foretell the arrival of a pleasurable or unexpected event.

Elopement

In ancient interpretations, dreaming of elopement was generally considered to be a bad omen because it indicated a clandestine union—one that was not approved of by family or society. Is there some kind of partnership—business or personal—that needs to be kept secret? Perhaps the dreamer wants to escape to a more romantic or exciting state that involves a union or partnership of some sort. Depending on the context of the dream, it could mean that you are running away from your predictable situation to one that is more exciting.

Wedding ring

The shape of the wedding ring associates it with the idea of eternity, and an encircling love. Dreaming that you give or receive a wedding ring may symbolise your desire for these things. More generally, this dream may represent the making of any kind of commitment or vow.

Jilting

Dreaming of being jilted suggests insecurity or change in your emotional life. If you are jilting someone in your dream, the dream probably suggests either guilt over treating someone inconsiderately, or a desire for more freedom in your life.

Divorce

This dream is not necessarily a dream about relationships, but about any division or split in your life. It may signal your need to escape from a particular situation or emotion that is no longer beneficial to you. If may also signify anxiety about money.

Honeymoon

Elopement

Wedding ring

Jilting

Divorce

Cross-reference

For Honeymoon, see Holiday p.214
For Wedding ring, see Ring p.403

Holidays

Packing

A dream in which you are packing a bag or suitcase can have several meanings. At the most basic level, this activity suggests a desire to put order into your life, perhaps even to perform some kind of stock-take of your 'possessions' or talents. But because packing is something we tend to do before taking a trip, this dream also suggests preparation for the next stage of your life journey. This dream may signal your desire for independence. It may also be prompting you to think about the things that are most necessary to you in life. If you are being forced to pack in a hurry, it suggests that you are not quite ready for change. If you are having trouble fitting everything into your suitcase, you may be having trouble deciding on your priorities. To 'send someone packing' suggests the desire to remove them from our lives, while 'packing one's bags' can be a metaphor for moving on from a bad situation.

Holiday

Dreaming of a holiday suggests our desire to slow down, relax, or take time out for ourselves. If the dreamer is feeling overworked or harassed, this is likely to be a compensatory dream that offers in imaginary form the relief that is not available in his or her waking life. Or, the dream could simply be telling you that you are too focused on a single issue or problem, and need to give yourself a break or cultivate more variety in your life.

Trunk

According to traditional dream interpretations, a full trunk denotes that you are careful with investments and make the best use of your resources, while an empty one reveals that you have been extravagant and have no reserves for difficult times ahead.

Tourist

To be a tourist in a dream is to see things from an outsider's point of view, or with a fresh perspective. It may also indicate that the dreamer feels unfamiliar with his or her new surroundings. If you are helping a tourist in the dream, it suggests that you will need to explain yourself more clearly and be of greater help to others in your working environment.

Luggage

Are you carrying any emotional baggage, that is, emotions and beliefs that you won't or can't get rid of? Luggage is a symbol of the things we take with us that we feel we need, despite the fact that we don't actually use everything we take. If you have been feeling the need to unburden yourself, the dream may be prompting you to travel light and only take what you need with you. Perhaps you need to leave your excess luggage behind in order to make progress in your waking life.

Packing

Holiday

Trunk

Tourist

Luggage

Passport

Passport

A passport is the proof of your identity. It is also the document that gives you entry into different places. As a result, dreaming of a passport may signal doubts or anxieties about 'who you really are'. It may also represent a desire to travel or to gain entrance to something. This doesn't have to be literal but may represent any aspect of the life journey (such as 'social mobility'), in which case the document in your dream may stand for those things or qualities that offer you a 'passport' to a different or better life.

Cross-reference

For Luggage, see Knapsack p.276
See also Travel p.274

Financial matters

Money

Money plays a very important part in our lives as it creates the conditions for our well-being. However, dreaming of money does not refer to the actual money in our lives, but to what we value. Time, energy and love are three things that are valuable to all of us and making sure you have enough of any is a concern. If you dream of holding onto money, you may be 'tight' or feeling emotionally insecure. Not having enough money makes us feel inadequate. It can also indicate a feeling of sexual impotency. Stolen or counterfeit money represents the belief on our part that we are being taken for granted and that we feel cheated in some way. Money also stands for power and our potential for success. Generally, this dream is asking the dreamer to pay attention to his or her values and to reassess them on a regular basis. Money also has to do with cost. What do your actions, which derive from your values, cost you?

Accounts

'Accounting' dreams are a warning that you stand to lose your money if you are too free in giving credit to the wrong people or institutions. If the accounts balance, then it is a good indication that a profitable venture is coming your way. Psychologically, it can also imply that you are 'accountable' for your actions. Do you need to 'pay back' a favour or repay someone with kindness? Working on accounts can also mean you are avoiding the work needed to solve financial problems.

Poverty

Dreaming of poverty doesn't necessarily symbolise money worries. It can also suggest that you feel emotionally or spiritually 'impoverished'. Perhaps a relationship is failing to provide you with the emotional sustenance you need. Poverty is more indicative of emotional deprivation in waking life. The dreamer is feeling lonely and perhaps a little bit of a failure. It's a warning that you need to reach out and talk about your feelings.

Purse

Traditionally, the purse is a symbol of femininity. Thus, if a woman dreams of a purse it may represent her feelings about some aspect of her sexuality. More generally a purse can also stand for the things that are valuable to us, such as money or relationships. Losing or mislaying a purse may suggest a fear of loss in these areas, while the action of putting something in a purse symbolises your desire to protect or secure something.

Income

Dreams about our income in whatever form (e.g. wages, tax) symbolise the things that sustain our day-to-day life. For example, if you dream of a pay rise, it could be a sign that your self-confidence has grown and that you want others to appreciate your value. Equally, to dream of a drop in income may suggest emotional neediness or insecurity. To dream of paying or calculating tax can suggest not only money worries, but also a sense of obligation to others.

Money

Accounts

Poverty

Purse

Income

Coin

Coin

Finding a coin in a dream symbolises good luck and foretells a boost in your confidence and self-esteem. But if you are looking for a lost coin, the dream signals a lack of confidence in yourself or another.

Cross-reference

For Income, see Work p.246

Financial matters

Tax

Taxes are associated with paying one's dues. Most of us regard taxes as a penalty fee for our standard of living or chosen lifestyles. Dreaming of a tax can suggest that you are feeling 'taxed' and unwilling to give a great deal of yourself to others. Perhaps you feel as if you are already giving enough and don't need to hand out more of your emotions and time.

Wealth

This dream probably symbolises a desire on your part to improve your status or living standards. The wealth in your dream, however, can also stand for any of the resources that are available to you. In traditional gypsy lore, a dream of wealth was believed to forecast sickness or even death. Dreaming of wealth can also be like a money dream—a feel-good dream—particularly if the dreamer is under financial stress in waking life. Often the subconscious mind will give the dreamer a means of escape through dreams.

Wages

If you dream that you are being underpaid, it is a sign that you feel underappreciated; while a dream of being overpaid suggests that you may be experiencing guilt about failing to act, or not doing enough in a given situation.

Wallet

A wallet can symbolise any aspect of our resources, not only financial, but also emotional, sexual or intellectual. To dream of losing your wallet suggests that you may have a concern with inadequacy in one of these areas. To dream of finding one suggests your desire for a windfall or piece of good luck.

Will

A will represents your intentions. This dream could be prompting you to order your priorities or decide on a course of action. Wills are also associated with death, so this dream could also be suggesting that you are about to enter into a new phase of your life. Because wills commonly make provisions for your relatives or offspring, dreaming of one may also reflect your concerns about looking after those close to you, such as children. It is common to have a dream about wills when we are about to take a long trip overseas and are leaving family behind.

Debt

Dreaming about debt may reflect financial worry at work or home. If you dream that you are in debt, it may suggest that you have been failing to return the love or attention of someone close to you. The symbolic meaning is that you owe somebody something and the time has come to pay. The debt is not necessarily associated just with emotions.

Tax

Wealth

Wages

Wallet

Will

Debt

Rent

Rent

Dreaming of paying rent represents paying for what we want in waking life. In other words, we pay our dues or our personal responsibilities. Collecting rent, however, is about what we are getting from others.

Cross-reference

For Will, see Death pp.208–9

Fame & fortune

Success

Dreaming of success is usually wishful thinking. It is a compensatory dream in which we try to make up for our feelings of failure and the lack of importance we feel in waking life.

Fame

Dreaming of being famous suggests your wish to be recognised for your talents. It may suggest that you need to give yourself credit for your own abilities rather than wait for others to acknowledge you. Once you realise your own potential, you will be able to stand out above the rest. If, however, you dream of others being famous, you may have an unfulfilled desire to be like them. On the other hand, you may be afraid of exposure and prefer to remain quietly in the background.

Wreath

Traditionally, wreaths were symbols of triumph and were bestowed on emperors or successful athletes. Today we are more likely to associate wreaths with funerals. The wreath in your dream may refer to the ending of a relationship or episode in your life, but it may also suggest a tribute. The expression 'being wreathed in smiles' plays on this association of the wreath with abundance or plenty.

Luck

If you dream of taking part in a raffle, you probably feel that it's time for luck to come your way. However, like gambling, it still involves a risk. In traditional gypsy folklore, a raffle was regarded as an indication of uncertainty.

Applause

Have you achieved something lately and now want to be recognised for it? This is a wish-fulfilment dream. But make sure that you are not being vain, but genuinely wish to be appreciated or given approval.

Success

Fame

Wreath

Luck

Applause

Treasure

Treasure

Finding treasure in a dream stands for the discovery of something of value to you, usually a precious part of yourself of which you had not previously been aware. This may be a quality such as the ability to love, create and forgive, or other similar attributes. If the treasure is difficult to reach, it suggests that your highest goals are not easy to attain and that you will be able to appreciate their value only by going through trials and setbacks. A treasure that is being stolen suggests that we don't feel worthy of owning what we consider greatly desirable.

Cross-reference

For Wreath, see
    Funeral p.208
For Luck, see
    Gambling p.185
For Treasure, see
    Jewellery/Jewels
    p.402

221

Crime & criminals

Murder

To dream of murdering someone is an expression of how you feel about someone or something in waking life. You want to get rid of the object or person so that you can be happy or have more control over your future. Try to work out what the person or object represents to you. It could well be that it's part of your own personality that you want to 'murder' or values represented by other people in your life such as bosses, co-workers, a partner or children. If you are murdered in the dream, it means that you feel as if you are being destroyed by some external force which is well beyond your control.

Mafia

The Mafia, as portrayed by the media, is a symbol of family honour, organised crime, secrecy and corruption. Consider whether it is really these qualities that the dream is attempting to convey to you and what role they play in your personal life. Are you lacking in close family ties? Are you carrying some kind of moral burden?

Stealing

In every culture stealing goods is an offence that results in some form of punishment. If you dream of stealing something, observe carefully what it is that you are taking. If you are 'needy' and are stealing to survive, you may feel justified in this behaviour. If, on the other hand, you are taking something without permission, it may be a sign that you feel undeserving and unloved and that this is the only way of getting what you want. If something has been stolen from you, it's possible that you feel cheated or not respected. You should also consider expressions such as 'steal someone's heart', 'steal the show' or 'steal someone's thunder'.

Thief

Thieving has to do with loss of property, whether of possessions or loved ones. The figure of a thief usually stands for the fear that something is being taken away from you. Thus, people speak of the death of loved ones in terms of their being 'snatched away'. One's heart can also be stolen and the thief may even be the part of ourselves that has stolen our youth, exuberance or beliefs.

Riot

To dream of witnessing a riot or being part of one denotes uncontrollable emotion in the dreamer. It may symbolise a need to overthrow oppression even if it means breaking laws in order to achieve a worthwhile aim. Consider what is causing you to feel this way in your life.

Murder/Murderer

Mafia

Stealing

Thief

Riot

Fraud

Outlaw

Trespasser/
Trespassing

Fraud

To dream that someone has cheated you indicates that you are too trusting of people and that you need to protect yourself better. If you are the one committing fraud, you should explore your reasons for feeling that you do not deserve to have things, so that you need to cheat to obtain them.

Outlaw

The outlaw in your dream probably represents the law-breaker in you—the reckless, rebellious or freedom-loving part of yourself that wants to throw off restrictions, whether they are legal, moral or social. This dream suggests that you want to reach the top, but don't want to go through all the red tape or legalities to get there.

Trespassing

Finding yourself in a situation in which you are a trespasser denotes that you are intruding and not respecting someone's privacy or boundaries. If someone is trespassing on your space in the dream, think about why you feel that your wishes aren't being considered.

Cross-reference

For Murder, see
    Killing p.230
For Fraud, see
    Legalities pp.228–9
For Outlaw, see
    Legalities pp.228–9
For Trespassing, see
    Barriers p.207

223

Punishment

Punishment

If you dream of being punished it is less likely to symbolise the desire of others to punish you, than your own self-critical or unforgiving attitudes towards yourself. Perhaps you are unable to live up to your own expectations. This dream may relate to a conflict or situation that dates from your childhood, a time when we often feel guilty or responsible for actions that may not be our fault.

Noose

Having a noose around one's neck is not the most comforting of dreams. It suggests a feeling of helplessness and vulnerability. It is also a dream of fear—fear of getting involved or 'hung up' on someone or something as well as trying to deal with repressed emotions.

Execution

'So, shoot me!' as the saying goes, may well apply to the execution dream. If you dream of your own execution, you may be experiencing a period of depression or low self-esteem. The execution imagery may well be representing self-pity or even self-punishment. If you see someone else being executed, the dream may be of a more judgemental nature. You may well be thinking that someone ought to be 'shot' or 'strung up' for their offensive action.

Guillotine

Do you feel that you are losing your mind? Or are you losing your head over someone? Despite the guillotine being a weapon used to execute people, we associate it more with the killing of our common sense. You may be cutting off a part of your personality. Do you feel irrational or impulsive?

Perhaps you have a desire to 'cut off' your head (rational thoughts) and make decisions based on the heart. The guillotine is also associated with revolution and passion. The dreamer may be acting out of haste to bring about drastic change. The warning is to use your head and not your heart to make decisions.

Handcuffs

These are powerful symbols of restraint, whether by our own self-doubt or negative qualities, or by a particular person or situation in your life. If you are trying to handcuff someone else in your dream, the dream suggests you have a possessive attitude towards somebody close to you. It may be a warning that your desire for intimacy has aggressive undertones and that you need to take a more relaxed approach.

Dungeon

A sign that you feel trapped or confined in an unrewarding situation, this dream may be telling you that you need to work on developing an escape plan if things are to improve. Jung believed that dreams about dungeons are associated with fears about getting in touch with the primal self.

Punishment

Noose

Execution

Guillotine

Handcuffs

Dungeon

Cross-reference

For Noose, see Rope p.413, Hanging p.206
For Dungeon, see Trapped p.199, Cage/Cell p.331

Punishment

Prison

The prison in your dream may stand for a situation you've created yourself. In this respect you can be both prisoner and jailer. This dream may be prompting you to think about any emotional traps you have created for yourself in your waking life, or patterns of behaviour that are preventing you from moving forward.

Jail

Like all images of confinement, being in jail symbolises the obstacles to our freedom. It may be the freedom to express yourself creatively, to move away from home, or to escape an emotional situation that has become imprisoning. This powerful dream could be a prompt to consider your feelings about your environment, and to think about how you might expand your horizons.

Jailer

If jails represent the obstacles to our freedom, the jailer is the figure who is at the source of these restrictions. He or she may stand not only for another person in your life, such as a parent or authority figure, but for your own inhibitions or negative attitudes. If the dreamer is the jailer then he or she creates their own obstacles in waking life.

Flogging

Any dream about punishment has to do with the dreamer's feelings of guilt. Do you think you deserve to be punished for some inadequacy or some action that you haven't been proud of? Perhaps you have a cruel taskmaster and you feel you are being driven beyond your limits? The taskmaster could represent you or someone in authority.

Prison

Jail

Jailer

Flogging

Banishment

Banishment

Being sent away from the company of others is one of the worst forms of punishment we can experience. Dreams of being banished usually draw on childhood experiences of ostracism or punishment. If you dream of being banished, it is likely that you are afraid of doing or having done something that will earn the disapproval of your friends or colleagues. However, it may also mean that you want time away from others because you are feeling socially under some pressure.

Cross-reference

For Prison, see Cage/
  Cell p.331, Trapped
  p.199
For Jail, see Cage/
  Cell p.331, Trapped
  p.199

Legalities

Warrant

Dreaming of a warrant symbolises a concern with issues of permission or legality. The meaning of the dream will depend on the type of warrant that appears in it. For example, if you are issued with a search warrant, it is likely that you need to examine your own or somebody else's motives more carefully. A warrant for arrest, on the other hand, suggests the need for either you or someone close to you to stop doing something that may be dangerous or possibly even illegal.

Jury

This dream symbolises issues of fairness and judgement. If a jury is judging you it could be a sign that you feel put under pressure by others, or that your actions are under scrutiny. If you are a member of the jury, the dream suggests that you are being required to make up your mind about a difficult issue.

Signature

Dreaming of signing your name on a document is an indication that you are about to make an agreement or have just made one. The signature also symbolises your desire to be recognised for your individuality, or to leave your mark on the world in some way.

Inquest

An inquest in a dream suggests the urge to investigate a past matter or emotion. Because inquests are associated with suspicious or mysterious events, this matter may be one that is associated with the dreamer's feelings of guilt or ambivalence. Either way, it suggests the desire to settle a matter once and for all, perhaps as the condition for putting it behind you and moving on.

Acquittal

To dream you are acquitted of a crime signifies that you are about to come into possession of valuable property and become wealthy. Others being acquitted will also experience prosperity in business. Guilty people being acquitted indicate a period of ups and downs in fortune.

Witness

Some situation in your life requires careful scrutiny. You may need to pay attention to the actions or motivations of those around you, or even your own. This dream also suggests that you may be required to give evidence of some kind or to testify before a 'higher authority', such as your conscience.

Contract

Dreaming of a contract or signing one suggests that you are having doubts or fears about a commitment in waking life. If you don't go through with the contract or agreement, it may be pointing out that you have a lot of hard work ahead of you. Are you concerned about taking a risk? It may also be that you don't trust people to keep their side of the bargain. Look to other symbols in the dream to interpret the meaning more fully.

Warrant

Jury

Signature

Inquest

Acquittal

Witness

Contract

Cross-reference

For Jury, see Judge
    p.286, Court p.326
For Signature, see
    Handwriting p.241
For Acquittal, see
    Crime & criminals
    pp.222–3

229

War, fighting & violence

Duel

Duelling is an activity that indicates conflict or competitiveness in a close personal or work relationship. But the duel is a very ritualised, formal kind of conflict, which may suggest that your aggression is either kept under control, or that you are playing according to the rules.

Massacre

Massacre is murder on a large scale. Dreaming of a massacre, whether you are a witness or take part in the killing, indicates a need for you to terminate or put an end to certain habits, values or attitudes that are no longer working for you.

Killing

The aggressive content of this dream could be a warning that you have been keeping your anger or resentment too hidden, and that it is doing you internal harm. This dream does not necessarily stand for aggressive impulses towards others. It may also symbolise your desire to eradicate some aspect of your own personality, in which case the dream could suggest that you have either low self-esteem or a negative attitude towards yourself or your life.

Suicide

Is something in your life ending abruptly? This could relate to a relationship problem or a work-related issue. Dreaming of suicide generally reflects the anger we feel towards ourselves. What parts of yourself are you trying to destroy? Perhaps you feel that you have little to live for in your life and that you and everyone else would be better off if you weren't around. In this case, the dream is an emotional plea from your subconscious to acknowledge that you can no longer cope with a particular situation on your own. If you see someone else committing suicide in your dream it could be that you wish this person would disappear from your waking life. Sometimes, however, the person in your dream can represent a quality in yourself that you wish were destroyed or overcome.

Torture

If you see someone being tortured in a dream, chances are that this represents past hurts and disappointments, usually emotional ones. Dreaming of being tortured suggests you are trying to come to some understanding about personal injury—be it pride or abandonment—that you haven't been able to forgive or forget.

Shooting

A gun is a symbol of aggression. Shooting someone means that you feel aggression towards some person or the part of yourself that this person represents. The gun also represents the male sexual organ and drive. If the weapon doesn't fire, the dreamer has feelings of sexual inadequacy. You may be using the gun to protect something that is of value to you. Killing someone may be a message that you have violent feelings towards this person and wish to eliminate him/her from your life.

Fighting

Depending on the dream, fighting tends to represent our need for independence and change. Dreaming of a physical fight is our subconscious way of dealing with anger, frustration and difficulty in expressing our feelings—whether the anger is aimed at ourselves or at others. Fighting also indicates defence—we fight for our values, our survival, our space, our health and our desire to win out against negative forces such as crime, pollution, injustice and people who attack us or our opinions. This is a dream of conflict that indicates the need for some sort of change. To dream of fighting may also suggest that you need to 'fight' more in your waking life for what you feel is rightfully yours.

Stab

A dream in which you are stabbed suggests that you are open to or 'wounded' by someone else's remarks or criticism. A 'stab in the back' is a betrayal, whereas a 'stab in the dark' is a wild guess. Generally, this dream indicates decisive action associated with some pain.

Duel

Killing

Suicide

Massacre

Torture

Shooting

Fighting

Stab

Cross-reference

For Killing, see
   Murder p.222
For Massacre, see
   Murder p.222
For Stab, see Knife
   p.393

War, fighting & violence

War

War symbolises any conflict, often including a loss of the ability to communicate. Dreaming of war may be an expression of feelings of anger you have tried to suppress ('fighting mad') or it may be a sign of an internal conflict ('at war with yourself'). Either way, the damage that is associated with war in real life suggests that you need to try and resolve conflicts before you or those around you get hurt.

Military

The military represents discipline, enforced regulations and obeying commands for the good of all. If you dream of being in the military, you may want to integrate some of these qualities in your own life situation in order to achieve a desired result.

Army

If you see a marching army it is a warning that a long journey is ahead of you, but with each victory there will be ultimate success. Fighting is an obstacle dream and it may be an expression of how you are feeling. If you see your life as a battle, it is a good idea to reassess what is making you feel this way. An army is often a symbol of discipline and obedience. Once again, you will need to think about where these qualities fit into your life.

Navy

To dream of being in the navy suggests your desire for organisation and structure in your life. Depending on what rank you see yourself or others, the dream reflects your status as you or others see it as well as your desire to improve on it. The navy also offers escape and travel. Is this what you are really longing for?

Battle

If you dream that you are involved in a battle or war it is likely to suggest that you are 'battling' difficulties, or striving to overcome opposing forces. Paying attention to the nature of your opponent in the battle may help you to identify what these forces are, so you can devise strategies for dealing with them.

Combat

We often feel as if life is a struggle, but the combat in your dream can show you how well you are dealing with contrary forces. You should take note of how evenly balanced the fight is, whether the enemy is overwhelming you, whether the fight is fair or unfair, and how well you manage to acquit yourself.

War

Military

Army

Navy

Battle

Combat

Soldiers

Soldiers

Dreaming of soldiers may express a need for discipline or a concern about a lack of it in your life. On a deeper level it may indicate an inner conflict as the dream highlights the ways in which we are at war with ourselves. If the dream is accompanied by negative emotions, however, it may be indicating that the dreamer's waking life has become too regimented and predictable.

Cross-reference

See also Conflict pp.178–9
See also Weapons p.374

Communicating

Loudspeaker

Hearing a loudspeaker suggests that there is something or someone trying to gain your attention. Is it going in one ear and out the other? What is it that you don't wish to hear, despite the loudness? Perhaps others aren't hearing you and your best way of communicating may be to be more assertive and outspoken.

Language

To dream that you are listening to a foreign or strange language and not understanding it denotes that you are finding it difficult to understand what someone around you is trying to communicate. This lack of communication may be affecting you in a relationship or at work. On a deeper level it may be your unconscious trying to communicate with you from within, speaking 'in tongues' in order to tell you something about yourself which you are not consciously able to understand.

Saying no

If you have difficulty in saying 'no' to people and their requests in your waking life, chances are you dream of giving this response to them in your dream. This dream reflects how you really feel. It is important that you take note of what you are saying 'no' to and apply it to your life situation.

Quip

A quip is a joking or clever remark, usually uttered 'off the cuff'. A dream in which one occurs can have several meanings. It may indicate that you feel vulnerable to being joked about or becoming a victim of the quick wit or insights of another. However, the quip in your dream may also stand for your own ability to provide insight on your behaviour or social situation. The dream could also be encouraging you to acknowledge your own wit or intelligence.

Question

If you have a dream in which you or someone else is asking a question, it is a sign that your subconscious is trying either to resolve an issue or acquire more information. This dream suggests doubt within some area of the dreamer's life. It may also indicate the desire for self-knowledge.

Sometimes our dreams can provide an answer to a problem in our waking lives. Because of this, some dream interpreters recommend that we think about an issue or problem before going to sleep, so that our subconscious is more likely to supply the answer in the form of a dream.

Talking

Generally, dreaming of talking denotes the dreamer's ability to communicate with others. Most of us dream of being unable to talk or not being understood by others. If you have difficulty speaking in your dream, it is an indication that you have built up emotions that you find difficult to express in speech. Speaking without being understood is frustrating both in dreams and real life. Sometimes the only sounds coming from the dreamer are babble. Do you have a communication problem? Are you frustrated that people aren't listening to you? Perhaps this dream is telling you to employ a new communication strategy. The dream may also indicate that you feel emotionally cut off from people around you.

Loudspeaker

Saying no

Quip

Language

Question

Talking

Cross-reference

For Language, see Foreign countries p.314, Abroad p.338

Communicating

Voices

Hearing voices in your dream, without knowing whom they belong to, can be frightening. In some cases, the voices may be representations of parts of yourself that you've discarded and which no longer sound familiar to you. The voice in your dream could also be your conscience—that little voice inside your head. Take note of what it is saying because it may be telling you what's best for you. To those who believe in the spirit world, the voices may be interpreted as belonging to a higher spiritual self or their spiritual guide. Trying to remember the words and tone of the voice will help you to understand your dream more fully.

Confession

If your dream finds you laying your soul bare, it could be a sign that you need to face up to something in your waking life. Alternatively, it could be an indication that you feel overly scrutinised or judged by others.

Fax/Fax machine

A fax machine is used for communication over distance. A dream of receiving or sending a fax stands for a message from a hidden part of ourselves that is coming into the a dream in a logical way—through modern communication equipment. This dream may also be a sign that we are trying to reach someone who is 'distanced' from us. Similarly, the fax machine may symbolise new ideas that the dreamer wishes to communicate to others.

Oath

Swearing an oath in a dream suggests that there is an issue of commitment or loyalty in your waking life. More generally this dream may suggest that you need to take something in your life more seriously.

Speaking on the telephone

We tell people to 'stay in touch' and 'keep in contact' and the most efficient and accessible way for most people to do this is by telephone. A dream in which you are calling someone up or answering the phone reflects your need to communicate and connect with others. Sometimes it can symbolise your desire to get in touch with various aspects of yourself. If you don't answer the telephone in your dream it suggests that you may not want to hear something. Is someone trying to get through to you? Calling an emergency number indicates that you need assistance with an emotional issue that is causing you stress or has placed you in a dilemma. If you recognise the number that you are calling, you may need to contact that person. Perhaps he or she has

been on your mind during your waking hours. Being unable to get through, either because the telephone line is out of order or because the number is busy, indicates your frustration with not being able to get your message across to someone in your waking life.

Voices

Fax/Fax machine

Oath

Confession

Speaking on the telephone

Cross-reference

For Confession, see Religion pp.146–8, Guilt p.159

Communicating

Vow

A vow is more of a spiritual agreement than a contract between two people. Perhaps you have made a vow to yourself about something that involves a stronger obligation than a mere promise. A promise can be broken without incurring the serious consequences that result when one breaks a vow such as a marriage or religious undertaking. If you dream of taking a vow, pay attention to what sort of vow it is. Does it involve others?

Yell

Sometimes our dreams frighten us so much that we wake ourselves up by shouting aloud. In this situation our shout is a response to the overwhelming emotions generated by the events of the dream. More generally, if you dream of yelling, or you hear someone else crying aloud in your dream, it symbolises the need to express powerful emotions and feelings.

Being dumb

Being unable to speak in a dream suggests your frustration that people aren't listening to what you have to say. This dream implies that you need to work on ways to get their attention, perhaps by rephrasing your concerns or presenting them in a more positive way.

Warning

A dream in which you are either giving or receiving a warning is a sign that something in your life is trying to get your attention. You may need to ask yourself whether something in your life spells danger, or whether an action you are about to undertake may hurt yourself or a person close to you. This dream may also be a warning to you to pay attention to a powerful emotion before it gets out of hand.

Antenna

Raising an antenna will mean better communication. The dream may be trying to tell you to listen more carefully to those around you so that you won't lose 'reception' with them, that is, that you will have an open channel of communication at all times.

Wailing

Traditionally, wailing is a way of releasing emotions at funerals and other emotionally painful occasions. If you have a dream involving wailing, it may be serving the same purpose. If you have been suffering from an emotion, grief or unhappiness that you have been unable to express, your dream may be trying to help you acknowledge the feeling and release it. The sound of wailing is also associated with sirens, and in this context hearing wailing in a dream can suggest your fear of an impending emergency or disaster.

Promise

A dream in which the making of a promise occurs is probably reminding you of an obligation you may have consciously forgotten—whether you owe something to another, or they are obliged to do something for you.

Advice

Receiving advice from someone in your dreams, particularly if it is from a wise old man or woman, is a sign that you need to listen to what others are telling you. You may also need to listen to yourself and your intuition.

Vow

Yell

Being dumb

Warning

Antenna

Wailing

Promise

Advice

Cross-reference

For Warning,
see Danger
pp.196–201
For Antenna, see
Satellite p.381
For Wailing, see
Crying/Weeping
p.160

239

Communicating

Letter

A dream of a letter is about communication, news, expression and reaching out. This also applies to e-mails. An unopened letter may represent the dreamer not listening to his or her intuition. Opening a letter suggests achievement, self-awareness and receiving news. If you receive a love letter, it may be wishful thinking, but it could also be a symbol of people's love for you. A bill in the mail indicates that whatever action we take will have to be paid for. If we are sending a letter or e-mailing, it could be a reflection of our need to communicate more clearly.

Writing

A dream in which you are writing symbolises communication—whether with others, or between the different parts of yourself. Perhaps there is a part of you that you are struggling to express to those around you. What the dreamer needs to communicate depends on the type of writing. Such a dream is often indicative of the dreamer's need to communicate the creative side of self in waking life. This dream can also represent your desire to order your thoughts, to make an impression on others, or to leave your mark in the form of a permanent record.

Books

Books can symbolise your accomplishments; the wisdom or success you have accumulated during your life. Reading books in a dream suggests a desire to find something out, to acquire knowledge, power or public recognition. Turning pages in a book could represent your desire to 'turn over a new leaf'. Looking for something in a book may also suggest that you are trying to remember or need to review an earlier event. Dreaming of books may also suggest your fear that some hidden aspect of yourself is about to be made known or 'published'.

Advertisements

If you see an advertisement billboard in your dream, take notice. You may need to pay attention to something you've been ignoring or treating poorly in your life. Be prepared for unexpected changes coming your way. Watching TV advertisements may suggest that you are prone to believing everything you hear and so there's a need for you to be more discerning. If you are aware of advertisements featuring in your dream it may be telling you that you'd like to be publicly acknowledged for something or that you need to sell yourself better in order to achieve the recognition you crave and deserve.

Handwriting

Because everybody's handwriting is unique, handwriting in a dream tends to symbolise individuality. If you are writing in your dream, it probably indicates your desire to express yourself creatively in some way. But if you are having trouble reading the handwriting, it could be a sign that you feel baffled by or unable to 'decipher' the personality of someone close to you.

Cross-reference

For Books, see Novels p.396, Reading p.187, Library, p.327
For Handwriting, see Signature p.228

Education

Education

Education is closely linked with knowledge, so dreaming of being back at school may be telling you to apply the knowledge you learned then to a present situation. It could also be telling you to upgrade your knowledge and skills to improve your lifestyle. To dream of a college or university education may indicate that you wish to pursue new knowledge that will eventually lead to a more fulfilling life. If it is a dream where you feel frustrated and uncomfortable in a learning environment, it may reflect your anxieties about being unable to conform to what is expected of you. This could be at home, work or in a social group such as a tennis or golf club where there are rules and regulations that you need to abide by.

School

Dreaming of school, most likely your old school, represents your learning and knowledge. Not only do we gain an education at school, however, but we also learn about group pressure, authority, social acceptance, competitiveness and all those things that shaped us as we were growing up. It is common to dream about school when you are about to undertake some type of new learning process. If you have this dream ask yourself whether you are preparing to embrace new attitudes, groups or knowledge.

High school

This dream tends to refer to our relationships with large groups of people, perhaps at work, or in a social context. Because it draws on memories of a time when we were younger and less independent, it can also suggest emotional immaturity, lack of confidence or a desire to impress others with our talents and achievements. This was also a time when we needed to fit into a group and when peer group pressure was at its highest. Perhaps you are experiencing these feelings in a real-life situation.

Tests

Dreaming of tests in general denotes an awareness of being judged by others. Tests represent a competition of abilities in which we are always measuring ourselves against others. A driving test is to do with issues of competence and skill. Any type of written test relates to problems with knowledge and problem solving. It may be that you are anxious about performing and that this anxiety or self-criticism is revealing itself in your sleep. If you dream of going for a medical test, the dream reflects a concern about your health. Have it checked out, just in case.

Study

To study is to focus on a certain subject with the aim of expanding your knowledge. Pay attention to what you are studying in your dream. The dream may be suggesting that you need to acquire a more in-depth understanding of an issue before you go ahead with a plan of action. If you have always longed to go back to study, this dream may be encouraging you to follow your desire (on the basis that it's never too late to learn).

Education

School

High school

Tests

Study

Cross-reference

For High school, see Groups of people pp.280–1
For Tests, see Driving p.264, Exams p.245

Education

Teacher

If you dream of a teacher who taught you in your school years, it may mean that something has resurfaced around the experience. Usually teachers are authority figures whom we are taught to respect. Did you clash with the teacher? Were your individuality and creativity repressed? Did the teacher embarrass you or expect you not to perform? These same fears may be revisiting you at a stage in your life when you are vulnerable and feeling more like a student than an authority figure. On the positive side, dreaming of being a teacher or being taught could be a sign that you are looking for more sophisticated knowledge and guidance on some issue.

Blackboard

Blackboards symbolise instruction: the desire to learn or remember something. They may also suggest that you are seeing the world too simplistically, in black and white. Or, you may feel anxious that something of value is in danger of being 'erased'. You may not be taking note of the lessons concerning you. Ask yourself what you have learnt.

University

As a university is a place of 'higher' learning, dreaming of being a student there highlights your need or desire for further education. You may be feeling stuck and bored with the limited knowledge available to you, in which case the university appears as a place where knowledge can be broadened and your potential for learning increased.

Exams

When you dream of being in an exam situation—usually unprepared, late or not being able to find the right room—you are having a typical anxiety dream. Self-worth, accomplishment worry and having to prove oneself are all issues that are cleverly disguised by the typical exam anxiety dream.

Teacher

Blackboard

University

Exams

Certificate

Lecture

Certificate

A dream in which you are given a certificate suggests your anxieties about your qualifications or confidence in performing a particular task. This dream may be trying to reassure you by giving you a positive message about your competence. If the certificate is illegible, however, or you have trouble unfolding or reading it, you may need to do more preparation before you can complete a task successfully.

Lecture

If you are giving a lecture in your dream it's likely that you wish to speak your mind on some issue that is close to your heart. If you are on the receiving end of a lecture, you may either pay attention and so gain knowledge, or feel reprimanded.

Cross-reference

For Exams, see Tests
  p.243
See also Children
  p.294
See also Youth p.303

Work

Work

Given the major part that work—or lack of it—plays in our lives, it's not surprising that it should appear in our dreams. Of course the work you find yourself doing in your dreams may be very different from your actual job. It's probably wise to interpret the meaning of this work symbolically, rather than trying to relate it to your actual occupation. For example, if you are working in a hospital in your dream, it may represent your concerns either with health or looking after others. Working in a kitchen might stand for a creative endeavour, while working in an office may signal 'official' activities.

Employment

We tend to associate the type of job we do with our self-worth and how we compare with our peers. Status is the desired result of being 'gainfully employed'. Dreams relating to employment can suggest a need for change, concern over performance of tasks or getting along with colleagues and staff. Depending on the context, dreaming of an employer indicates issues of independence, rebelliousness and proving yourself.

Interview

Like dreams of examinations, dreams of interviews tend to represent anxieties about being tested or made to perform. It is also common to dream of an interview before a real one is actually scheduled to take place. In this case the dream is ensuring that you are prepared for this event. This is true even when the dream is negative—in which case the dream is allowing you to express your worst fears, so you can go into the real situation with confidence and make the best of it.

Resigning

To resign is to give up. Whatever the reason, you need to work through your emotional response to this dream. It may be telling you to try harder and not give up or be reinforcing the view that you have done as much as you can.

Office

This dream may be a sign that you have too much responsibility at work, or that you have a project or problem that you can't leave behind when you go home. Take note of how your colleagues react to you as this can indicate if you feel satisfied at work.

Falling

This is one of the most common dreams and one that we all have at some stage in our lives, usually at a time when we are feeling insecure and lacking in confidence. It is a typical anxiety dream that suggests our sense that we have no control. It has been interpreted as a dream of sexual surrender, where the fall and landing symbolise sexual intercourse. It also stands for the fear of failing—whether through 'falling into temptation', 'falling from grace' or 'letting ourselves and other people down'. Falling is also associated with isolation and the need to feel supported, especially if the dreamer is feeling misunderstood or not accepted for who he or she is.

Going to the edge and falling could be a warning that you are overworked or that you've set yourself such high standards that you are likely to fail. Dreaming of another person falling suggests your wish to be rid of them in your waking life. To see a house falling down suggests that you are struggling to let go of old attitudes and beliefs. If you witness something fall, you may be concerned about a potential danger.

Many people dream of falling and wake up before hitting the ground. Others fall and land—usually they are still alive in the dream and have felt no pain through their fall, despite their injuries. If you fall without hurting yourself, you will have minor struggles with your problem. If you are hurt, it will take you longer to build up the strength to face your fear and deal with it. On the more positive side, the dream may be giving you some good advice—to let go of old negative habits or dogmatic beliefs and enjoy life more.

Queue

Skipping

Levitation

Floating

Falling

Cross-reference

For Skipping, see
    Children p.294
For Floating, see
    Afloat p.102

Movement

Migration

Dreaming of migrating indicates your need to find greener pastures and achieve your goals in an environment where you will not be judged by old standards. If on the other hand the migration is forced, the dream may be expressing your frustrations at having to change your ways of thinking and abandon your comfort zone. Your attitude within the dream holds the key to the message it is trying to convey.

In general, dreaming of migration reflects uncertainty about the steps the dreamer is about to take. However, it also suggests that beneath that uncertainty there is the promise of prosperity.

Climbing

If you feel as if a current situation is an uphill struggle, this dream symbolises the need to persist if you are to reach your goal.

Wading

Wading, like baptism, suggests the desire for cleansing or symbolic rebirth. Wading through water often suggests that the dreamer, though in touch with his or her emotions, is not really coming to grips with them. Wading in muddy water is a result of not facing up to emotional issues. To interpret this dream you should pay attention to whether the water in your dream is clear or muddy.

Wings

Dreaming of wings suggests a desire for freedom, independence, and the ability to achieve flight or 'lift off'. The association of wings with angels also gives them a meaning of protection. If you dream of a broken wing, it suggests that something is preventing an idea or project you are involved with from 'getting off the ground'. It may also stand for the obstacles that prevent you from becoming independent.

Rocking

Rocking is associated with babies, sleep and comfort. Dreaming of rocking, therefore, is to do with a desire to return to this blissful state. Rocking the boat, however, refers to disturbing the peace or bucking the status quo.

Crossing

To dream of a road or level crossing suggests that you are approaching a point of transition in your life.

Wandering

A dream in which you are wandering suggests a period of uncertainty and doubt about your goals. Wandering can be a necessary part of the process of self-discovery or making up your mind, so this is not necessarily a negative dream.

Kicking

Being kicked in a dream suggests that you fear hostility or ill will from others. If you are the one doing the kicking, the dream may be acting out aggressive impulses that you have tried to ignore. A kick in a dream may also be reminding you of something you have forgotten. If the dreamer is aimlessly kicking, they are trying to break free from some constraint in real life. In this instance, kicking may represent self-preservation rather than just being a symbol of aggression.

Migration

Wading

Wings

Climbing

Rocking

Crossing

Wandering

Kicking

Cross-reference

For Climbing,
  see Hills p.94,
  Mountains p.96
For Crossing, see
  Crossroads p.333
For Rocking, see Baby
  p.295

259

CHAPTER EIGHT
Travel

Dreams of travel are a general indication of how you feel your life is progressing, and the direction you are taking. Since life is seen by many people as a journey, these dreams can help you to understand whether you are in control of that journey or whether you need to make some changes. As well as considering what type of vehicle you are travelling in, the environment can be important in the interpretations of these dreams, for example, whether you are travelling on calm water or bumpy roads.

Vehicles

Car

Like other forms of transport, cars are a symbol of where we are going on our life journey. Are you in control of the car or are you a passenger? Are you clear about where you are going, or does the car seem to be driving you? Do you have passengers, or are you alone? Are you travelling fast or slowly? These factors can help you to assess the current state of your 'drive' and confidence. A dream in which you are driving may be telling you wish to be somewhere else.

Bus

The bus journey in your dream may suggest how quickly or directly you are moving towards your goals. It makes a difference whether you are a passenger or the driver. If you are a passenger, it could be a sign that you don't feel you are in control of your life. If you are enjoying the ride, however, it may suggest that you would like to enjoy the freedom of being without responsibilities. If you are driving the bus, you probably feel responsible for others, perhaps at work or in your family.

Taxi/Cab

A taxi represents the help that you receive but have to pay for. Because a taxi is a means of transport, dreaming of being in one indicates that you are going places or being taken somewhere. Just be careful that you aren't being taken for a ride. The way in which you travel in your dreams reflects the course you are taking in life.

You could be worried about the meter ticking over (can you afford your current lifestyle?) or anxious to reach your destination (will you ever arrive?). To help you interpret this dream it's important to take note of the state of the car, the nature of the journey or the driver, and how you felt during the trip.

Motorbike

The image of the motorbike arouses feelings of adventure, freedom and escape and is associated with rebellious youth. Dreaming of riding a motorbike represents our physical energy and independence as well as sexual drive. If you are feeling confident and are in control of the motorbike, your daring and sense of adventure will pay off. If, however, you are not in control of the vehicle, it could be wishful thinking on your part to be free and daring, because you don't have the confidence to carry it off. You may be yearning for past youth or regretting the time you spent being 'responsible', or in mourning for your own 'reckless spirit'. Accept it and move on.

Car

Bus

Taxi/Cab

Motorbike

Truck

Ambulance

Truck

Dreaming of driving or of being a passenger in a truck indicates ambitions that are to do with work and large corporations. The larger the truck, the more ambitious you are and the greater the load (responsibility) that you are having to carry.

Ambulance

An ambulance is linked with urgency and speed. Attention should be given to whatever is troubling you so that your plans may come to fruition in the least possible time. If you wish to interpret it as a prophetic dream, it is wise to pay attention to your health and welfare.

Cross-reference

For Motorbike, see
    Youth p.303
For Ambulance, see
    Speed p.255
See also Road p.264

263

Road & rail travel

Road

Like a path, a road in your dream describes your direction or approach to something in your life. Dreaming of being at a crossroads represents the choices confronting you. If you see the road behind you, it symbolises your past, whereas the road ahead is your future. An unpaved road is 'off the beaten track' or the 'road less travelled'. This means it could just be sidetracking you from your true path. On the other

hand, it may be a difficult road, but in the end more rewarding. A narrow winding road with lots of bumps and holes is a symbol of hardship and difficulties along your way. Change your existing conditions and the road will be easier to travel on. Going the wrong way up a one-way street is an anxiety dream. It suggests that you are up against the norms of society. How long can you last without running into some problem?

Driving/Driver

Driving in your dream is a sign of your desire to take control over your direction. If you are having trouble making the vehicle go where you want it to, however, the dream suggests that you suffer from contradictory impulses or are unresolved about what direction to take.

Acceleration

If you are speeding up in your dream, it could be a sign of the need to take things more slowly, or to think through a matter more carefully. If the accelerator is jammed or out of control, the dream may be warning you of bad habits that are likely to get out of hand if you don't slow down.

Wheel

The wheel stands for mobility and the ability to deal with life's challenges. The wheel of fortune also associates this object with the variable fortunes or 'ups and downs' we are likely to encounter in life. If you dream of losing a wheel, it may indicate that you lack energy or motivation for some enterprise.

Large car/Hearse

If you are driving a large expensive car like a Rolls-Royce or Mercedes, take it as a sign that you will shortly receive a worthwhile proposition, or that your material or emotional life is about to improve. If the car you are driving is a hearse, it is a sign that emotions or matters from the past are weighing you down. However, this dream also suggests that you may be about to off load whatever it is that is troubling you.

Brakes

If you have to brake suddenly, it indicates that you should be prepared for obstacles ahead. This dream can also foretell a 'break' in your life, whether it is a lucky break, or simply a transition of some kind.

Backseat driver

If your dream contains a pushy passenger who's trying to tell you where you should go, watch out! Chances are that someone is trying to manipulate you or that you feel pushed in a direction you don't want to go. This dream may be telling you that it's time to identify 'the backseat drivers' in your life, and take control of the wheel.

Caravan

A caravan represents adventure and travel, not necessarily physical, but also in the mind or imagination. Take this as an indication that it's time to consider either a holiday or a new approach to a familiar situation.

Road

Driving/Driver

Acceleration

Wheel

Large car/Hearse

Brakes

Backseat driver

Caravan

Cross-reference

For Road, see Tar
    p.382, Path p.339,
    Crossroads p.333
For Hearse, see
    Funeral p.208
For Caravan, see
    Holiday p.214

Road & rail travel

Bicycle

Cycling symbolises the dreamer's personal projects or aspirations. If you are riding your bicycle in the air, for example, it may suggest your desire to gain a larger perspective on your life and surroundings. Like all dreams with movement in them, dreams in which you are riding a bike tend to reflect how you feel about your progress in life. Take note of the surroundings through which you are cycling. Are you passing through attractive countryside, or are you lost in difficult terrain? Is your progress easy or an uphill struggle all the way? If your present progress is difficult, but you can see something attractive ahead, your dream could be reminding you that even if you are finding your life difficult at the moment, something better may be waiting for you just over the horizon.

Carriage

This traditional and romantic form of transport suggests either romance (whether of the 'runaway' or the more sedate variety) or a desire for a traditional marriage.

Tyre

If you have to stop and change a tyre, it suggests that expenditure on your current lifestyle may be in danger of 'blowing-out' of all proportion.

Headlights

If you dream of approaching headlights, it is likely that you feel as if your actions or feelings are under scrutiny or are being unfairly judged.

Railroad

Generally a railroad or railway in your dreams represents your life journey or the direction that events in your life are taking you. You may be wondering whether you are on the 'right track'. If there's only one track in your dreams, it may indicate that there is only one option in your life or that you are inflexible in your thoughts. If there is more than one track, you need to make a decision which way to go. A railway station means that you're about to move into something new in your life and leave the old behind. You may be leaving a relationship or moving into a new environment.

Bicycle

Carriage

Tyre

Headlights

Railroad

Cross-reference

For Carriage, see
   Horse p.57,
   Wedding p.210
For Railroad, see
   Journey p.275

Travel on water

Rowing a boat

If you have no difficulty rowing and the boat is not upset, life ahead is looking positive. If this is not the case, you need to be more organised and coordinated to achieve your goals.

Lifeboat

You may be feeling a need to be saved in this dream. If you reach a lifeboat in time, it could indicate you'd be successful at the last minute.

Boat

Of all modes of transport, boats are one of the most suggestive. Perhaps this is because they carry us through water, a symbol of the emotions. The boat in your dream may be a symbol of your hopes and fears for the immediate future. Pay attention to the water surrounding you in your dream. Is it still and reflective, or are you buffeted by storms, or even afraid of falling overboard and being drowned? These details may be forecasting the emotional 'weather' you are currently experiencing in your journey through life. If the boat is drifting, it may be a sign that you worry about not being in control of your life. If it is in danger of capsizing, you may need to act decisively to avoid a bad situation. To dream of a boat is also symbolic of significant emotional change from negative to more positive emotion, particularly if the boat is moving through calm waters.

Canoe

To be 'paddling your own canoe' is a symbol of independence and your ability to manage your own affairs. If you share the canoe with another, it suggests that you and a romantic or business partner need to 'pull together' if you are to reach your goals.

Oar

An oar is a navigation device, so its appearance in a dream indicates a goal that you are trying to reach. It suggests that you will be able to guide your own destiny, but that doing so will require skill and care. If you lose or drop an oar in your dream, take it as a sign that you need to keep a firmer grip on your assets. You don't want to be 'up a creek without a paddle'.

Raft

Dreaming of floating on a raft represents temporary safety until rescue is at hand. Water is a symbol of emotion; therefore, being on a raft at sea highlights your present emotional state—one that is filled with difficulty and uncertainty. If you reach your destination unharmed then you will achieve your goal and overcome your emotional upheaval. If the raft comes apart, it is a warning to be careful and not move on until you have 'mended' it.

Rowing a boat

Lifeboat

Boat

Canoe

Oar

Raft

Submarine

Submarine

A submarine is a more positive dream image than any other sea-going vessel. That is because it represents our ability to delve deeply into our subconscious while also functioning in the real world. Moreover, because the dreamer has the protection of the submarine, he or she will feel safe about delving more deeply into the subconscious mind.

Cross-reference

For Lifeboat, see
    Rescuing p.176
For Raft, see Floating
    p.256, Afloat p.102
For Submarine, see
    Navy p.232

Travel on water

Sailing

Sailing represents the way we take charge of our life. The meaning of this dream will depend on how you choose to face life's decisions. Do you 'sail against the wind'? That is, do you fight and struggle to get what you want? Perhaps everything is 'plain sailing', in which case you tend to go with the flow to achieve your aims. Sailing is also about freedom and in your dream may be alerting you to your desire to break free from restraints.

Sails

If sailing is about taking charge, sails symbolise the energy and power that move us.

Ferry

If you dream of being on a ferry, expect a major change to occur in your life. The ferry has ancient associations with being carried along the River Styx towards death. However, this journey is not a physical death but the ending of a phase in your life, whether to do with a relationship, a value system, or an activity. The ferry is symbolic of the vessel that carries you towards this transition.

Fleet

To dream of a fleet of ships reflects our hopes and aspirations. If the fleet is coming in it means that the dreamer may very well gain what they are hoping for.

Wreck

A wreck is a traditional symbol of misfortune or failure. If you dream of one, it suggests that you fear the failure of some enterprise or project, possibly due to circumstances beyond your control. This dream warns you to be prepared for trouble ahead.

Anchor

Spiritually, the anchor represents hope and sanctuary. In everyday life it is a symbol of stability and safety. It may indicate that you need to remain 'grounded' in order to weather a storm or a difficult situation ahead. On the negative side, to be anchored means to remain stagnant in one place and be afraid of taking risks.

Sailing

Sails

Ferry

Fleet

Wreck

Anchor

Cross-reference

For Sailing, see Sailor p.290
For Wreck, see Failing p.176
See also Water pp.98–103
See also Ocean p.102

Air travel

Aeroplane

An aeroplane indicates a swift journey, transporting you from one location to another. If you fear air travel, dreaming of being a passenger can be pointing you to some fear involved in travel. Freud regarded flying as a sexual dream—one of wild abandonment and desire for freedom. If you feel that you have no control over the plane, then it may suggest that there are issues in your life's journey that need to be addressed. If you are at ease with flying in a plane, it may indicate that you wish to rise above the rest and find an escape. A pilot means that you are in control of where your life is heading.

To dream of an aeroplane crash is not necessarily a prophetic dream telling you of some catastrophe to come, but it can be a dream that reveals your feeling of helplessness in the face of things that you seem to be beyond your control. As planes are associated with travelling over long distances, the crash may be telling you that there will be a major change in the distant future.

Zeppelin

A Zeppelin is basically a balloon filled with gas, so if you dream of one it probably symbolises something or someone in your life who is 'full of hot air'—possibly even 'a gasbag'. Because Zeppelins are also associated with disaster and accident, due to events such as the Hindenburg tragedy, this dream could also express your fears of an accident, or anxiety that a situation may be about to 'go up in flames'.

Propeller

Like engines, propellers stand for our drive, our stamina and the energy with which we make things happen in our life. Propellers are associated with flight, which suggests that our energies in this instance may be required to 'lift' us beyond our present obstacles or situations.

Aeroplane

Zeppelin

Propeller

Parachute

Parachute

Parachutes represent protection, especially against falling or failing. Dreaming of one may signal that you are ready to tackle a new challenge or activity, or that you seek greater freedom in your life. If, however, you dream of falling and your parachute refuses to open, the dream symbolises your fear of failing in an important enterprise. Perhaps you are insufficiently prepared, or you don't trust those around you to offer support when you most need it. The dream may also be suggesting that you are putting up too many protective mechanisms. Perhaps it is time for you to make the leap?

Cross-reference

For Aeroplane, see
Journey p.275,
Flying p.255
For Parachute, see
Falling p.257

273

General travel

Travel

To travel is to seek a change from our usual environment. We talk about 'travelling through life' to indicate both the process of ageing and our self-development through experience. If you are travelling alone in your dream, it implies that you wish to be more independent. However, it could also suggest that you are solitary or feel alienated from others. Travelling with other people represents sociability and the way we get along with others. If you are going on a business trip, the journey is a symbol of where your career is taking you. Going on a holiday, however, suggests your need to 'get away' from the pressures of daily life and from people who constantly make demands on you. This dream is encouraging you to give yourself 'time out' so that you can recuperate.

Fare

Dreaming of paying a fare of any kind suggests that we have paid our dues in order to achieve our goal and that we are now ready to reap the rewards.

Fork

Dreaming of a fork in the road means that you will have to make a decision on an important matter. Symbolically, the fork in the road represents a junction on our spiritual path where guidance will be needed to make a decision as to which direction to take.

People can appear in our dreams under many different guises. They may be people well known to you in real life, or people you don't know but recognise by their profession or uniform such as a policeman, lawyer or acrobat. You may even have dreams about mythical figures —giants, princesses, mermaids and so on. Generally, dreams about people, however they appear, reflect some aspect of how you see yourself or how you feel other people see you or behave towards you.

Groups of people

People

Sometimes the people in our dreams represent actual people in our waking lives. At other times they stand for something or somebody else: disguised versions of people we do know, or aspects of ourselves. You may be able to 'unmask' the true identity of the figures in your dreams by paying attention to the clues in your dream. For example, someone who treats you harshly in your dream could represent a person in your life who has treated you this way. In general we tend to dream about the people in our lives for whom we have strong but mixed feelings. The figures in your dreams may also stand for your own thoughts or feelings. In this case their interactions within the dream may be helping you to explore your feelings about a particular issue. If one character in your dream merges into or becomes another, it is likely that they represent aspects of an idea or feeling. Try to analyse who or what the people stand for in your life. For example, if you dream of an actor, it may reflect that you feel someone close to you is behaving artificially. Are these people drama queens? What are their genuine selves? Dreaming of distant relatives such as grandparents may refer to issues belonging to your family background or roots. These figures might also be disguised versions of people closer to you, such as parents. Dreams of authority figures can indicate an issue either with an actual authority figure in your life or with your internal qualities of conscience, sense of responsibility or discipline.

Crowd

Dreaming of a crowd highlights your feelings of being hemmed in and your need for space in which to express yourself.

The elderly

Seeing old people in your dreams suggests wisdom and it's a good sign. It may mean that you have achieved some sort of enlightenment or that through hard work you will achieve your goal. To worry about your own age could mean that you are burdened and feeling older than you are. Consider seeking medical help or using relaxation methods to give you an energy boost.

Tribe

If you dream of a tribe, it may represent a social group that you belong to such as a club, religious association, family or other group of people with whom you share common interests. Do you desire acceptance from some group? Do you feel that you don't stand out as an individual? Work out whether the tribe is primitive or not, and what its rules are. It may be worth asking yourself if you are feeling alienated in your waking life and, if you are, joining a group with whom you share a common interest.

Friends

Friends appearing in your dreams indicate the need for you to explore the qualities that friends bring into your life, such as love, support, loyalty, comradeship and fun. If they tend to be negative qualities—such as competition, jealousy and possessiveness—it is time to reassess the friendship. Friends can also represent aspects of your own personality that you need to acknowledge more. Perhaps you need to be a better friend either to yourself or to someone else.

People

Crowd

The elderly

Tribe

Friends

Harem

Harem

In Western European culture the harem has traditionally been a symbol of exotic pleasures. To dream of a harem is likely to signal your desire to explore your sensual nature. For a woman this dream may also suggest the need to belong to a community of women or 'sisterhood'. For a man it could be an escape from a situation in which he feels put under pressure by a female partner or partners.

Cross-reference

For Friends, see Acquaintance and Companion p.298
For Harem, see Sexual behaviour pp.164–7

Gender

Man

A masculine figure that appears in our dreams indicates parts of our personality—the things that we possess and those that we want. An older man can represent wisdom or a father figure. A man in a woman's dream can represent the masculine side of her nature—that is, the logical, strong, assertive elements that she requires to survive in the world. It may suggest that a woman wishes to get in touch with the masculine side of herself in order to cope better with what is at hand. A man dreaming of a man is in fact dreaming of himself. To understand how someone feels about the masculine side of their personality, consider these idioms: 'be a man', 'make a man of', 'odd man out', 'man to man'.

Woman

If the dreamer is a woman, the female figures in her dream may represent aspects of herself, including those aspects that she does not immediately recognise or identify with. By projecting these feelings onto another female figure, the dreamer is able to express herself in a less confronting manner. If the dreamer is a man, the female figures in his dream are likely to represent not only his relationships with the actual women in his life, but his relationship with the part of himself that is more 'feminine' or intuitive. How the woman is dressed or appears in the dream often indicates whether or not the dreamer is happy with that aspect of self. A well-dressed woman suggests that the dreamer is happy with the aspect of self that they identify with.

Girl

If you are female, and you either dream of yourself as a girl or see a girl, the dream generally relates to the more emotional, young and vulnerable aspect of yourself. It may also reflect how you feel about a sister or daughter. For a male this dream is a reflection of his undeveloped emotions. Regardless of whether the dreamer is male or female, this dream suggests a need to be in touch with the more feminine aspects of self.

Man

Woman

Girl

Boy

Boy

If you are female and you dream of a boy, it may represent the more masculine aspects of your character—the dream may be asking you to get more in touch with these parts of your character. If you are an adult male, the dream may represent the need to be more 'boyish' or playful in waking life.

Cross-reference

See also Family
    pp.294–7
See also Behaviour &
    feelings, Chapter 6
See also Children
    p.294

Jobs

Acrobat

To watch acrobats performing means that you must be careful or you are likely to have an accident. If the acrobat in your dream is unable to perform his or her act, this signifies that you will escape whatever misfortune was intended for you. If you are the acrobat, it means you will experience difficult times but you will eventually overcome the difficulty. If the acrobat has a mishap then it may mean the dreamer's plans will go astray.

Actor

To dream of meeting with actors is an indication that trouble in the domestic sector of your life is probably occurring. The meaning of the dream will depend on the character portrayed by the actor, and whether the performance is tragic or comic. If you dream of a comic performance, you are generally happy with your present life and will continue to be so. If, instead, you dream of a tragic performance it may indicate that tough times are ahead. Shakespeare's words—'all the world's a stage and men and women are merely players'—may well apply to your next 'stage' in life. From a psychological perspective being an actor can represent uneasiness about present situations in life.

Boss

The boss in your dream may be standing in for anyone with authority in your life, such as your parents, or your own inner sense of duty or obligation. This dream is likely to suggest attitudes towards power: either yours or that of others.

Captain

If you play the part of a captain in a dream, it is an indication of your willingness to take on the role of authority. You may feel that you are already occupying this role in waking life. If someone else is ordering you around, however, the dream suggests you are unhappy with authority figures.

Carpenter

If you are doing carpentry in your dream or watching someone else doing it, it is a sign that some part of your life needs work or repairing. It may also signal that the overall structure of your life requires attention.

Acrobat

Actor

Boss

Captain

Carpenter

Admiral

Caddy

Admiral

To dream of a high-ranking naval officer may be an indication that something of importance will be coming your way, perhaps elevating your own status. It might represent an important event outside one's control that will bring about significant personal change as well as change in lifestyle.

Caddy

If a caddy is following you in your dream, it may be a sign that a friend or work associate is acting in a subservient role to your ambitions or personality. They may be looking up to you for leadership and guidance. If you are the caddy, the dream may suggest that you are feeling unhappy with your status as 'helper' in which you play a secondary role.

Cross-reference

For Actor, see Entertainment pp.248–9
For Boss, see Work p.246
For Carpenter, see Tools p.406

Jobs

Dentist

A dream of going to the dentist suggests that something you have been putting off for a while needs your attention. If the dream is very anxious, or you are losing your teeth, it suggests your fears about helplessness, loss or impotence.

Doctor

Because doctors are seen as authority figures who have responsibility for healing, to dream of one tends to signal a desire for a cure to take place. It can also be a sign that a cure has happened.

Judge

A dream of a judge is likely to symbolise our own tendency to judge others or ourselves. This dream could indicate a tendency on your part to be too harsh on yourself. It may also be a warning that your attitude towards others risks being unsympathetic, or overly 'judgemental'.

Hairdresser

Dreaming of a hairdresser can have several meanings, depending on the context and the emotions that accompany the dream. On the one hand, it can mean that you are looking for physical intimacy, on the other hand, that you wish to be taken care of by others. Being at the hairdresser's can also suggest your anxiety about the way that you appear to others. Do you feel unprepared for some social event or situation that is coming up?

Guard

A guard is a symbol of both protection and imprisonment. Depending on the dream, the guard is a warning to you of some kind. Either you need to be on your guard in relation to some action, or you feel that you are being kept away from your heart's desire.

Inventor

If you dream of this figure, there is a good chance that there is a problem or project in your waking life to which you are trying to find a solution. Is the project brimming with ingenuity or does nothing appear to be working? The progress experienced by your dream inventor will help you to evaluate the obstacles you are likely to face.

Detective

If your dream involves a detective, it is a sign that you need to investigate a matter or emotion more closely. If the detective is following you, it is an indication that you feel watched or pursued. This dream can also signify your consciousness that you have behaved in a dishonest or underhand manner.

Dentist

Doctor

Judge

Hairdresser

Guard

Inventor

Detective

Cross-reference

For Dentist, see Teeth p.113
For Doctor, see Disease & illness pp.120–7
For Guard, see Jail and Jailer p.226

Jobs

Lawyer

Dreaming of a lawyer is associated with one-sided arguments and contracts. Lawyers often possess negative associations in a dream, acting as a psychological warning that you are surrounded by people that are false, untrustworthy or hurtful. You should beware of committing to any legal agreement without professional counselling or proper understanding of whatever it is you are entering into.

Pawnbroker

Dreaming of a pawnbroker usually symbolises anxiety about lack of means. These may not only be financial, but also to do with time or energy. This dream may suggest that you feel obliged to temporarily give up something you value, such as a talent or a hobby, until you find yourself in a situation where you can reclaim it.

Policeman

If a policeman appears in our dreams, we may have subconsciously called him or her to report a crime against us, to punish someone who has injured us, or to retrieve something that we have lost. More negatively, the police can appear in our dreams in response to our own sense of guilt about having behaved badly or 'broken the law'. Policemen can be frightening figures who often relate to childhood fears of authority, or suggest that we still carry some guilt for something that happened in the past.

Nurse

Nurses are depicted as the angels of mercy, dedicated to 'nursing the sick back to health'. Seeing or being a nurse in your dream represents a need for care and nurturing, in relation to your physical as well as emotional well-being. A nurse also represents the healing process, someone who 'revives' those on their way out of this world. This is generally a good sign. However, as with any symbols connected with health, it is a good idea to check your health.

Pilot

Dreaming of a pilot suggests either confidence about your direction in life, or an active search for guidance. It can also symbolise the dreamer's desire for protection. Are you looking for a 'safe harbour', or are you concerned about landing safely?

Lawyer

Pawnbroker

Policeman

Nurse

Pilot

Cross-reference

For Lawyer, see
   Legalities pp.228–9
For Police, see
   Crime & criminals
   pp.222–3
For Pilot, see
   Aeroplane p.272

289

Jobs

Waiter

The behaviour of the waiter in your dream will help you assess the way you feel about your treatment by those around you. Thus, a waiter who is slow or rude suggests your belief that those close to you are not treating you with enough respect or consideration. If you are scolding the waiter, it is a sign either that you are prepared to demand the respect you feel you deserve, or that you feel self-conscious about the demands you are placing on others. Similarly if the dreamer is the waiter he or she may feel that there are too many demands on them in waking life, particularly by those close to them.

Psychologist

If you have a dream about a psychologist, it's a sign that you feel the need for 'counselling' of some kind. In this respect the psychologist in your dream is most likely to represent your own capacity to interpret your current emotional state and devise strategies for improving it.

Vet

A vet is a symbol of our need for creature comforts. This dream suggests that our basic (animal) needs are not being properly met.

Sailor

The sailor represents ease of movement and our ability to weather the storms of life, particularly those involving emotional turmoil.

Chemist

To dream of a chemist usually signals your sense that some vital ingredient is missing from your life. What's the missing component? The nature of the substance that you are trying to obtain from the chemist may help you to discover what this is.

Prostitute

A dream with a prostitute in it will mean different things depending on the circumstances of the dream and the dreamer. More symbolically, this dream can suggest that the dreamer—male or female—feels 'prostituted' or used in some way: a dream that probably denotes dissatisfaction in a job or relationship. For men, dreaming of a prostitute can signal a desire for sex or taking what they want in a way that isn't complicated by emotional ties. For a woman, it may signal either a desire to express her sexuality outside traditional moral restrictions and roles, or a desire to gain power or money. It may also indicate some guilt about her sexual desires or the fear that others don't respect her.

Waiter

Psychologist

Vet

Sailor

Chemist

Prostitute

Cross-reference

For Waiter, see Restaurant p.358
For Prostitute, see Sexual behaviour pp.164–7

Jobs

Clown

To see a clown in a dream or to dream of being one suggests a fear of not being taken seriously.

Optometrist/Optician

An optometrist in a dream is often associated with your own need to see things a little more clearly, particularly on an emotional level. If you've been having difficulties with your eyes lately, then take the dream literally. You may need glasses.

Juggler

The significance of this dream symbol is pretty clear. You are probably in a situation where you are conscious of having to keep a number of different balls in the air. If the dream is accompanied by a sense of exhilaration and accomplishment you are probably enjoying the challenge. It you are terrified of dropping something it may be a sign that you are overextending yourself and need to cut back on your activities or commitments. However you feel, the juggler in your dream gives you the chance to look at yourself and your performance from a more detached perspective. Generally, if the dreamer is uncomfortable with what they are juggling in the dream it may be a subconscious message to lighten the load.

Cashier

Not surprisingly, the appearance of a cashier in a dream tends to reflect money worries, or anxieties about your business transactions. To help you interpret these you should pay attention to the attitude of the cashier, whether he or she is friendly or hostile, what you are purchasing, and whether the price demanded seems reasonable or too high.

Servant

If you are tired of being at someone's beck and call, whether it's that of your boss or your family, chances are that you are feeling like a servant. This dream can also suggest that you are feeling subservient, that is, subject to constant scrutiny and criticism. Think about whether this is an accurate indication of how you are feeling at present.

Gardener

The gardener is the nature loving, wise aspect of ourselves that takes a 'down to earth' approach to life and is the keeper of the natural order of things.

Clown

Optometrist/
Optician

Juggler

Cashier

Servant

Gardener

Cross-reference

For Optometrist/
   Optician, see Eyes
   p.112
For Gardener, see
   Garden p.66
For Cashier, see
   Money p.216

Family

Family

We spend our formative years with our family and that means that our attitudes, values and opinions are based on what we were taught. Whether or not we go against these values, our pattern of behaviour is moulded on what was displayed in our family unit. The absence of a mother or father is an important issue that often traumatises individuals.

However, dreaming that your parents are dead or are absent in a family reunion could indicate that you have gained independence and are no longer reliant on their dominant role.

Children or siblings in dreams often represent aspects of ourselves. A helpless child or sibling in danger of drowning is really a symbol of the part of you that is in need of help. A

father usually represents authority while a mother stands for relationships and the nurturing part of you. It may well be that the family member you are dreaming of actually represents that person. However, if you dream of conflict in the family, it may be a reflection of conflict within different parts of yourself. Take note of the emotions that arise in the dream.

Grandparents

Grandparents in a dream are representative of love, wisdom, protection, security and tradition. If you dream of searching for a grandparent, you are likely to be searching for the qualities that they stand for.

Children

Like babies, children usually stand for something precious to the dreamer, or symbolise his or her responsibilities. If the children are crying or badly behaved, it is a sign that you feel doubt about your capacities to deal with a current situation. It could also be that you are feeling resentful of duties at home or at work. If the children are happy, the dream is a positive indication of harmony in your emotional life.

Parents

Dreaming of your parents usually symbolises your attitudes towards authority. This dream may signal a guilty conscience, or your resentment or acceptance of some authority figure or figures in your life. Because our parents played a crucial role in protecting us when we were children, their appearance may also be a warning that you need to take care in a particular life situation. Some dream interpreters believe that parental figures in dreams stand for the 'male' and 'female' parts of ourselves. In this context, the father in our dream traditionally stood for discipline, power or social authority, while mothers represented love, encouragement and the things that nurtured us.

Family

Grandparents

Children

Parents

Baby

Baby

In dreams, babies usually represent something precious to the dreamer, such as a talent, relationship or a situation that needs protection and care. If the baby is sick or in distress, and you are unable to comfort it, it may be a sign that you are afraid of losing someone or something through your inability to nurture it adequately. A happy baby suggests a joyful sense of adventure or new beginnings. In dream lore babies are often identified with the dreamer's soul life, or 'inner child'. A healthy baby can also mean growth in a relationship or situation and the opposite if the baby is ill.

Cross-reference

For Grandparents, see
    The elderly p.280
For Children, see Boy
    and Girl p.283
For Baby, see Cradle
    p.371, Rocking
    p.259

Family

Father

Fathers usually represent respected authority figures. Depending on the circumstances in the dream, seeing your father could suggest either that you are struggling with the authoritarian side of yourself, or that you feel inexperienced (inadequate) in some aspect of your life.

Husband

This figure does not necessarily represent your actual husband (especially if you are unmarried!) but may stand for someone in your waking life who occupies a protective or supportive role towards you, particularly if they are male.

Wife

Dreaming of a wife signals a concern with issues of family and relationships. This dream could be prompting the dreamer to pay more attention to family members. Alternatively, it could symbolise the dreamer's desire for greater security or closer emotional relationships with others.

Twins

Gemini is the astrological sign of the twins. The twins symbolise our dual natures—the mixture of good and bad that can be found in all of us. If you dream of seeing twins, the dream may be pointing out the two opposing aspects either of yourself or of a particular issue. Often the message of the dream is the dreamer's need to reconcile the two. Search the symbolism of the dream carefully for clues on how this may be done.

Mother

The mother represents the nurturing and protective aspects of ourselves. How we relate to people in any relationship is symbolised by this figure. If it is a negative dream, the mother image may be possessive, jealous and lacking in emotional bonding. Assess whether the dream is indicating that you need to apply the positive maternal instincts to your life, or whether you need to acknowledge the negative aspects and integrate them for a more balanced outcome.

Widow/Widower

Dreaming of being a widow if you are a married woman is a sign of fears of abandonment, or a wish to escape the constrictions of a relationship. For a married man the situation is reversed. If you are not married, it is likely to represent any potential loss.

Father

Husband

Wife

Twins

Mother

Widow/Widower

Uncle

Girlfriend

Boyfriend

Uncle

Unless the dreamer has been recently thinking of or has visited an uncle, dreaming of this relative usually represents issues to do with family tradition and values. An uncle is generally regarded as the male authority figure next in importance to the father. So, dreaming of this figure may reflect your need to be free of a domineering influence. Examine your feelings about your uncle/s to undersand the meaning of this dream.

Girlfriend

If you are a man and dream of a girlfriend or ex-girlfriend, the dream is usually more about the balance of the masculine and the feminine in the dreamer than the actual relationship itself. If a girlfriend appears in a woman's dream, it is a reflection of the type of friend the dreamer would like to be.

Boyfriend

Dreaming of a boyfriend or ex-boyfriend generally indicates your feelings about attachment and romance towards this person. If you dream of an unlikely person that you'd be involved with, you may need to be more open in your relationships to men in general and realise that there is no ideal lover.

Cross-reference

For Widow/Widower
  see Death
  pp.208–209
For Father, see
  Parents p.295
For Mother, see
  Parents p.295

297

Archetypes

Acquaintance

To dream of people you know is a good dream. However, the degree of your relationship with the acquaintance, and the manner in which you conduct yourself in the dream, determines what message your dream is sending you. For example, if you are having a pleasant conversation with the acquaintance, then you can expect your business affairs to run smoothly and your domestic life to be stable. If you are engaged in a heated and loud discussion with the acquaintance, then you can expect a series of humiliating and embarrassing events to surround you. Making a new acquaintance in a dream could indicate that a change in your life is about to occur.

Cannibals/Cannibalism

These primitive symbols of fear tell us that something is 'eating us'—either from within, or from something that is threatening in our environment. If your dream features cannibalism, you may need to face up to a situation or emotion that you have been avoiding. It may be that your work environment is one that embodies the term 'dog eat dog'.

Companion

The close companion in your dream is likely to represent your own attitude towards yourself, and the degree to which you are protecting and nourishing your own projects and emotional life. As the saying goes, 'be your own best friend'.

Leper

Lepers were once known as 'the untouchables' because of the risk of contamination they posed. If you dream that you are a leper, you may be feeling rejected by people, or sense that an aspect of your life has been contaminated. Dreaming of seeing a leper suggests that you need to acknowledge imperfections in others around you.

Gypsy

Gypsies are often thought of as a nomadic, mystical race who lead a carefree, unconventional lifestyle. Do you want more freedom in your life? Do you feel stifled and wish to express yourself in a more creative and less conservative manner? A dream of gypsies is often related to the dreamer's own feelings of restlessness and need to be released from the burdens of life. The message is the need for 'time out'.

Acquaintance

Companion

Cannibals/
Cannibalism

Leper

Gypsy

Adversary

Enemy

Adversary

To see your opponent or adversary in a dream could indicate conflicting forces in your waking life. If it involves confrontation, you may be having some difficulties in getting your point across and people just don't support your views. By not giving up and trying hard you can overcome these problems. You may also need to face your opponents in life in order to move forward.

Enemy

An enemy is an opposing force and in a dream the image of an enemy can come in many shapes and forms. But unlike an enemy in real life, the enemy in a dream could be anyone or anything—sometimes it could be the dreamer's opposing side (his or her own worst enemy). You need to reflect on what conflicting emotions or issues are present in your life and whether the best tactic is to fight or walk away.

Cross-reference

For Acquaintance, see
  Friends p.281
For Companion, see
  Friends p.281
For Leper, see
  Banishment p.227
For Enemy, see
  Conflict pp.178–9

299

Archetypes

Martyr

A martyr is a glorified victim. Religious martyrs have traditionally been depicted as heroes/heroines who have gone to their deaths for their strong beliefs. Dreaming of a martyr reflects your admiration for this type of extreme behaviour in which you become a victim in order to prove your point. If you feel that you are a victim in the sense that everyone expects you to perform certain duties, but you perform them grudgingly, it may be time to review the role you have either taken on yourself or that others have given you.

Refugee

If you dream of being a refugee, it suggests your feelings of being out of your comfort zone (eviction) and an urgent need for acceptance. Do you feel like a stranger in some situation? Perhaps you are trying to adapt in order to survive.

Hero/Heroine

The hero or heroine in our dreams often reflects our own initiative or potential for growth and change. If the hero or heroine in your dream is someone completely unlike you, the dream may be offering you the opportunity to get an objective view of your own goals, potential and actions. Alternatively, this figure could represent those qualities you most admire in others and wish you could achieve yourself.

Hunchback

Dreaming of a hunchback suggests that you or someone around you is carrying too great a burden and that their life is at risk of becoming pushed out of shape or 'deformed' as a result. It may be associated with a feeling of being shunned or shut out in waking life.

Idiot

To dream of an idiot can suggest a sense of frustration at being unable to communicate. This type of dream can also indicate that you are using your intellect rather than your heart in real life. You may want to go with what you feel.

Martyr

Refugee

Hero/Heroine

Hunchback

Idiot

Hermit

Hermit

It's likely that the hermit in your dream symbolises either your own need for solitude, or your fears about loneliness. As in the tarot, the hermit can suggest the wisdom and spiritual awareness that can come from reflection or withdrawal from material pursuits. It can also suggest a fear that some activity or quest is unbalancing your life and forcing you to become too socially withdrawn. You should use the feelings that accompany this dream to help you to interpret its meaning. If there are negative feelings associated with the dream, the dreamer is taking a mature or wise outlook in their current situation.

Cross-reference

For Martyr, see Religious figures pp.150–3

Archetypes

Pirate

Being captured by pirates usually symbolises feelings of lack of control and vulnerability. For a woman this dream may represent a fear or anxiety about the aggressive behaviour or controlling attitudes of the man or men in her life. On the more positive side, pirates are also associated with adventure and action. If you dream of being a pirate it may suggest that you want a more active role in life, perhaps even one that is outside social conventions or the norms of what is expected of you.

Arab

To see an Arab in your dream suggests that you are concerned about your involvement in business transactions with someone outside your usual business clientele. Dreaming of being an Arab represents concerns about changing fortunes.

Dwarf

These diminutive figures usually stand for a neglected or minor aspect of ourselves that needs our attention. This dream may be a warning to you not to overlook aspects of your personality that are in danger of shrinking or remaining stunted because you are refusing to take them seriously enough.

Officer

Officers are authority figures, and as such may symbolise either another person in your life or the part of you that is responsible for creating order and discipline. This dream can signal a desire for guidance on your part; alternatively, it can suggest that you feel overregulated.

Alien

An alien is someone not belonging, something or someone that is foreign. To dream of aliens suggests that we need to face part of ourselves that 'alienates' us from others. Ask yourself whether your ideas or views are too strange or 'alien' for others around you to appreciate. If you dream that you're abducted by aliens, it may indicate that you have a fear of changing and adapting to a new environment. Moving to a new job, interstate, overseas, a new home or a new status in relationships such as becoming widowed or divorced may induce these type of feelings.

Pirate

Arab

Dwarf

Officer

Alien

Youth

Youth

Youth stands for potential, growth and the possibility of transformation. The youth in your dream may stand for yourself at that age. Alternatively, he or she may represent the qualities symbolised by the idea of youth. This dream could indicate a period of stocktaking on the part of the dreamer: an attempt to recall and evaluate the decisions made at a crucial period of life. However, it could also signal a general openness to change, growth and transformation.

Cross-reference

For Pirate, see Sailing p.270, Treasure p.221
For Alien, see Space p.443

Archetypes

Devil

Dreaming of the devil represents the need for us to confront an issue in our lives. If you see yourself in this role, it is a warning to think about your own actions and the way in which they impact on those close to you. The devil is also symbolic of an over-concern with earthly pleasures—either sexual or material. You are placing too much emphasis on these areas and the dream indicates that it's time for you to get in touch with your emotions.

Maniac

When we describe a person as a maniac, we generally label them as threatening. There are 'maniac' drivers (lacking in control) and there are those who are passionately driven by some possibly irrational desire. Depending on the context of the dream, it may indicate that you are afraid of this aspect of yourself or of a situation around you. You may be hoping for some calm, order and control in your life.

Pesterer

In dreams, as in waking life, pests are things that bother us and won't go away. The person who is pestering you in your dream may stand for an actual person, but could also represent a thought or emotion that has fastened onto you and won't leave you alone. If something or someone is pestering you in your dream, it's worth thinking about the things in your life that exert a negative influence, or the thoughts that you seem to be having trouble dismissing.

Victim

Seeing yourself as a victim denotes that you have given yourself this role by holding back your potential. Be more proactive in your approach to life, and adopt a more positive attitude. Only you can get yourself out of the role of victim.

Devil

Maniac

Pesterer

Victim

Fortune teller

Fortune teller

Fortune-telling is associated with looking into the future for guidance and trusting in the opinion of those equipped with more knowledge. If you dream that you consult a fortune-teller, consider whether you are impatient to gain knowledge of some future event. Keep in mind that you are trusting someone who appears to have the knowledge, but that in fact only your actions can affect the future. This can also be a warning dream that tells you to beware of false prophecy, and to find out something for yourself rather than believing what someone else tells you.

Cross-reference

For Devil, see Hell
    p.147, Evil p.447
For Maniac, see
    Insanity p.124

305

Archetypes

Neighbour

A neighbour reflects the qualities you see in your neighbour (or someone close to you) as well as your relationships with others. Dreaming of having a good neighbour is a sign of well-being and tranquillity. If your neighbour is fighting with you, take a look at what's causing the dispute and resolve it, as it usually reflects your own personal relationships with people around you.

French

French culture and people are associated with sophistication and elegance, so dreaming of a French national, or that we speak the language or are part of the culture, represents a desire to embrace these qualities.

Orphan

Dreaming of an orphan signifies your fears of being abandoned, unloved or rejected. This is a dream that suggests vulnerability and uncertainty about your place in life. It is probably a sign of the dreamer's desire to be loved and accepted. If you dream of adopting or taking care of an orphan, it probably signals your desire to nurture or protect a part of yourself that feels vulnerable or unloved.

Hermaphrodite

People who possess both male and female sexual organs indicate a concern with balancing the feminine and the masculine parts of our sexuality.

Leader

If you dream of being a leader and taking control of others, it suggests that you are taking responsibility and initiative in your life, or that you have a desire to do so. If you are being led, you are not taking responsibility for your actions. A leader is also an authority figure. Your attitude towards the leader in your dream may reflect your true feelings about a person with authority in your life.

Royalty

Princess

The princess is the female equivalent of the prince. This figure represents either your own characteristics, or those of a young woman to whom you are close.

King

The king in your dream may stand either for an authority figure, such as a parent or boss, or for your own desire for prestige or homage.

Queen

In some dream interpretations the figure of the queen is regarded as an archetypal symbol of the dreamer's mother. But the public role of a queen also suggests that this dream may be about your desire for public recognition, admiration or respect. Traditionally, dreaming of a queen was believed to foretell success for the dreamer.

Prince

A prince is an archetypal symbol for a young man, so the prince in your dream probably represents one of the important males in your life, whether a brother, lover or friend. If you are a male and have this dream, your prince may also symbolise the aspects of yourself that you feel most positive about.

Neighbour

French

Orphan

Hermaphrodite

Leader

Princess

King

Queen

Prince

Cross-reference

For French, see Foreign countries p.314, Language p.234
For Royalty, see Palace p.326, Throne p.373

Mythical beings

Mermaid/Merman

Mermaids are mythical creatures said to dwell in the sea, but able to breathe on land. This duality in their nature makes them symbolic of our desire to be able to connect the rational with the emotional, allowing us to be more at peace with our environment. To dream of mermaids may mean that the dreamer needs to let go of the rational and instead take a leap of faith.

Enchantress

An enchantress/fairy/witch image represents magic, illusion and seduction. The dream suggests that you should not be fooled by appearances but guided by your common sense instead. As the saying goes, 'all that glitters is not gold'.

Ogre

An ogre is an authority figure seen in his or her most negative light as overbearing, threatening or 'monstrous' in some way. If you dream of such a figure it may be a sign that you have a problem with an authority figure in your life—perhaps a parent or boss. The ogre may actually be you, so it may be a good time to reflect on how you are dealing with others.

Imp

The imp in your dream might represent your own mischievous side. In this case it may stand for your own sense that you have been misbehaving or acting against the interests of others. However, this figure might also symbolise a person or force that is trying to stop you from achieving success.

Giant

As children we saw adults as giants. Our parents seemed frightening in comparison to our small stature. This dream may be indicating that you feel powerless, or that whatever issue you are facing seems too big for you to handle. Perhaps that is why you are reverting back to your childhood fear of adults. Recognise your own power and outwit the problem—just as David did with Goliath.

Nymph

A nymph represents parts of ourselves, whether we are male or female, that are seductive, youthful and elusive. The dream may suggest that these are desired qualities you wish to make use of in your life.

Fairy

Fairies usually represent wishful thinking and belief in the possibility of magic existing in the world, rather than reliance on the practical.

Vampire

This terrifying creature of the night is created by our fears of being drained to the point at which we lose our life. The expression 'to be sucked dry' is an example of how the demands that are made on us can feel as if they are physically 'killing us'. The vampire is associated with evil and anything that is negative in our life, so if we dream of being attacked by one it indicates that we feel seriously weakened by another person's will. On the other hand, if you have this dream over the Halloween period, it may simply mean that the activities and images of your waking state have activated your imagination.

Mermaid/Merman

Enchantress

Ogre

Imp

Giant

Nymph

Fairy

Vampire

Cross-reference

For Vampire, see Bat p.45, Blood p.108, Evil p.447
See also Mythical animals p.59
See also Magic p.141

Identity & appearance

Transparency

When someone says that they 'can see right through you', they usually mean that they can see you clearly for what you are. If you dream that you are transparent it may suggest that you feel vulnerable and fear that your thoughts and feelings are exposed for all to see. Try to accept this feeling and resolve to deal with it more 'clearly' when you are feeling less threatened.

Name

If you hear your name being called in a dream, it suggests you should be paying attention to your individuality and personal nature. If your name has been changed, work out why you'd like to be someone other than yourself. Perhaps you sense a change in how you see yourself. Other people's names highlight our need to look at those qualities we admire or dislike in those people. In doing this, you may discover a new aspect to yourself.

Imitation

A dream in which you are mimicking someone else suggests insecurity about the value of your own skills or contribution. This can be a particularly difficult dream for those who work in creative fields and feel the pressure to be 'original'. However, imitation is a part of all creative work, and this dream can be a reminder of the debt one owes to others. Take note of what is being mimicked as this might be highly valued by the dreamer and perhaps there is a need to explore this in real life.

Ugliness

To dream of an ugly person or see yourself as ugly means that you are looking at parts of yourself that, for some reason, you find unattractive.

Disguise

To be wearing a disguise in a dream suggests that you are refusing to look at a matter or situation head-on. If others in your dream are disguised, it may be an indication that you feel excluded, or are anxious that others are not dealing with you honestly.

Adoption

If you dream that someone adopts you or that you have adopted a child, it could mean that you will be taking on some family responsibility. It could also mean you have been searching for your ideas to be adopted or that you may need to do so.

Transparency

Name

Imitation

Ugliness

Disguise

Adoption

Cross-reference

For Transparency, see Invisibility p.142
For Name, see Calling p.170
For Adoption, see Orphan p.306

CHAPTER TEN
Places

This chapter explores the significance of place in our dreams. This can be on a large scale in terms of whether you dream about being in a different country, on a medium scale in terms of what type of buildings are in your dream, down to small details such as whether your dream took place in an attic or bathroom. The location of a dream is also important—many dreams, for example, are located underground in tunnels, pits or holes which can represent feelings of being trapped.

Countries & regions

Foreign countries

Dreaming of being in a foreign country highlights the need for a different mental or emotional attitude to be applied to a situation. It also indicates that new experiences are ahead of you.

Egypt

Egypt is regarded as a mysterious and exotic place linked with ancient knowledge and great wealth. Depending on the dreamer's association with Egypt, it may signal a need to get out of the rut and pursue interests that are more related to adventure and mysticism.

Orient

In the West, the Orient is associated with the exotic, with ancient wisdom and mystic tradition. Some dream interpreters go so far as to associate the Orient with the dreamer's unconscious. A dream of the Orient or of a person from the Orient may signal your desire to explore any of these areas. Alternatively—especially if a compass is involved—the dream may signal your desire to 're-orient' yourself in a relationship or work situation.

Africa

Africa is associated with adventure, wild animals and dangerous landscapes. Dreaming of this ancient and complex continent suggests that you long for something with these qualities in your life. It may not be necessarily be restricted to travel but to parts of your life that lack excitement, urging you to expand your horizons and adopt a new perspective.

Europe

Travel, culture, history, fashion, architectural and artistic beauty, the seat of Western civilisation—all these ideas are associated with Europe so that dreaming of living or travelling there suggests a personal longing for these elements or connections. If the dreamer has connections with Europe, it may also represent a desire to explore his or her roots or more traditional life.

America

America is mostly associated with material wealth, success and freedom of the individual. It may suggest that these qualities are missing in your life and that you may need to be more ambitious through your own effort and determination. An urban environment highlights the stress and the competitive edge that comes with city living, while a rural setting may indicate a desire for freedom and enterprise.

India

For a Western person, India has a range of associations. It can be associated with the exotic and colourful, with the desire for spiritual awareness, with respect for the sacred, and with the desire to unite the disciplines of mind and body. India is also associated with the extravagance of the Raj, with the non-violence and spiritual example of Gandhi, and with social problems such as overpopulation, poverty and sickness. Thinking about the personal associations that this large and varied country holds for you will help you to interpret its significance in your dream. For example, dreaming of India may express your desire to travel, but it could also suggest your quest for higher awareness.

National flag

A flag represents beliefs and principles that you hold in common with other like-minded people. It is a symbol of common good, patriotism, loyalty and comradeship, and provides an object for people with common beliefs to gather around or follow. Dreaming of a flag could be a sign that you need to reflect on your principles and where you stand on issues that affect you and those people around you.

Foreign countries

Egypt

Orient

Africa

Europe

America

India

National flag

Cross-reference

For Foreign countries, see Abroad p.338
For Egypt, see Pyramids p.327
See also Language p.234

Buildings

Tower

Calling someone 'a tower of strength' implies that they can be of great support during a crisis. To live 'in an ivory tower' on the other hand, is to be removed from the world and immersed in your personal space. Whichever of these two expressions best reflects the meaning of your dream will depend on how you see your role in life. Either way, the tower stands for the things that you have created in your life. Are you a helper of others or do you stand back and not get involved?

Mill

To dream of a mill suggests difficulties in the dreamer's waking life. A mill represents the process of extracting what is important in your life. In order to extract and turn it into nourishment, the mill uses the potentially painful method of crushing. This dream suggests that your own experiences may be painful as a result of this extraction process, but that the pain will be worth it, as you will be transformed for the better. It suggests that you need to retain what is positive but throw out anything that is negative in your current circumstances.

Buildings

In dream lore, buildings are said to represent the dreamer's self in relation to his or her current environment. Different parts of buildings can also mean different things.

Apartment

If the apartment is small, dingy and uncomfortable, it suggests that your financial situation is bleak and future prospects are not good. It also means that your family or partner is taking up 'too much space' in your life. However, if the apartment is spacious and lavish, there will be a substantial increase in your financial affairs and your family life will also improve. Try to recall as many vivid images as you can, so that the meaning of the dream can be more accurate. The state of the apartment may be reflective of the dreamer's self or emotional state.

Property

Property stands for our inner resources. A dream in which you are selling property suggests your desire to obtain recognition for your achievements, or to market your talents. If you are trying to buy property, it may mean that you are keen to develop your inner resources, or that you wish to establish yourself more securely.

House/Home

This dream is about your private life and emotions. You should pay attention to where it is situated. Is it in a location you feel happy, dissatisfied, secure or unsafe in? What can you see out of the windows? These details may provide clues about where you feel you are in your present life, and where you would like to be.

Tower

Mill

Buildings

Apartment

Property

House/Home

Cross-reference

For Tower, see
    Platform p.333
For Mill, see Grain
    p.182, Wind p.92,
    Water pp.98–103

317

Buildings

Garage

Whether you see the garage as a tool shed, workshop or car park, it represents your passions, motivation and the resources available to you. It is a symbol of your energy reserves, and the things you don't need but you can't let go of, 'just in case'. If you dream of a car repair garage, you need to take care of your ambition or drive.

Laboratory

Dreaming of a laboratory indicates the dreamer's need to be objective about some issue. If you are a specimen in a laboratory, it may be that you feel that you are being judged, monitored and controlled by those in authority around you. However, if you are a technician or a scientist, you have control over the experiment you are conducting. Depending on the outcome of the dream, a successful experiment usually suggests that whatever you've been working on will have a positive outcome. If the experiment is a failure, the dream may be trying to tell you that you need to be more objective and calculating in your approach.

Igloo

This dream image is probably a symbol of the way you feel about either your domestic situation or your inner self. Made of blocks of ice, the igloo can suggest coldness, frigidity and the barrier you put up. More positively, it can also be a symbol of refuge in a hostile landscape. The inside of the igloo will explain which meaning is relevant.

Hut

Like hotels, huts suggest a temporary residence or insecurity. This building may also convey the dreamer's sense of having a reduced lifestyle or income. More positively, dreaming of a hut may suggest your desire for a holiday or for a simpler, less cluttered lifestyle.

Warehouse

To dream of a warehouse suggests a concern about your internal reserves of energy or resourcefulness. The amount of activity in the warehouse should help you decide whether you can interpret this dream positively or negatively.

Public house/Bar

If you dream of being in a bar or a public house, it suggests that you need people around you for socialising. Perhaps you are feeling isolated in your private life and need to make new friends. Generally a dream about this public place is to do with how we relate to group situations.

Hotel

Dreaming of a hotel indicates a short-term situation, such as a relationship that we realise subconsciously is unlikely to last, or a brief holiday or escape. For business people or travellers on the other hand, this dream is more likely to express attitudes towards their work.

Garage

Laboratory

Igloo

Hut

Warehouse

Public house/Bar

Hotel

Cross-reference

For Igloo, see
    Snow p.91, Ice/
    Iceberg p.80
For Public house/
    Bar, see Groups of
    people pp.280–1
For Hotel, see Holiday
    p.214, Travel p.274

Buildings

Lighthouse

A lighthouse is to warn ships that may be in distress, or have lost their bearings, and guide them to calmer waters. Because it is positioned near water, it symbolises the emotional difficulties that lie ahead. The light guides the dreamer by helping him or her to see what type of danger is ahead so it can be avoided. avoidedavoidedavoided.

Factory

Dreaming of a factory indicates the state of activity and production in your life. It may be telling you that if you work at a steady pace, even though the activity is repetitive or stifling, you will ultimately reach your goal. However, it may also indicate that you need to get away from the daily grind and strive for a more challenging job or lifestyle. This dream may be interpreted either way, depending on the dreamer's state of mind. Alternatively, the dreamer could be experiencing a lack of control in his or her working life. If you feel alienated or even a little exploited in your job, then there is definitely a need to consider how you could improve your current working conditions.

Cabin

Whether a cabin in the woods or a ship's cabin, this is a symbol of refuge and comfort set in the wildness of nature. As a result, it serves as a symbol for feelings of security in which excitement is never far away. Taking the opposite view, to dream of a cabin can also be indicative of feelings of being closed in, similar to symptoms of 'cabin fever'. It's up to the dreamer to interpret the symbolism that relates most closely to his or her experiences.

Windmill

The windmill is a traditional device for harnessing the energy of the natural environment. For this reason dreaming of a windmill relates to the way in which you are using your talents or resources. If the sails are turning freely, you probably have a store of creative energy. If, on the other hand, they barely turn at all, something has robbed you of your energy or motivation.

Observatory

An observatory is a place designed to bring distant things into close view. Is there an issue or emotion that you have been trying to keep at a distance, and that you need to examine more carefully? Alternatively, dreaming that you are observing the stars through a telescope can suggest your aspirations to a higher intellectual or spiritual state. It can also suggest your desire to be promoted or to rise to a prominent position.

Lighthouse

Factory

Cabin

Windmill

Observatory

Cross-reference

For Lighthouse,
    see Light p.450,
    Boat p.268
For Factory, see Work
    p.246
For Observatory, see
    Stars p.85

Parts of buildings

Pillar

A pillar or column can symbolise our spinal column or backbone. In this context the condition of the pillar reflects the support available to you, or your ability to remain upright in difficult circumstances. An alternative interpretation is that it may suggest a desire to be a 'pillar' of your community. The pillar can also symbolise the male sexual organ, and describes it as representing the driving or forceful aspects of your personality.

Walls

Walls symbolise our ability to construct our lives, and to make sense of the world by erecting divisions between our different activities. But as structures that divide and impede vision, they can also suggest the things that frustrate us or stand in the way of our desire for an uninterrupted space or view. The dreamer may be feeling vulnerable and the walls in the dream may reflect the boundaries constructed in life as a self-protective mechanism. Sometimes such a dream suggests it is time to pull down some of these boundaries so that you can obtain what it is that you presently desire.

Arch

An arch in a dream is symbolic of distinction and gaining a new status. In Roman times, arches were erected after victories and named after Roman Emperors to mark the event. At some traditional weddings, the bride and groom walk under an arch together as a sign of a new status as a married couple. If you're about to take on new responsibilities or move into a new phase of your life, you may see an arch or doorway. Don't be afraid to go through, as your courage and effort will be rewarded.

Floor

The floor represents support. It is the base structure on which you build your house (life). If the floor is weak, your support structure will also be weak and unable to see you through life's difficulties. If you are cleaning, polishing or repairing the floor, it suggests that you are willing to put effort into improving your standard of living. A slanted floor indicates that you are off-balance and deviating from your original plans. This may result in you not being able to achieve your goals.

Chimney

As a conductor of heat from inside to outside, the presence of a chimney in our dream can help us to assess the ways in which we deal emotionally with others.

Steeple

A steeple is generally associated with the mind and also with our spirituality.

Door

If you are passing through a door in your dream, it's a sign that you are ready to tackle your inhibitions, or make progress in respect to a certain area of your life. Closed doors, on the other hand, suggest either that someone is shutting you out, or perhaps that you are not ready to explore your own fears and desires.

Pillar

Walls

Arch

Floor

Chimney

Door

Steeple

Cross-reference

For Steeple, see Church/Temple p.149

323

Parts of buildings

Ceiling

A ceiling represents what is above you, the horizon or limit of a particular matter. If the ceiling is peeling or leaking, it is a sign that your life lacks security or that some part of it requires urgent attention. If it is high and lofty, this should be taken as a positive indication of your capacity to think or express yourself freely. If it is made out of glass and you're a woman, consider the expression 'breaking the glass ceiling'. If you are unfamiliar with this term, it is an expression that describes women's feelings of frustration at being able to see the possibilities for success in a working environment, but being unable to achieve them due to a variety of factors. When a woman breaks the glass ceiling, it means that she has broken through opposition and sexism and achieved success.

Roof

The roof represents the peak or our view from the lofty summits, high up, removed and totally objective. We utilise this objective state of mind to either reach spiritual growth or to protect ourselves against emotional involvement. To dream of being under the roof suggests that you are protected. However, if the roof is leaking watch out for possible dangers. The leak may imply that you are feeling emotionally vulnerable.

Windows

Dreams about windows are about your view or perspective on what is going on around you. Opening a window reflects your wish to let other people come into your life or influence you in some way. If you are on a high floor, you are looking at life from up high: that is, you are objective and think rationally about the view or situation. A window in the basement is looking at your primal self and therefore you're exploring your emotions about an issue. If you are climbing out of a window you are possibly trying to avoid some type of emotional commitment.

Structures

Obelisk

An obelisk can be a symbol of your inner nature and strength. This dream could be allowing you to assess the way your personality has been 'shaped'. The shape, size and decoration of the obelisk will help you to interpret the way you feel about yourself. An alternative meaning suggests that you are overly distant or cold (like a statue) in your relationships. This can represent the various inner depths of the dreamer, including the dark and cold side of one's nature. Such a dream may be a warning that you are using your strength or projecting yourself in a cold and unfeeling way in waking life.

Bridge

These structures are symbols of the power of human ingenuity to overcome obstacles and forge connections. Crossing a bridge suggests progress from one state to another. This progress has the potential to be both dangerous and exhilarating. For example, if you fear losing your balance and fall off the bridge, it is a sign that you doubt the power of your own abilities to carry you successfully through a project or undertaking. If you experience exhilaration in your dream, it suggests you are anticipating a new challenge and are prepared for risk and adventure.

Ceiling

Roof

Windows

Obelisk

Bridge

Cross-reference

For Windows, see
    Looking p.193,
    Curtain p.370
For Obelisk, see
    Statue p.428
For Bridge, see Falling
    p.257

Public & grand buildings

Court

Not surprisingly, dreaming of being in court denotes your anxiety about being judged. This dream could imply a guilty conscience or fear of discovery. It may also reflect your feelings of being unfairly treated and your desire for justice. If on the other hand you are being 'courted', it is a sign that someone is interested in you either professionally or romantically.

Palace

Dreaming of a palace suggests your desire for advancement, increased prosperity or an improvement in living conditions. If you are comfortable in the palace, it may be a sign that these things are within your grasp. If you feel out of place, however, or the people in your dream are ignoring you, it may be a sign that you lack the means to turn this dream into a reality, or don't feel that you deserve it.

Post office

This is a dream of communication—probably long distance. Dreaming of a post office could symbolise your desire to get in touch with someone who is far away, either because they are in a different country or city, or because they belong to your past. Alternatively, it could be prompting you to make contact with something or someone that you have pushed away from your conscious mind.

Hospital

Dreaming of a hospital usually indicates either the desire for healing, or anxieties about your own health or well-being or those of someone close to you. The events taking place in the dream, and the behaviour of the doctors and nurses, will help you to decide which meaning is indicated.

Airport

An airport is a symbol of transition. A busy airport represents your desire for escape and freedom, while an empty one indicates that your own plans may be delayed.

Public buildings

In general, these buildings are likely to tell you about your social or work relationships.

Pyramid

Pyramids are associated with death, mysticism and the focusing of mental and spiritual energy. This dream may reflect your thoughts on questions of death and the afterlife. Alternatively, it could indicate your desire to focus on and integrate the different parts of yourself. Pyramids are also associated with preservation. In this case, it may be a subtle warning that the dreamer needs to centre

their spiritual and material selves in order to find balance in the waking world.

Library

Seeing a library in your dreams represents your total life experience. Each book contains the skills, the experience and the knowledge that we have learnt throughout our life so far. The dream may mean that you need to research a subject more thoroughly before going ahead with a decision. Or, it could reflect your quest for learning. Are you in someone's 'bad books' or should you be studious and 'hit the books'? Returning a library book indicates that you are willing to pass on your knowledge to others.

Museum

A museum is a place where memories are stored and precious things are preserved. It represents the living past, family and heritage. Perhaps we are trying to connect with this past in order to come to terms with who we are and what our values are based on.

Court

Palace

Post office

Hospital

Airport

Public buildings

Pyramid

Library

Museum

Cross-reference

For Palace, see Royalty p.307
For Court, see Judge p.286
For Airport, see Aeroplane p.272

Rooms

Rooms

Some interpreters of dreams believe that the different rooms in a building actually symbolise different aspects of the dreamer's personality.

Balcony

Balconies are associated with the thrill and perils of romance. They also suggest aspiration: reaching for something desirable. If you are high up on a balcony with a good view, it may suggest your desire to be less involved and to take a more detached perspective on a matter or situation. If you are in danger of falling, the dream denotes anxiety about your hopes and aspirations.

Bathroom

As the Christian ritual of baptism suggests, bathing is a symbol of purification, regeneration and preparation for a new day. Water is also a symbol of our emotions; so if you dream of having a bath, it may be a sign that you need to pay more attention to your feelings. However, if you have trouble getting out of the bath, maybe you are too immersed in your emotions.

Similarly, if the water is going cold, perhaps it's a sign that you are lingering too long over some activity or relationship. Dreams in which you are embarrassed about bathing in public suggest a fear of exposing your inner self and emotions to others.

Attic

This room can stand either for your memory or intellectual life, or for matters that you have been trying to store away from your conscious mind.

Bedroom

This dream is likely to symbolise the way you feel about your emotional or sexual life. The bedroom is associated with privacy, relaxation and sensuality.

Rooms

Balcony

Bathroom

Attic

Bedroom

Kitchen

Basement

Kitchen

The kitchen represents family life, the heart of the matter, and the place where your emotions are most at home.

Basement

This is where you keep your most secret fears, or those parts of you that are still hidden or undeveloped.

Cross-reference

For Bathroom, see Personal grooming pp.136–7
For Bedroom, see Bed/Mattress p.370

Rooms

Vault

In a dream, a vault that contains valuables, such as a bank vault, represents the place where we house our resources. These may be emotional, physical or practical. The dream may be prompting you to take care of these resources so that they are not stolen. A burial vault, on the other hand, is associated with death and loss. In a dream this loss is most likely to be the loss of something that was once stored in our memories.

Passages/Corridors

As conduits between the different parts of a house, these spaces tend to symbolise the transitions we make between different aspects of our personality, or contrasting life stages.

Hall

To dream of a large, hall-like building or space tends to suggest some emptiness or vacancy in your life. Perhaps you lack friends or a social life, or don't have enough activities to fill your time. Alternatively, if the dream is a pleasant one, it may signal your desire to have more space, or feel less pressured by those around you. If the hall is filled with people, it is likely that the dream represents the public aspects of your life.

Study

An office tends to reflect our feelings about our work or professional lives—especially if we work in one in our waking lives. Whether or not you feel comfortable in this office—whether the other workers are friendly, are ignoring you or trying to boss you around—may reflect how satisfied you feel at work.

Pantry

As you might expect, a pantry symbolises the things that nourish you and keep you going. In a dream a pantry is likely to represent the emotional resources that you are able to draw upon, both from within and from those around you. In this context, interpreting the dream requires you to take note of the condition of the pantry: is it well stocked, or are there empty shelves?

Because pantries tend to be a feature of old-fashioned kitchens, this dream may also have significance in terms of your childhood. For example, the pantry in your dream may represent the nourishment or basic resources that you received from your parents and family when the foundations of your current life were created. An empty pantry would suggest that they have given all they have to give. It's basically a warning that the dreamer needs to restock resources.

Cage/Cell

Feeling 'caged in' and wanting to 'break out' are reflections of frustration coming from different areas in your life. Dreams of caging a wild animal suggest the desire to overcome threatening obstacles, whether they come from others or from within yourself. If you are the one who is caged in the dream, be alert for a potentially negative situation at work or in your emotional life.

Vault

Passages/
Corridors

Hall

Study

Pantry

Cell/Cage

Cross-reference

For Study, see Office p.246
For Cage/Cell, see Trapped p.199, Prison p.226, Captivity p.200

331

Locations & places

Alley

The setting in a dream can give you an indication about your 'inner landscape' and where you're at. If the alley is clear and bright, then you have a reasonably easy road ahead, despite some 'narrow misses'. However, an alleyway that is cluttered, dirty, with a dead end, is a warning of conditions to come or how you're viewing your present circumstances, either in your private or working life. If the place seems familiar but in actual fact is unknown to you, perhaps you are not solving a recurring situation. Are you feeling trapped? Or are you perhaps lost? How you feel about being in the alley is a good indication of how you should interpret the dream.

Backstreets

Backstreets carry with them connotations of illicit activity or concealment. If your dream is accompanied by pleasurable feelings, it may suggest your sense of indulging in a secret or guilty pleasure. If the dream has anxious or threatening feelings, it is likely to indicate that you feel involved in something 'shady' and are fearful of the consequences should the activity become public knowledge. This type of dream indicates an inner desire to break loose, to explore the deviant side of the self, particularly if the dreamer feels they are being good to others and not themselves in real life.

Outside

The outside or exterior of your dream house tells you how you feel about appearances; the side of you that you present to others. Being outside, looking in on a building with no means of entering, indicates the dreamer feels if he or she is an onlooker in his or her own life. Empower yourself and take control.

Crossroads

Important decisions and danger are symbolised by a dream of crossroads. Their presence in a dream warns you that care is required when making a decision—you are facing an important crossroads in your life.

Alley

Outside

Backstreets

Crossroads

Platform

Platform

Generally, dreaming about a platform provides us either with a jumping off place to something new, or a chance to look around and view our surroundings from up high. This dream can suggest preparation for a change or a desire to assess your current situation from a more objective point of view. Because platforms are associated with height, this dream may also suggest your feelings about being promoted or 'elevated' above others around you. Depending on your feelings in the dream, this situation could be a source either of nervousness and anxiety, or of excitement.

Cross-reference

For Crossroads, see
Fork p.247
For Platform, see
Tower p.316

333

Locations & places

Harbour

Generally, a harbour is a symbol of security and of the desire to be protected. Harbours are places of safety and calm where you can take refuge from the storms and heavy seas you are likely to encounter in your life journey. Because of these associations, dreaming of a harbour may also symbolise a reassuring relationship, whether with a partner, parent or friend.

Quay

Quays or docks are strongly associated with meetings or departures. For this reason dreaming of one is likely to suggest either the process of leaving something behind, or the desire to begin a new phase in your life. The circumstances within the dream will help you make sense of its meaning, while your emotions will reveal your attitude towards this change.

Canal

These slow-moving passages of water are symbols of communication, calmness and reflection. Their appearance in a dream is a sign that you need to be willing to slow down and even drift for a while so that you can reflect more deeply upon your life and progress. It can also be an indication that different aspects of your self—such as your business and romantic sides—need to be in better touch with each other.

Marketplace

A market is a place of commerce and trading, and as a symbol represents 'public' space and dealing with people in general. Dreaming of a market may suggest that you need to be more commercial in your ventures and look for the resources that will allow you to pursue this goal. Dreaming of a stock market could be an indication that you need to carefully consider financial decisions.

Harbour

Quay

Canal

Marketplace

Town

Town

Towns are places where there is a strong sense of community and a great deal of social interaction going on. Dreaming of your hometown suggests that you feel comfortable with doing things the way you have been since childhood. On the other hand, if you see yourself in a strange town, it may mean that you don't yet feel comfortable in a new environment. The new town may also stand for a side of yourself that you haven't accepted yet. Deserted towns represent past social contacts or values that are no longer of use to you ('ghost towns'). If you are lost in a strange town, it may mean that you are looking for a new direction in life. This dream suggests that you may be forced to rely on the advice and kindness of strangers in order to find your way.

Cross-reference

For Harbour, see Boat p.268
For Quay, see Departing p.252
For Canal, see Travel on water pp.268–71

Locations & places

Shelter

A shelter represents our search for protection. If we dream of sheltering someone, it may mean that we are really trying to protect parts of ourselves from potential hurt and disappointment. Being sheltered by someone else signifies our belief that we are protected by a divine source.

Address

If you dream of an address that has significance to you, your dream is trying to draw your attention to, and make you deal with, a situation that happened in your past but is still troubling you in your present life. If the address evokes feelings of safety and happiness, then you can take your mind back to that period and see if something is missing. If the address evokes feelings of unhappiness, this signifies that you wish to escape from the past but are being reminded of how you behaved at the time and that you now have an opportunity to correct it. Writing down an address usually means luck and predicts that good news is coming. A new address indicates a major change. A negative association with an address may signify that there is a feeling of alienation or lack of belonging and thus a need to move on in reality.

Camp

A camping ground offers us a temporary refuge or stopping place in a longer journey. If you dream of such a place, it may symbolise your desire to take some time out to gather your strength. But it is also a reminder that you can't afford to relax for too long, because a longer process or journey demands your attention. Dreams of camping also reflect the desire for adventure—getting away from the hustle and bustle of city life and living with nature's challenges.

Tunnel

Seeing a tunnel in a dream indicates a wish to delve deeper into the unconscious and explore the deeper parts of ourselves. Crawling through a tunnel is reminiscent of our birth experience, the tunnel resembling the birth canal. Perhaps you feel a need to crawl back into the safety of the womb and only emerge when you are ready to make contact with those on the outside. The tunnel could also signal a 'fresh start' or a re-birthing of your ambitions and desires. Because a tunnel is a passage with two definite ends, it can also represent our life's journey. Those of us who break through the obstacles and blackness of the tunnel usually emerge to find a positive outcome (light at the end of the tunnel). On a more punning level, the dream may be pointing out to you your own 'tunnel vision'. It may mean that you need to be more aware of other things that are going on around you, rather than just focusing on the one.

Fair/Fairground

The fair brings back our childhood memories of fun, excitement, rides and prizes. It suggests a letting go of social restraints as we indulge in a more imaginative state. The dreamer may need to get in touch with the childlike aspect of his or her personality. Your subconscious may be telling you to let go of the restrictions and boundaries you've set up in your life, to embrace creativity, and to see things through fresh eyes. The fair is also a symbol of social and public life, with an assortment of characters as well as the 'swings and roundabouts' of life in general.

Shelter

Address

Camp

Tunnel

Fair/Fairground

Cross-reference

For Address, see
  Envelope p.397
For Camp, see
  Caravan p.265
For Tunnel, see
  Underground
  pp.342–3

Locations & places

Threshold

If you are carried over the threshold in a dream, it signals the beginning of a new relationship. An alternative interpretation is that a threshold indicates new responsibilities in the near future.

Yard

The yard is the outside part of a dwelling that divides the inside of the house from the street or neighbours. For that reason it tends to symbolise the parts of your life that exist between the private and public arenas. A dream in which you are sweeping or tidying a yard suggests your desire to present a favourable image to the world. It may relate somehow to the saying, 'clean up your own backyard', indicating that before you comment on how others lead their lives, you should make sure that your own is in order.

Hearth

A hearth or fireplace symbolises the need for security, whether the context is our family life or our relationship with ourselves. This image is a symbol of emotions or passions that are contained and directed so as to provide warmth for us and those close to us. But if the fire is getting out of hand, it could be sign of your fear that some powerful emotion is in danger of threatening your cosy or familiar existence. If, on the other hand, the fire is in danger of going out, it suggests that there is an emotional problem or 'cooling' of feelings between you and someone you are close to.

Abroad

This dream signifies that a change is needed in your life. You are feeling very unsettled and have a real desire to break the chains and be free of the confines of your present circumstances and environment. The idea of travelling to a foreign destination invites new prospects and changes in your present work, choice of lifestyle and people involved in your life.

Path

How does your path in life appear in your dreams? Is it difficult, winding, full of dangers and obstacles? Or is it smooth and well-trodden, shaded by trees, or surrounded by attractive gardens or 'prospects'? These details suggest your current state of mind about your overall progress in life. Are you playing it safe by following in others' footsteps and sticking to a familiar route, or are you prepared to venture into uncharted territory, where the way is less certain but may also be more rewarding?

Surroundings

Surroundings in dreams are important indicators of our feelings and attitudes. If you are in a dreary setting, it probably reflects your feelings of depression, while bright and airy places suggest contentment and security. Chill surroundings tend to represent emotional coldness while a warm and relaxed environment indicates that the dreamer feels safe and sheltered. See the entries on individual settings and climates for more specific examples.

Threshold

Yard

Hearth

Abroad

Path

Surroundings

Quarry

Quarry

Dreaming of a quarry suggests the work that has to be done if you are to access the valuable insights that you hold in your subconscious. Alternatively, the desolate, abandoned appearance of a quarry may suggest that you feel exhausted or overextended: stripped of your resources. In this case the dream suggests that you need time to recover if you are to recoup your vital energies. If the dreamer is working in a stone quarry it can be indicative of feelings that he or she is nothing but a slave to others' needs in waking life. In this case, the message is to be good to yourself.

Cross-reference

For Threshold, see
  Door p.323
For Hearth, see Fire
  p.81
For Abroad, see
  Foreign countries
  p.314

339

Barriers

Moat

A moat in a castle, usually medieval, is a symbol of our need to defend ourselves emotionally against intimacy. As the castle is a fortress—a defence system against anyone penetrating it—the drawbridge is movable. We choose to open our castle grounds when we are confident or to close up when we feel under attack or vulnerable. Because the moat has water, our emotions are what we are trying to protect.

Gate

A gate is a symbol of transition or change from one stage to another. When we walk through the gate we are entering another state. In dreams this may mean a transition from one period of life to another, such as from adolescence to adulthood, from the single state to being married, from school to employment or even from life to death. The pearly gates of heaven are a symbol of the passage across the threshold of life into the realm of death. If you dream that the gate is locked and you are trapped either inside or out, you may need to look at other symbols in your dream. Ask yourself whether the gate is a barrier or an opportunity for new things.

Fence

A fence is an artificial structure built to restrict and control movement, particularly of animals. A dream of a fence is a classic obstacle dream, often inviting an interpretation that reads it as a symbol of control over our inhibitions or our 'wild' self. As boundaries, fences can also represent our own boundaries within society, in relationships and at work. Often it's the conflict of work encroaching on our personal lives that is symbolised by a fence, and suggests our need to build a wall of resistance to keep them apart. We can also feel 'fenced in', confined, and 'stuck' in a place we may want to move out of. Fences also symbolise protection of property and of self, and the desire to keep out unwanted intruders. A fence between you and someone else is an expression of your desire to stay on your own turf and remain separate.

Maze

Dreaming of a maze represents a confusion of feelings and ideas that make it difficult for us to find our way or make progress. Beliefs and old values influenced by authority figures can block our ability to think clearly, making us feel as if we are lost in a maze of our own doubts and irrational fears. If you dream that you make it through the maze to the exit, it means that you will overcome your fears and become a wiser, more confident person.

Moat

Gate

Fence

Maze

Labyrinth

Ditch

Labyrinth

A labyrinth is a confusing network of passages. Exploring the labyrinth is a symbol of exploring our deeper selves, especially our fears that we keep hidden from others. Depending on whether you are lost in the labyrinth or you reach the exit, take note of the outcome. Should you be asking for help to find your way out? Are you facing your fears or running away from them without a resolution, forever roaming the labyrinth of your mind to escape them?

Ditch

Barriers such as these tend to symbolise the obstacles that prevent us from reaching our goals. A ditch may suggest your fear of getting bogged down if you try to move forward. Alternatively, if in the dream you are stuck in the ditch it may suggest that you feel exposed, and are anxious about being seen to be putting yourself forward. Dreaming of a ditch usually indicates that it's time to change in order to avoid routine in life.

Cross-reference

For Labyrinth, see Passages/Corridors p.330
See also Restrictions pp.206–7

Underground

Underground

Dreaming of being underground signals a withdrawal from all the aspects of life that cause us to be agitated. Perhaps we need to stay underground for a while to think about an issue and should only resurface once the decision is made. Being in a subway suggests that you are about to take a trip inside yourself, to discover who you are and what you really believe in. However, dreaming of being underground is not necessarily about the need or wish for withdrawal. It can also indicate the need to reflect on certain aspects of life at a deeper level. You may need to reflect before making a decision. If the dream is set in an underground house or shelter it is likely to be about primal fears. This dream suggests that you don't feel safe, and may be threatened by people or situations in your life.

Pit

Dreaming of a pit is an obvious reflection of the dreamer's fear of falling or becoming trapped. The expression 'pit of despair' denotes an emotional situation that is very difficult to climb out of. In this respect the dream may symbolise the dreamer's need for outside help and support if he or she is to escape a negative emotional situation. Pits can also symbolise fear of death—not necessarily physical, but the symbolic 'death' of some relationship or phase of your life. A pit also represents the ruts or holes we make in waking life.

Tomb

A tomb is a final resting place, so entering one is an exploration of how we feel about death. This may not be an actual death, but an ending of some phase of your life. If there are bodies in the tomb, these may indicate aspects of yourself that you have put to rest. For example, they could be the ambition you gave up on or a world trip you couldn't take. In general, anything related to death signifies a renewal or awakening of some sort. In consequence, this dream is actually related to rebirth.

Abyss

To dream of an abyss or any hollow space foretells of trouble and difficulties ahead. Quarrels, threats, loss of control and failure are all associated with this type of dream. If you fall into an abyss, you can expect your fears and disappointments in any given life situation to be realised and be overcome only with a feeling of loss. However, if you manage to avoid falling into an abyss you will overcome your troubles and recognise your potential, which will lead to self-acceptance and success.

Mine

'Working in a salt mine' is a saying we use to convey the repetition of the work place. Mines are a symbol of places where we work, but can also signal the process of going within ourselves and examining our potential. Are we a 'gold mine' waiting to be discovered? In general the mineral associated with the mining will reflect the meaning of the dream. For example, dreaming of a salt mine suggests persecution or even dictatorship.

Hole

Generally speaking, a hole can stand either for a trap or bad situation in life we fear falling into, or for a place of refuge that appeals to our impulse to hide or feel protected. Holes in clothing, on the other hand, tend to represent our sense of our own failings, the things that are incomplete or missing from our personalities or lives. A pothole in a road may represent the need to stay alert and watch for dangers that lie ahead.

Underground

Pit

Tomb

Abyss

Mine

Hole

Cemetery

Cemetery

Dreaming of a cemetery may indicate your desire to take a rest or time out. But this dream may also be a warning that some part of you, whether a talent, emotion or activity, is at risk of 'dying' if you don't put it to use. To dream of a cemetery can also denote an awakening or a need to seek higher knowledge so that you realise your talents and desires.

Cross-reference

For Tomb, see Death
        pp.208–9,
        Funeral p.208
For Cemetery, see
        Death pp.208–9,
        Funeral p.208
See also Tunnel p.336

Stairs & lifts

Steps/Stairs

To get somewhere 'step by step' is to make progress with effort and consistency. Are the steps hard to reach in your dream? If you are climbing up the steps, it means that you will make steady progress in your present situation. Going down steps symbolises descent into your subconscious. It also represents your past (you've already been up these steps before). These steps symbolise the efforts we must take to achieve a certain goal or reach a state of greater enlightenment.

Escalator

Like a lift (below), going up an escalator suggests that you are reaching your full potential or goals; while going down an escalator indicates the reverse. The positive aspect of the escalator is that if one is persistent there will be success at the end. Have you ever seen young people run up the escalator that is going down and still manage to get to the top? Unlike the open escalator, the lift is enclosed and therefore this is not possible to achieve. Unfortunately the lift is either taking you up, down or is stuck in between floors.

Lift/Elevator

Lifts indicate our emotional highs and lows. Going up suggests that you are elevated, 'uplifted', given support, rising to success and tapping into your spiritual self. Going down in a lift is symbolic of going within ourselves, tapping into our unconscious state and discovering what is hidden there. If you feel trapped, or there is no way to control the lift, you need to work out what it is that is blocking your emotions. A lift or elevator can suggest the aspect of ourselves we are most in tune with. If you are going up in a lift, it is likely that you are comfortable with the rational and intellectual side of your personality and thoughts. To go down in a lift, on the other hand, suggests a willingness or ability to explore your subconscious.

Broken buildings

Demolition

Generally speaking, this dream represents the way you feel about change. If you are in charge of the demolition, it is a positive sign that you are initiating the change and feel in control of it. But if something is being demolished around you, then the dream suggests that you feel powerless to control or direct the changes in your life. Demolition also represents the need to tear down current circumstances and build something more positive. The message is to look at what you have built in your own life that is not working. Perhaps you need to think about tearing it down and starting again.

Scaffold

Dreaming of a scaffold is a sign of a change that is about to enter your life. Given that a scaffold is a temporary structure, this may only be a temporary or short-term change. However, it will be a change nevertheless.

Ruins

If we see ruins it is usually as a result of vandalism or a natural disaster. If it is due to vandalism or carelessness, then it points to our own destructive urges. How did we create this state? If it is not of our own doing, but we need to pick up the pieces, then we must accept it and move on just as we do with all of nature's disasters.

Falling buildings

Not surprisingly, dreams of falling buildings suggest that the dreamer is at risk of being overwhelmed by problems or responsibilities.

Steps/Stairs

Escalator

Lift/Elevator

Demolition

Scaffold

Ruins

Falling buildings

Cross-reference

For Steps/Stairs, see
    Descending p.253
For Lift/Elevator, see
    Descending p.253
For Ruins, see
    Disaster p.200

CHAPTER ELEVEN

Food & drink

Dreaming of foods can be seen as a need for nourishment on either a basic, physical level or on a more complex, emotional level. The type of food you dream about also has its own symbolism, for example, apples are associated with 'forbidden fruit' while pomegranates are a symbol of fertility and resurrection because of their many seeds. The act of eating or drinking is linked with feelings of satisfaction and sustenance, which again may be giving you clues to your emotional feelings rather than just your simple physical needs.

Fruits, nuts & grains

Fruit

Fruits are associated with reproduction and ripeness ('coming to maturity'). We talk about the 'fruits of our labour' to indicate the prosperity that follows a time of hard work. Each individual fruit is thought to represent some aspect of sexuality, fertility or the life force.

Cherries

These popular and richly coloured fruits are traditional symbols of romance and sensual enjoyment.

Bananas

Bananas are unique in their elongated shape, and represent male sexuality. To dream of a big, yellow banana signals that you need to slow down your pace of life and take better care of your health, especially your diet. It could be your body's way of telling you that you're missing out on some essential vitamins and minerals.

Apples

Apples are the 'forbidden fruit' described in the Bible, and in religious symbolism represent the fall of mankind or the origin of sin in the act of taking a bite of what is forbidden. Over the centuries the apple has also become a symbol of sexual or maternal love, as in the expression 'the apple of my eye'.

Lemons

We associate lemons with something being 'bitter' or—as in the case of a car that is described as 'a lemon'—an object that has given us endless trouble and is defective in some way. Consider how these two definitions apply to what is happening in your life and how you feel about it.

Dairy

Ice cream

Eating ice cream in a dream usually symbolises a desire for pleasurable or sensual sensations. However, if the ice cream is too cold or you find yourself concerned that it's going to melt, this dream could stand for some of the worries that prevent you from fully enjoying your sensuality.

Tea

Champagne

Wine

Alcohol

Ice cream

Cream

Cheese

Milk

Cream

This luxurious food is a symbol of prosperity and well-being. It can also symbolise something that has been obtained illegitimately, as in 'the cat that got the cream'. To dream of it suggests your desire for personal advantage, however it is gained.

Cheese

Dreaming of cheese could be a sign that you have been overindulging in rich food or social events. You may need to take more care in your diet or lifestyle.

Milk

Milk is a symbol both of sustenance and kindness. Your dream may be highlighting the fact that you are not taking care of your basic human needs. However, milk can also manifest itself as a less desirable trait: being taken advantage of is referred to as 'being milked' and if you 'cry over spilt milk' you are meant to take the consequences that are a result of your actions.

Cross-reference

For Champagne, see Celebration pp.202–204
For Milk, see Baby p.295

Sweet foods

Honey

This substance represents an intense experience of sweetness or pleasure. By extension, it can also refer to someone we love or who gives us pleasure.

Pancakes

Dreaming that you are eating pancakes or watching someone making them suggests a desire for emotional nourishment or fulfilment. It may be a sign that these things are lacking in your current relationship or home life. If you are pouring syrup on the pancakes, it may be a sign that you need more 'sweeteners' or inducements in your life.

Chocolates

Like cherries, chocolates are associated with romance and sensual pleasures. Dreaming of them may suggest your desire to be spoiled or indulged. It may also be reminding you of a special occasion coming up such as birthday or anniversary. Check your diary.

Jelly

Dreaming of this wobbly substance suggests an issue that is hard to get your teeth into. Perhaps somebody is avoiding a confrontation, or you yourself can't seem to define an issue or problem that is bothering you. To dream of jelly may also suggest a sense that you are failing to be firm on a particular issue or problem. At worst, dreaming of jelly denotes a sense of unreliability or 'spinelessness'.

Cakes

Dreaming of eating cake is usually a positive dream; a sign that you like to feel indulged or approved of by others. It could be a sign that you feel a particular need to be pampered or nourished, especially if you've deprived yourself of the 'sweet' things or 'extras' in your life.

Easter egg

Easter is a Christian time of renewal and rebirth. Dreaming of this time could suggest symbolically a desire to return to our younger days. The Easter egg represents spring and new birth. Think about the part of your life that you wish to revive or the new ideas that you'd like to give birth to.

Honey

Pancakes

Chocolates

Jelly

Cakes

Easter egg

Sugar

Sugar

As sugar is both pleasurable to our palate and a cause of tooth decay, interpreting its symbolic meaning requires you to understand its dual nature ('sickly sweet'). Sweets suggest rewards, while to be 'sweet on someone' is to have romantic feelings towards them. Is your life lacking in 'sweetness and light'? If so, inject some pleasure into it and treat yourself to some sweet outcomes. Putting sugar on something bitter can also make it easier to swallow. To dream of sugar can also be an indication that something in your life is not pleasing to your palate—in other words, that it is not good for you.

Cross-reference

For Cakes, see Birthday p.204
For Easter egg, see Spring p.438

Vegetables & salad

Vegetables

If you dream of vegetables, you should make sure that you are getting all the vitamins and other nutrients you need. Sometimes in our conscious state we tend to think that we should eat more vegetables but don't make a regular habit of it. The subconscious picks up on this and we dream about it.

Carrots

To dream of this vegetable may be a sign that you need to take better care of your health, especially where vitamins are concerned.

Salad

A craving for a salad in a dream indicates your body's need for the vitamins provided by the variety of ingredients in the salad. Pay attention to the vegetables and their vitamin groups. On a broader level, dreaming of food denotes a desire for nourishment in general. Eat well and be prepared to pamper yourself a little.

Pumpkins

This bright orange vegetable is associated with Halloween and with autumn. In your dream it may symbolise the coming to fruition of a plan or an idea.

Peas

In ancient times, the Greeks interpreted a dream of peas as an omen of business success. Today the expression 'alike as two peas in a pod' tends to associate this vegetable with things that look alike, or share common characteristics. This dream could be prompting you to think about someone you resemble, such as a family member or close friend. It could also reflect your anxieties about being too conformist, or fears of losing your individuality in a social group or relationship.

Cabbages

This vegetable is a basic symbol of nourishment; perhaps a type of nourishment we didn't enjoy very much as children. But the complexity of a cabbage when cut in half suggests the complex layers of our emotions. We can think of it in terms of layers that grow as we ourselves grow and mature over time. In this context, the emotions that accompany the dream may provide the clue to its meaning.

Onions

Onions are multi-layered vegetables and can often represent parts of ourselves.

Potatoes

The meaning of this dream is probably going to depend on the way you feel about this vegetable. For most of us, however, the potato is a staple food—not glamorous, but nourishing. For this reason it tends to represent a domestic situation that is secure and comfortable, but not necessarily exciting.

Olives

Olives are emblems of peace and kindness, as the oil pressed from the olive can be used for many purposes.

Vegetables

Carrots

Salad

Pumpkins

Peas

Cabbages

Onions

Potatoes

Olives

Cross-reference

For Pumpkins, see Seasons p.438

Eating & drinking

Drinking

To be drinking something in a dream may signify either your need for sustenance or your desire to 'imbibe' some emotional or spiritual truth. If you are worried about becoming drunk, however, it is a sign that you lack social confidence or are worried about embarrassing yourself in front of others.

Restaurant

A restaurant or café represents our need for company. We may be searching for emotional satisfaction or need to have an intimate relationship. The association with food suggests the need for emotional nourishment.

Dinner

This dream suggests that you need to pay attention to your closest family or social relationships. Perhaps you need more sustenance than you are receiving, or maybe you are failing to provide others with nourishment?

Eating

To be eating in a dream suggests that you are satisfying your hunger, not necessarily for food, but also your other needs—whether emotional or sexual. To refuse food is to refuse the opportunity for growth and positive change. Sharing food at a table is a sharing of yourself with others. The dream may be interpreted in relation to the circumstances—how was the food consumed? What type of food was it?

Fasting

Fasting is usually associated with cleansing. When we fast, our bodies are cleansed of toxins. A dream of fasting may be drawing your attention to a need for some type of cleansing in your life. Ask yourself what is toxic in your current life. It may also be telling you that you are 'going without' to punish yourself or to make a statement about a grievance of some sort. This dream may take the form of a hunger strike rather than fasting.

Intoxication

This dream reflects anxieties about your consumption (not necessarily of alcohol) or about habits that threaten you with loss of control, whether in relation to money or your emotions. More positively, being intoxicated in a dream could be a sign that you are preparing to relax, enjoy yourself more, or behave less responsibly for a change. This dream can also symbolise a desire for a change in attitude and perspective.

Thirst

If we need to satisfy a thirst it means that we have a desire to satisfy our basic needs. Normally, these are spiritual and emotional needs which, if unsatisfied, will lead to us 'wasting away' in some way. Think about whether you are refusing to satisfy some inner need and how you can be kinder to yourself.

Hunger

A dream in which we are hungry can be simply a projection of our physical state. More symbolically, the physical experience of hunger can stand for something we lack in some other sphere of our lives—whether it is a hunger for love or intimacy, for fame and celebrity, or for money and wealth.

Appetite

A lack of appetite indicates a diminishing of other drives in your life such as your libido or ambition to succeed. It may be a warning that your health is not as good as it should be. Having an appetite for food or drink can be a sexual desire or a need to consume what is around you—especially financially. Take care not to overspend and try to manage your money carefully.

Picnic

The picnic in your dream probably represents your romantic or social life. Is your life like a picnic? When interpreting it consider whether or not you are enjoying the experience. These things could include the weather, the company, the food, and irritating factors such as ants or mosquitoes.

Drinking

Restaurant

Dinner

Eating

Fasting

Intoxication

Thirst

Hunger

Appetite

Picnic

Cross-reference

For Intoxication, see Drugs p.128, Alcohol p.352
For Hunger, see Starving p.199

Food, miscellaneous

Meat

Meat is associated with flesh and as such is a symbol of physical gratification.

Ham/Cured meats

Eating this meat in a dream could signal your sense that you are living on the 'pigs back'. Because ham and other cured meats such as salami are prepared by a process of 'curing' the dream may also reflect concerns about health. These represent our need for preservation.

Popcorn

A dream in which you are eating popcorn may reflect your wish for more excitement in your life. This dream may occur before you are due to attend an event or entertainment.

Yeast

Yeast is used as a raising or lightening agent in bread, and as such symbolises the forces in our lives—such as ideas or the influences of others—that can change our personalities or the situations we are in, usually for the better.

Wafer

Wafers are a delicate form of biscuit used to represent the body of Christ in the Christian service of Communion. These associations suggest that the wafer in your dream is likely to represent something in yourself or your life that is delicate, easily broken, and which demands respect or even has sacred value. The expression 'wafer-thin' reinforces the association of wafers with fragility.

Pie

In traditional gypsy interpretation, a dream in which the dreamer was making pies foretold happiness and prosperity. Today we are probably more inclined to interpret this dream as a sign that you want to get at the 'meat' of an issue. If the pie is too hot for you to eat, it probably symbolises your frustration that something is preventing you from getting your teeth stuck into an issue or activity. It also depends on what kind of pie; for instance, apple pies are associated with all things good and wholesome. Eating an apple pie might indicate that you are looking for the good in something.

Herbs & spices

Salt

Salt makes a difference to our lives, adding zest to our food and pleasing our palates. It represents the finer qualities that we incorporate into our daily grind. Salt is a staple food, which spices things up but can also be an aggravation (as indicated by the expression 'rubbing salt into a wound'). Salt can symbolise status or goodness, as in the saying 'salt of the earth'. It may represent these qualities either in ourselves or in someone around us.

Pepper

Dreaming of this pungent spice may suggest that things are about to become livelier ('pep up' your life). But because pepper can make us sneeze, it may also signal irritation with a person or with a situation.

Spice

Spice is usually associated with zest and pleasure ('spice of life'). Does your life need spicing up?

Garlic

Garlic was once regarded as so potent that evil spirits would not approach the wearer. In many countries, garlic garlands were hung over doorways for protection. Today, the meaning of garlic has changed in a practical direction. Garlic has been recognised as a natural herb with strong detoxifying qualities that guarantee better health. Depending on the nature of the dream, seeing or eating garlic indicates your desire to ward off something, which could be illness or perhaps other people.

Meat

Ham/Cured meats

Popcorn

Yeast

Wafer

Pie

Salt

Garlic

Pepper

Spice

Cross-reference

For Yeast, see Bread p.360
For Wafer, see Holy communion p.147

361

Objects

Most dreams contain some type of object which can be of help in relating the dream to your everyday life. The object may play a primary role in what happens such as playing a musical instrument in an orchestra, flying a kite or receiving a prize in a competition but often the object may be simply part of the background and therefore easily overlooked. Have you considered what you were wearing in the dream, for example, or what material your clothes were made from? If you were making a cup of tea, think about whether or not the kettle boiled over. This type of detail can give vital clues that you may otherwise miss.

Clothing

Clothing

Having new clothes in a dream is a positive sign, suggesting that you are about to embark on a new period of self-expression and heightened self-esteem. To dream of getting dressed suggests that it's time for a change. If people are looking at you critically, however, or you are forced to dress in public, the dream suggests anxiety about your ability to perform in a new role.

Dress

If you are a woman and you dream of a beautiful new dress, the dream suggests that you want a more active social life or even romance. This dream can also suggest that you are anxious about the way in which you appear to others, or symbolise your desire to be thought attractive or fashionable by those around you.

Cloak

Mystery, adventure and concealment can all be symbolised by the dream of a cloak. This dream can be a sign that you or someone close to you is deliberately or unconsciously attempting to hide something. Consider the term 'cloak and dagger', which has long been associated with notions of secrecy, danger and undercover violence.

Cap

If you are doffing your cap in a dream, it implies a sense of inferiority. In olden days it was customary to do this to those in authority. But putting on a cap can also signal your desire to be prepared for and protected against any unexpected event or circumstance that may arise.

Button

If you dream of a button or buttons, it may be a sign that you or someone close to you is afraid of rejection or of being left behind or 'mislaid' in some way. On the other hand, if in the dream you are sewing on a button it could be a sign that you are trying to communicate with somebody, or bring some person or experience into your life.

Clothing

Dress

Cloak

Cap

Button

Coat

Hat

Coat

If you are wearing or putting on a coat in your dream, it is a sign that the next part of your life will be accompanied by protective influences. It also suggests a 'cover up' or that you are protecting yourself from the world or others around you. Think about how this fits in with your waking life situation.

Hat

Putting on a hat in a dream can signal the awakening of your creative impulses or your desire to find a solution to a problem. It can also symbolise completion, as in the expression 'to cap it all off'. Hats can also represent positions or roles in life. Changing hats in a dream means that you want to change your position in life.

Cross-reference

See also Materials & fabric pp.424–5

Clothing

Shirt

Dreaming of a shirt or blouse signifies the state of our emotions. One can be a 'stuffed shirt' who is unable to accept new ideas. At the same time, someone can be so generous that they give you 'the shirt off their back'. Think about other symbols in the dream such as the colour, texture and condition of the shirt to arrive at a more precise interpretation.

Pocket

A pocket is a place we store things to keep them safe, and it is also a hidden place. For these reasons a pocket in your dream can symbolise secrecy: those thoughts and feelings you keep hidden from others, and the possessions you want to keep safe. Pockets are also associated with sexuality, and this meaning could be reflected in your dream. Being 'out of pocket', on the other hand, suggests lack in some area of your life, while 'lining your pockets' indicates that you are seeking to provide for your own advantage, perhaps at the expense of others.

Apron

Are you tied to your mother's apron strings? Or perhaps you crave those times when you felt safe in your mother's arms. An apron can represent the need to be nurtured or that you need to connect to the nurturing side of your nature. It is also a sign of being domestic, so throwing away the apron can be telling you that you want to get away from domestic issues or the mundane.

Label

Dreaming of a label is about self-image and how others see you. It may be that you are trying to establish a new identity or break out of a role that you are no longer happy with. If you dream of labelling things, it means that you are searching for order or wanting to establish some sort of order in your life. If you are re-labelling something, it could be that you miscalculated and 'labelled' someone wrongly.

Shoes

New, shiny shoes give us confidence in a job interview or important social occasion. For this reason they are associated with our position in life. Walking without shoes indicates that you are going through a tough time, while taking shoes off signifies that you are leaving the past behind you. Shoes keep us grounded and are a symbol of moving forward as well as a reminder of our need to be sympathetic to others as in the phrase to 'stand in someone else's shoes'.

Hood

A hood is most commonly used for concealment or protection and as such is associated with our desire for these things. If someone else in the dream is wearing a hood, the dream could be expressing your frustration with someone near you who you feel is hiding their feelings from you or refusing to deal with you openly. Because a hood can have a menacing aspect, dreaming of someone who is wearing one may also point to an aspect of yourself that you fear to explore. Are you afraid of revealing your ideas or parts of yourself?

Shirt

Pocket

Apron

Label

Shoes

Hood

Cross-reference

For Shoes, see Walking p.254

367

Clothing

Uniform

A uniform, whether it's a school student's, nurse's or soldier's, represents identification with a particular role. For example, if you dream of a soldier, it may be a sign that you feel 'at war' with yourself or others around you. Wearing a school uniform indicates your wish to fit into a group and most likely belong to the 'in' crowd. Think carefully about the type of uniform in your dream and interpret it with the help of other symbols.

Veil

The veil represents mystery and the hidden. In many cultures women are veiled to hide them from the gaze of men who are not from the family circle. In Western society a bride is veiled before the final wedding vows are sealed with a kiss. This ritual is a reminder of the transition from a single to a wedded state. If you are wearing a veil in your dream, think about whether you are going through a major change—emotionally or physically—or whether you are trying to keep people from seeing parts of you that you would like to keep hidden. Such a dream is usually indicative of something in the dreamer's life that is not predictable. There is an air of uncertainty surrounding recent decisions with the result that the outcome is veiled in mystery.

Fashion

Fashion that is ever-changing and dictates what we wear plays a significant role in our lives. Dreaming that you are taking an interest in fashion, either in a glossy magazine or shop window, may suggest your desire for outward change. People pass judgement on what we wear— label, quality and style—and we use fashion to convey these qualities. Are you really what you wear, or are you putting on a show to convince others?

Underwear

Seeing someone in underwear really means that you are catching a glimpse of vulnerable parts of yourself. If you dream of being embarrassed in your underwear, the dream indicates your anxiety of being 'found out'. It could also mean that you are trying hard to conform and be someone that you are not. To be seen in your underwear is to be seen for what you really are. This dream can also be interpreted as symbolic of the dreamer's feelings regarding his or her sexuality.

Zip

Dreaming of a zip symbolises your relationship or your connection with others, especially the degree to which you feel able to be 'open' with them. The state of the zipper in your dream—that is, whether it is open or closed—may represent how open or closed you are with your friends. However, if the zip is broken or stuck, this dream (like those in which we appear naked) is more likely to express a fear of social embarrassment or exposure.

Uniform

Veil

Fashion

Underwear

Zip

Cross-reference

For Uniform, see
    Soldiers p.233,
    School p.242
For Veil, see Marriage
    p.210

Furniture

Chair/Sofa

These are for resting and relaxation, so they usually express the dreamer's passive attitude or openness. This dream may be suggesting that you need to take more rest and be open to new methods of relaxation.

Cushion

This is a symbol of the things we use to protect or 'cushion' ourselves in life. If someone is trying to take a cushion away from you, or you can't get comfortable, it could be a sign that you feel uncomfortable or vulnerable in your waking life.

Lamp

In traditional symbolism, the lamp represents the spark of life. It brings clarity and shows the way ahead. A brightly lit lamp denotes a strong sense of purpose and direction, while a dim lamp indicates uncertainty and disillusionment.

Curtain

If the curtain is blowing open, dreams containing curtains are a positive indication of new possibilities or insights, especially in relation to your spiritual life. If you are closing curtains in your dream, it may be that you are avoiding a difficult or unpleasant issue.

Bed/Mattress

Beds are symbols of rest, comfort and security. They are also associated with intimacy and relationships. If the bed is in an uncomfortable or dangerous situation (on top of a cliff, for example, or in a place where people are watching you) your dream could be telling you that you feel vulnerable or 'exposed' in your relationships with others. If you feel protected and happy in the dream environment, it is more likely to suggest your desire for an emotional or sexually fulfilling experience or relationship. If, in your dream, you are frightened by something under the bed, the dream may be trying to draw your attention to something that has been unconsciously threatening your relationship with another, or with yourself. Traditionally, dreaming of making a bed was interpreted as a sign to expect visitors.

Lying in bed is also a passive activity, whether a person is recovering from an illness or just daydreaming. As a result this dream could be an indication of some form of depression.

Cabinet

Like most enclosed spaces, cabinets represent the inner aspects of your personality. In the case of the cabinet, which is associated with the collection of valuable or unusual objects, the association is with memory.

Carpet

The pattern and colour of the carpet will help you interpret this dream. If it is plain and ordinary, it may reflect your sense that your current life is dull and lacking in contrast, whereas a highly patterned carpet denotes a life that is eventful and passionate.

Cradle

An empty cradle symbolises your anxiety about losing someone or something precious to you through neglect or accident.

Cupboard/Wardrobe

These are where things are kept hidden, locked away and out of sight. Hidden memories, our ability to be open to people and a sense of isolation are all possible meanings of these pieces of furniture. The cupboard has a sexual significance, through its ability to represent the womb. If we have 'a skeleton in the closet' then we have secrets and desires which are hidden from those people around us. The term 'coming out of the closet' is used to describe homosexuals when they decide to acknowledge and inform the 'outside world' of their sexuality.

Chair/Sofa

Cushion

Lamp

Curtain

Bed/Mattress

Cabinet

Carpet

Cradle

Cupboard/ Wardrobe

Cross-reference

For Curtain, see Windows p.324
For Bed/Mattress, see Bedroom p.329
For Cradle, see Baby p.295

Furniture

Chandelier

This is a symbol both of prosperity and brilliance. However, if you are worried about the chandelier falling on you, it is a sign that you feel potentially overwhelmed by your current lifestyle.

Mirror

Like water, mirrors symbolise the process of looking into the unconscious in order to discover who we really are. If you dream of looking into a mirror it suggests that you are concerned about your image—about what others think of you and also about how you 'face' the world. There may be anxiety over appearance, ageing, health and attitudes. Perhaps you are too anxious about your image and don't spend enough time reflecting on who you are comfortable being. A mirror provides a reflection of ourselves, which is not necessarily a true representation of who we are inside. Rather, it symbolises what we would like to project onto others. If you dream of a mirror, your feelings within the dream will tell you whether or not the projection is an accurate one.

Table

A table is a symbol of social interaction. We eat at the table, either at home or at a restaurant, and at the same time gather around it to socialise with family, friends and colleagues. Dreaming of a table, therefore, is about order, ritual, communal activities and your place in society. Take note of where you are sitting at the table. If you are at the head of the table, this is a positive reflection of your self-image and status. Being at the far end of the table, away from familiar people, indicates that you need to polish up your communication skills.

Toilet

Dreaming of a toilet is associated with the relieving of physical discomfort in private. In dreams, the room itself reflects the dreamer's need for privacy, in order to release personal feelings and emotions without anyone observing. Dreaming of going to the toilet suggests that you need to flush away those things that are no longer important to you. If the toilet is blocked it probably means that your emotions are blocked too.

Throne

A throne represents absolute power and authority. If you dream that you are sitting on a throne, the dream suggests your right to exercise this power and authority. However, if someone else is on the throne, it is likely that you consider someone else to be more worthy of that position. An empty throne implies that you are not ready to accept a position of responsibility.

Chandelier

Mirror

Table

Throne

Toilet

Desk

Desk

Dreaming of a desk can symbolise our anxieties about work or study. It can be a sign either of overwork, or of our belief that we need to work more consistently if we are to achieve our goals. The desk may also represent a need for organising your thoughts in order to achieve those goals.

Cross-reference

For Mirror, see
    Reflection p.192
For Throne, see
    Royalty p.307
For Desk, see Work
    p.246

373

Weapons

Weapons

In a dream, weapons represent the dreamer's aggressive urges. These are not necessarily directed against others, but sometimes at parts of ourselves. If you have trouble making a weapon work, the dream suggests your feelings of impotence or inadequacy. See also, individual weapons.

Cannon

This is a symbol of extreme aggression, and often a sign that someone is threatening you in a rather exaggerated or obvious way. A cannon in a dream could also be a sign that you are overreacting to a perceived threat and are at danger of making yourself look ridiculous.

Gun

A gun is seen as a symbol of aggression. Shooting someone means that you feel aggression towards some person or the part of yourself that this person represents. The gun also represents the male sexual organ and drive. If the weapon doesn't fire, the dreamer has feelings of sexual inadequacy. Depending on what the circumstances are in the dream, the gun can be interpreted in many ways. You may be using the gun to protect something that is of value to you. Killing someone may be a message that you have violent feelings towards this person and wish that he or she wasn't in your life.

Bomb

Dreaming of a bomb suggests that you may be feeling 'explosive' at the moment. Are your emotions in check? What explosive situation are you dealing with? It may have to do with a relationship or with matters at work. If the bomb explodes in your dreams, it indicates that a sudden and unexpected event will take place as a result of deep feelings that have been brewing. We refer to people being 'walking time bombs' when their emotional and psychological states of mind are not balanced. On a deeper level, it is generally believed that a bomb represents your fear of death.

Weapons

Cannon

Gun

Bomb

Rifle

Dagger

Rifle

A rifle represents protection and because of its long shooting range is more likely to be associated with distant dangers. It may mean that the dreamer is afraid of being attacked from a vulnerable position and needs a sure 'weapon' for self-defence.

Dagger

If someone is using a dagger in your dream, it is a sign that you fear cutting comments or criticism. If you are using a dagger, it may mean that you feel you need to behave aggressively in a particular task or important business deal.

Cross-reference

For Bomb, see
   Explosion p.201
See also War,
   fighting & violence
   pp.230–33

Weapons

Sword

Dreaming of a sword represents our sense of courage and strength. If we take up the sword and fight, it symbolises our desire to fight for what we believe is right. The dream may bring out the warrior in us, whereas in waking life we may not be willing to actively pursue justice and retribution. A sword is also associated with power or authority. If the sword has a double edge then it may serve to remind us that power can either be used as a positive or negative force in our lives.

Spear

The spear is a masculine symbol of power. It is associated with the dreamer's own assertiveness and dominance over a situation. Do you need to get straight to the point?

Torpedo

Like a rocket, a torpedo bears a physical resemblance to the male organ and, as a result, suggests sexual drive. As a weapon, the torpedo suggests how the sexual drive can lead to excessive aggression if not directed in a responsible way.

Sword

Spear

Torpedo

Tank

Nuclear weapon

Tank

To dream of a war tank denotes a need to defend yourself from a position of safety, represented by armour. If you have this dream you should ask yourself whether you feel threatened at the moment and why you need to employ such drastic measures to fight for your beliefs.

Nuclear weapon

We are living in a nuclear age, where we face injury and death by the use of nuclear weapons, particularly bombing devices. This creates anxiety about our safety and our future, as well as that of the next generation. This dream usually reflects those anxieties and fears, particularly after incidents are reported in the news.

Cross-reference

For Nuclear weapon, see Explosion p.201

Machines & technology

Calculator

To see someone in your dream using a calculator suggests that you feel somebody around you may be untrustworthy. If you are using a calculator, chances are that a current situation is forcing you to behave more rationally or coldly towards your friends than you would like. This dream can also reveal money or business worries. If you can't find the answer, something in your life is not adding up.

Disc

In a dream, a computer or compact disc often stands for our desire for information or knowledge. This is often a work-oriented dream, and may be a sign that something is puzzling or eluding you in your work. A music or audio disc, on the other hand, tends to represent the desire for relaxation or time off.

Machines/Machinery

Dreaming of a machine represents our body's functions and drives: breathing, ageing, moving and our inner workings, such as emotions, wishes, desires—all those parts of us that motivate and move us. Machines also suggest that 'automatic' aspect of our lifestyles and the habitual things we do without using our creative force for the full enjoyment of life. You need to examine all the symbols of the dream in order to come to a conclusion about this dream. Are you taking the machine apart? Perhaps this indicates your need to try to get at something that isn't working. If you see a mechanic in the dream, he or she may represent a doctor (helping to fix the machine or body). Dreaming of a well-oiled machine means that you wish for things to run smoothly in your life, without any nasty surprises.

Dynamo

A dynamo is a symbol of controlled energy. To dream of one either signifies your ability to take on a task that requires constant application, or that you have been working too hard at something, feel 'run-down' as a consequence, and need to recharge your batteries.

Engine

The engine is a symbol of one's drive or energy. It includes the body as a machine, sexual energy and the drive to succeed. This dream needs to be interpreted in light of all other symbols in the dream. For instance, if you see a steam engine it could indicate 'full steam ahead' with a plan. A broken down engine on the other hand may suggest the state of your physical health and that you need to listen to your body's needs.

Computer

A dream with a computer in it is likely to represent productivity at work or in a creative enterprise. It can also symbolise your desire to be better organised. Dreaming of computers may also mean that you are overworked and are in need of human contact and fun.

Engineering

Dreaming of engineering works or of an engineer points to some aspect of your life that needs structuring or major adjustment. It is a positive dream because it gives the dreamer the feeling of being in control and using whatever assets are available to create the structure.

Cross-reference

For Engine, see Car
  p.262
For Computer, see
  Work p.246

Machines & technology

Robot

In today's age of automation, it's not uncommon to dream of robots. A robot is a symbol of efficiency, emotional detachment and control. These may be qualities that you feel are missing from your life and wish to incorporate more into your daily schedule. On the other hand, a robot's job is repetitious and unappealing. Perhaps you feel stagnant and unappreciated either in your job or at home. Consider which of these meanings are closest to your situation. This dream may also be warning you that you are living a 'virtual life', and that you need to make time to reconnect with family and friends.

Pump

Pumps are generally used to channel a resource such as water from its source underground to the surface. Perhaps there is some issue or emotion that you need to bring to the 'surface'. Alternatively, you may have a talent that you are trying to uncover. In this case the action of pumping suggests that achieving this will require some effort.

Telescope

If you are using a telescope in a dream, it means that you are taking a closer look at something. Because a telescope enlarges and enhances the object, this dream can also be a warning not to make something bigger than it is.

Robot
Pump
Telescope
Satellite
Piston
Radar

Satellite

A satellite is a sign of communication. As a global means of communication it represents the desire to communicate on the most extensive scale. This dream may be suggesting either that you need to get in touch with a deeper or more universal level of yourself, or to reach out to more people.

Piston

A piston is a symbol of drive and energy, especially in a sexual context. The way the piston is working in your dream will help you to assess your energy levels in real life.

Radar

A radar represents intuition, so if you dream of it, you are picking up on signals other people are giving out.

Cross-reference

For Satellite, see Antenna p.239
For Pump, see Water pp.98–103
For Telescope, see Stars p.85

Materials

Tar

Dreaming of road tar indicates movement or travel. If the tar is fresh and sticky, you may be feeling stuck and unable to move on to your journey. Tar can also be repaired, so despite its black colour, its appearance in a dream can be a positive sign that all is not lost.

Gravel

Gravel is dangerous to skid on, whether you're driving on it or scraped your knees falling on it as a child. The message of the dream may be to not take risks at the moment, but to wait until you are on solid ground.

Wood

Wood is an organic substance, and can signal our desire to be in touch with our basic instincts or to enjoy a more 'natural' or simpler lifestyle. More symbolically however, when we describe something as wooden, we usually mean that it lacks expression or life (to have a wooden heart is not to have feelings). In this context, wood can denote a situation or person who seems to be lacking in emotion or warmth.

Glass

Glass is a transparent barrier that allows us to see what's on the other side. For this reason it represents the invisible barriers that we put up ourselves or that others impose on us. These barriers might be emotional distance, social barriers, fears or a lack of self-confidence. When professional women refer to the 'glass ceiling' and their difficulty in breaking it, they mean that they can see what they could possibly achieve but that the glass (tradition/ male dominance) is a barrier that needs to be broken or opened up. If you dream of breaking glass it may indicate a broken promise, relationship or a shattered dream. This distressing dream may be turned into a positive one if you take it as a sign to free yourself of emotional restrictions and be ready for a new direction.

Cement

Unless you work in the building industry, a dream in which you are laying cement is likely to signal your attempt to cover something over. If the cement won't cover the surface it's intended for, or the work is very hard and exhausting, you should take it as a sign that the matter you are attempting to hide won't go away easily. If the cement goes on easily, it is a sign that you are prepared to move on.

Plaster

A plaster ceiling can symbolise your aspirations, or what you look up to in life. Plaster falling on your head suggests insecurity about the things that are 'above you' such as authority figures or future events. A sticking plaster (Band-Aid) symbolises the desire to patch a relationship or emotion, or to protect a vulnerable part of yourself from getting hurt.

Tar

Gravel

Glass

Wood

Cement

Plaster

Wallpaper

Wallpaper

Wallpaper tends to symbolise our surface or facade: the part of ourselves we present to others. If you dream of putting up wallpaper, it could be a sign either of your desire to hide something, or to change the way others see you. Stripping away wallpaper suggests a desire to make a positive change in our lives.

Cross-reference

For Tar, see Road
    p.264
For Glass, see Window
    p.324, Ceiling
    p.324
For Plaster, see
    Ceiling p.324

383

Household items

Cup

This container is a symbol of our emotional life. It will help you to interpret the dream if you note whether the cup is full or empty and whether you are giving or receiving it. A cup also represents gifts of the spirit, such as joy, happiness, health and inspiration.

Dish

A dish that is full tends to symbolise fulfilment in our emotional or family life, whereas an empty one suggests that something is missing or incomplete. A broken dish can suggest family arguments or conflict or even foretell the loss of a relationship.

Pan

A saucepan is likely to symbolise either your creative life ('what's cooking') or your domestic situation in general. If the pan is 'bubbling over', there's a good chance that your creative or home life is also full of energy and ideas. If you can't get the pot to boil, however, some crucial ingredient or motivating force may be missing. We use the expression 'flash in the pan' to describe an inspiration that is unlikely to last. There is also the expression 'out of the pan and into the fire', warning the dreamer to be more cautious in present situations.

Napkin

White dinner napkins are associated with formal dining and celebration. If they are crisp and clean, it is a positive sign that you are looking forward to an occasion. If the napkins are mismatched or soiled, it indicates that you may have problems in dealing with an occasion that requires you to be on your best behaviour or to put on a facade.

Jar

Trying to open a jar in a dream suggests a desire to enjoy the fruits of your labours. If the jar opens easily, the dream suggests confidence about your ability to overcome your obstacles. An empty jar symbolises disappointment and impoverishment, whether it represents yourself (in which case it may be a sign that you are depressed or lacking in energy) or a lack of nurturing in your life.

Table linen

Linen suggests the finer things of life. A linen tablecloth suggests fine dining and more formal family celebrations. Dreaming of a white, crisp tablecloth may suggest that you long for the finer things of tradition.

China

To dream of china, particularly bone china, suggests the need to exercise great care and delicacy in a social matter.

Cup

Dish

Pan

Napkin

Jar

Table linen

China

Cross-reference

For Napkin, see
   Celebrations
   pp.202–4
For Table linen, see
   Table p.372
See also Eating &
   drinking pp.358–9

Household items

Vase

A vase is associated with the feminine and with creativity— as the holder or receptacle of what is valued as beautiful. We are frightened of breaking a vase, and consequently take more care than usual around one—especially if it's not in our own home. This may be because we see it as fragile and precious to the owner and therefore to be treated with respect. A vase containing flowers is the item we first think of when we invite guests to our home or need to impress homebuyers. It represents beauty, creativity and growth. Consider whether any of these qualities strike a cord with you.

Antiques

Antiques are a symbol of that which is old and valued. Buying antiques can mean that you need to embrace good old-fashioned standards and stick to your old tried and true solutions. It is also thought to be an omen that an inheritance is coming your way. Selling antiques means a loss of value, whether it's monetary or moral values. The mood and circumstances of the dream are important in interpreting this dream.

Urn

Today when we think of an urn, we tend to envisage the urn used for holding the ashes of a loved one. As a result the urn is usually associated with death. Perhaps the urn is a reflection of our attitude towards death—do we visibly keep it around in a place where it can be viewed to remind us of our own mortality, or do we hide it out of sight?

Tape

If you dream of taping together something that is broken, it implies that you will be required to mend a friendship or a relationship. Dreaming of a tape measure suggests our need to perform. How do we measure up to others or our own expectations? Dreams of recording tape are associated with self-expression and communication, while dreams about red tape symbolises bureaucratic issues.

String

Do you hold the 'purse strings' in your family? Are you holding onto the 'apron strings'? Perhaps you are 'stringing someone along'? Like these sayings, your dream can have a variety of meanings. String not only holds things together (whether a relationship or a business), but is also a metaphor for controlling the family finances, connecting with others and not being fully honest.

Box

A box is traditionally associated with the feminine aspects of the personality, especially in its physical aspects. Boxes suggest containment, but also the desire for expansion. If the box in your dreams is empty, it's a sign that something is missing from your waking life. This dream could be warning you to mistrust the promises that someone has been making to you—whether in business or your romantic life. If you're struggling to open a box in your dream, it suggests that you've become bogged down in the pursuit of your goals, and need to think about adopting a different approach. If the box contains something frightening, it's a sign that you need to face up to some problem that you may have been trying to ignore.

Cross-reference

For Vase, see Plants p.66
For String, see Rope p.413

Household items

Padlock

A padlock suggests the desire to secure something— whether it's a person or an emotion. Perhaps you fear losing touch with a friend or partner, or there is an emotion you don't want to look at too closely. Alternatively, you may feel silenced. If you are opening a padlock in a dream, it suggests that you are trying to get in touch with emotions that may have been 'locked away'. Perhaps you are open to new experiences, or are preparing to 'speak out'. The dreamer definitely needs to unlock the padlock and explore those feelings.

Knob

A dream with a knob in it, such as a door handle, stands for anything in life that you may have been trying to ignore, but which keeps reminding you of its presence by sticking out. This dream may be telling you that you have to seize whatever it is, and explore it.

Plumbing

If you dream of problems with your plumbing, chances are that there is a 'blockage' somewhere in your emotional life. This dream could be a sign that you are bottling something up, or that the different aspects of your emotional life are not balanced or are out of sync. If you are calling a plumber in your dream, it suggests your desire to solve a problem or remove an obstacle. The expression 'to plumb the depths' suggests going to the heart of a matter, even if it is difficult or unpleasant.

Keyhole

Freud regarded keyholes as symbols of the vagina, an interpretation that gave any dream in which they appear an automatically sexual meaning. More generally, keyholes can suggest our desire to spy on others, or to penetrate their privacy. For this reason if you dream that you are trying to look through one, it may suggest that you are indulging your curiosity about somebody's private life too freely, or are at risk of gossiping about his or her affairs. Alternatively, it may suggest that you yourself feel that your privacy is at risk from the curiosity of others, or that you fear being exposed to scrutiny.

Key

The key in your dream may symbolise your attempt to find a solution to a problem or situation that has been bothering you. If the key breaks in the lock, or refuses to open it, the dream suggests that you can't see a way beyond your difficulties. In an emotional context, the appearance of a key in a dream may be a sign that you have been keeping your feelings too locked up. In this case the dream may be telling you that you need to release some of them. Interestingly, in traditional Chinese lore, the key is a symbol of discretion.

Padlock

Knob

Plumbing

Keyhole

Key

Cross-reference

For Padlock, see
    Prison p.226
For Keyhole, see
    Prison p.226
For Key, see Prison
    p.226

Household items

Candles/Candlestick

These can symbolise both celebration, and the exploration of your spiritual side. If the candles are on a birthday cake, this may be a reminder of an important date or anniversary. As a device that holds a light, the candlestick in your dream suggests the basis of an insight or investigation. What's the reason for that spark of light? If you are carrying the candlestick, it could be a sign that you are ready to explore a previously hidden part of yourself.

Broom

If you dream of sweeping the floor, it's likely that your life has become cluttered with obstacles and you need to get rid of them in order to move on. Perhaps you've become emotionally attached to someone who's making demands on your time and energy, or you've taken on too many commitments at work. This dream could also signal that you're being held back by outdated emotions from the past and that it's time to 'take out the trash'. Of course, it could just mean that you are aware that you need to clean your house!

Pillow

The pillow symbolises comfort, support and rest. The pillow in your dream may represent your desire for one or all of these things. Alternatively, it may stand for an actual person whom you rely on to support you through difficult times. If you want a pillow but can't find one, the dream suggests that you may be denying yourself basic forms of comfort or support. This dream suggests that you need to take more care of your emotional needs.

Garbage

The act of throwing out garbage represents getting rid of what you no longer need or what you consider to be useless. Depending on the type of garbage you see—in other words, whether it is furniture (values), food (nourishment) or flowers (beauty)—you may be discarding valuable parts of yourself. On the other hand, you may feel that it's time to let go of some parts of yourself that you have outgrown or which are no longer useful to you. In general, this type of dream indicates that the dreamer is discarding what is no longer productive in his or her waking life.

Quilt

A quilt represents your desire for emotional warmth or security. Specific quilts may carry special associations for the dreamer. For instance, if you dream of a quilt that you remember from your childhood, the dream suggests a desire to recapture the security and love you associate with that time. If the quilt in your dream is torn, soiled or on fire, it is a sign that you fear change or loss in your emotional or domestic life.

Broom

Candles/
Candlestick

Pillow

Garbage

Lamp

Quilt

Cross-reference

For Broom, see
    Sweeping p.180
For Candle, see
    Birthday p.204
For Pillow, see Bed/
    Mattress p.370
For Quilt, see Bed/
    Mattress p.370

Appliances & utensils

Scales

In the zodiac, the scales represent the sign of Libra, which symbolises the need for balance and order. Depending on the dream, scales can represent either a person who is a Libran or the dreamer's need to acquire more self-control or to make a decision. Scales also represent justice or fairness of dealings. The dreamer could be weighing up the pros and cons in preparation for making a fair or 'balanced' judgement.

Kettle

Like a hearth, a kettle is a symbol of domestic life and comforts. For this reason dreaming of one can symbolise your desire for a cheerful social or domestic life. However, if the emphasis in your dream is on the kettle boiling, it may suggest that your emotions have been building up and are about to reach 'boiling point'.

Oven

Ovens are associated with heat, and also with domesticity and the things that sustain us. The oven is also a source of amazing transformation: an appliance that changes unappetising, raw food into something delicious. In this context, the oven in the dream may suggest your own potential for transformation or change. The expression 'a bun in the oven' is used to describe pregnancy, giving the oven the added association with sexual creativity and new life.

Sieve

The sieve symbolises the sorting out of the good from the bad. This dream suggests that the dreamer has the resources to make the right decisions and needs to trust his or her own gut instinct.

Refrigerator

Consider whether you have stored up resentments that have resulted in cooling your emotions (you may appear 'cold-hearted'). Perhaps you have put something in cold storage until you are ready to take it on. Usually, a refrigerator represents self-preservation. When we are hurt, particularly if we are women, we withdraw our warm emotions and give the 'cold shoulder' as a way to protect ourselves from further heartbreak.

Knife

Generally speaking, dreaming of a knife symbolises your aggressive, active side. However if the knife refuses to cut, the dream is more likely to indicate your sense of frustration or impotence. If, by contrast, the knife cuts something easily, it could be a sign that you will soon overcome some difficulties.

Television

Dreaming of watching television reflects a desire for escapism and distraction from your present situation. If you are watching the news, listen carefully to what is being broadcast. It may have a specific meaning for you.

Corkscrew

The presence in a dream of this common gadget may symbolise the birth of a new idea or project. If you have trouble using it, it is a sign to prepare for potential difficulties. If, on the other hand, the cork comes out with ease, the process should be relatively effortless.

Fork

A dream of stabbing someone or being stabbed with a fork represents the force that drives us, often in a negative manner. The three-pronged fork is traditionally associated with the devil and is therefore a warning of trickery. However, in general, the fork is a symbol of indecision as indicated by the idiom, 'taking a stab in the dark'.

Cross-reference

For Scales, see Zodiac pp.144–5, Weighing p.174
For Knife, see Cutting p.171
For Television, see Entertainment pp.248–9

Gifts

Gifts & giving

To dream of being given a gift suggests your openness to what others have to offer. It can also mean that you feel supported or approved of in your waking life. If you are giving a present, the dream suggests your desire to connect with someone around you. The emotions surrounding the dream will indicate how well the dreamer feels that his or her efforts are appreciated. 'Give and take' is a phrase used to describe a healthy relationship, so if you dream of giving something to someone it usually suggests that you are giving something of yourself. Examine your feelings about giving in the dream. If you begrudge giving something away, then you may need to be more sharing, whereas if you're too eager to give or 'dump' on others, you may need to reassess your reasons for this dependency. If the receiver does not appreciate your giving, it indicates that you are not in tune with what the other person needs.

Charity

To dream of giving money to a charity suggests that people are making too many demands on you. It could also be a warning that you don't give too much of yourself in real life.

Prizes & trophies

Garlands

Garlands have traditionally been associated with honour and recognition. They have been awarded to champions and heroes for performing extraordinary deeds. Dreaming of receiving a garland may be an indication that you feel a need to be recognised by others for your talent and effort.

Prize

Dreaming that you are receiving a prize or watching someone else receive one usually suggests a desire for recognition or rewards. This dream may also indicate an improvement in your well-being or self-esteem.

Medal

A medal is a symbol of achievement. As humans, we all want to be appreciated for our efforts, and winning a medal or award is an acknowledgement of our talents. Other feel-good emotions associated with a medal are respect and achievement. This may be a wish-fulfilment dream or it may be pointing you to the fact that you are not feeling appreciated and you need something that will prove your worth.

Trophy

A trophy is a sign of a well-deserved achievement. Your dream may be pointing out that you wish to be validated for your efforts or that you need to set a goal for yourself that you want to achieve.

Cross-reference

For Gifts & giving, see Birthday p.204
See also Celebration pp.202–4

Books & stationery

Calendar

A calendar in your dream may be prompting you to remember something, either in the future or the past. Do you need to remember an anniversary or birthday? If you are putting up a calendar, it's a sign to be prepared for an event or change in your life. Marking a calendar in a dream indicates impatience for a particular date or event to arrive.

Novel

If you dream of reading a novel, try to remember the theme or genre. Books generally try to introduce us to new points of view and provide us with escapism. If your novel was an adventure or romance, the dream may be suggesting that you should include more of those elements in your life. It may also indicate your need to investigate or probe further into issues and perhaps change your perspective or approach to a particular situation. This dream may also have a punning meaning, in which the dreamer feels as if he or she has produced or taken a 'novel' approach to something in life and, as a result, is an innovator—much like a novelist.

Newspaper

Dreaming of a newspaper suggests becoming aware of some issue or news that was not known to you before. Usually, it indicates finding out something about yourself. Delve further to see what type of newspaper you dreamt of and which section you were reading. If the feeling associated with the dream is negative, it may mean that the dreamer feels as if his or her life has been sensationalised, or placed under some sort of scrutiny.

Scroll

A scroll is an ancient form of knowledge. Dreaming of a scroll indicates that you have tapped into a hidden knowledge—perhaps about yourself or indicating some new insight.

Dictionary

To dream that you are consulting a dictionary suggests that you are looking for some missing ingredient that will help to make your life more complete. The word you are searching for could be an important clue as to what this missing thing is. Such a dream indicates the need for meaning in our current situation, particularly if we have been feeling a bit perplexed in waking life.

Envelope

An envelope denotes either good or bad news. If the envelope is unopened in the dream the dreamer is fearful of the news. The dreamer is probably waiting on news in waking life and is fearful of the outcome.

Calendar

Novel

Newspaper

Scroll

Dictionary

Envelope

Paper

Paper

Dreaming of paper usually symbolises communication and self-expression. If the paper in your dream is blank, it may suggest problems in these areas. Similarly, if it is covered in illegible writing, it is likely that you are having trouble either communicating with others, or expressing your own needs. Wrapping paper tends to symbolise the way you present yourself to the world. But if you are having trouble removing the paper, some deeper issue or emotion may be escaping your attention. An alternative meaning is associated with the term 'paper-thin'. This would indicate that the dreamer doesn't feel secure, that things can easily be torn, secrets can readily be discovered and so forth.

Cross-reference

For Novel, see
    Reading p.187,
    Books p.240
For Paper, see
    Communicating
    pp.234–41

Toys & games

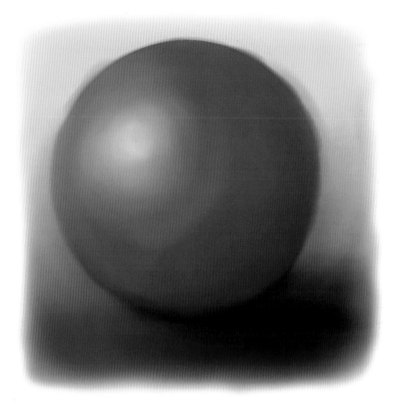

Ball

If you dream of throwing a ball to someone else, it could be a sign that you want to shift some responsibility onto another. If in your dream you're watching a ball game without joining in, it's a sign that you're standing on the sidelines of life; afraid to take the initiative because you think you may not have what it takes. In this case, your dream may be telling you that you need to place more confidence in yourself. But if you're right in the middle of the ball game, then it's a sign that you are a participant who is confidently dealing with what comes your way.

Cards

Depending on the context of the dream, cards are symbols of either risk, or sociability. If you have a winning hand, it is a sign of confidence in your ability to achieve a particular goal. If your are losing, it is a warning to proceed with caution, whether in business or romance.

Dice

Dice are symbols of risk or chance. Their appearance in a dream may be a sign that you are hazarding something on a single event or person. The numbers that turn up on the thrown dice may also have significance.

Hoop

This perfectly round toy signals our need to find balance, completion and harmony in our lives. It may also suggest nostalgia for childhood. Less positively, it may represent the sense that we are going round and round in circles when we should be making progress in life.

Doll

Dolls in dreams often represent children or the emotional aspects of childhood. If the doll is broken or abandoned, it may be a sign that you are anxious either about the welfare of an actual child for whom you are responsible, or that you feel that your own dependent or childlike qualities are at risk. If there is a negative association with the dream, it can mean the dreamer might feel as if they are treated like a child and not taken seriously.

Puzzle

If you find yourself trying to solve a puzzle in your dream, there's a good chance that something is also 'puzzling' you in waking life. The way you go about solving the puzzle in your dream may give you a clue that helps you to resolve this issue.

Ball

Cards

Dice

Hoop

Doll

Puzzle

Cross-reference

For Ball, see Football
    p.190
For Cards, see Games
    p.185
For Dice, see Games
    p.185
See also Children
    p.294

Toys & games

Balloon

If you dream of balloons, it could be a sign that you're longing for change. You're sick of your tired old routine and you want to rise up above the crowd and float off to new pastures. If the balloon is brightly coloured, expect a celebration in the near future. If the balloon is having trouble staying aloft, it's likely that you're feeling frustrated about your progress. To dream of balloons can also suggest that the dreamer has an inventive mind, which is not being used to its full potential.

Toy

Toys are associated with childhood and 'childishness'. Do you need to take things more seriously? This dream may also mean that you are 'toying' with people's emotions and need to think carefully about your actions. On the positive side, playing with toys can suggest that you are eager to explore your creative side and that the 'child within' is ready to come out and play.

Puppet

Puppets don't have control over their own movements, so if you dream of one it is a sign that you feel either manipulated, or driven by forces that are beyond your control. By dramatising your feelings of powerlessness, this dream could be trying to tell you to take back control.

Kite

Flying or watching a kite is usually a symbol of aspiration or of a new project or enterprise. Whether you are having trouble keeping it aloft or admiring it in flight will help you to assess the sorts of obstacles you face.

Balloon
Toy
Puppet
Kite
Quoits

Quoits

In the game of quoits, players are required to throw a ring over a peg or pole. It is a game that requires the need for accuracy and the ability to judge distances. Dreaming of it may symbolise the need for similar skills in some situation that is taking place in your waking life. But because quoits is also a game associated with childhood, summer and situations such as luxury cruises, dreaming of it may also signal a desire for relaxation or recreation. Playing a game of quoits generally reflects a need for the dreamer to be accurate in waking life but he or she may also be taking the fun out of life. The subconscious message in this dream is to find fun in whatever you do.

Cross-reference

For Balloon, see Air/ Sky p.78
For Toy, see Children p.294, Baby p.295
For Kite, see Flying p.255

Accessories

Jewellery/Jewels

In a dream, jewellery and precious stones are likely to symbolise the things you value most in life. These could include your own talents or creative abilities, those whom you love, or even abstract qualities such as courage, determination or fair-mindedness. Dreaming of finding jewels or treasure suggests your desire to achieve or produce something worthwhile. In this case the dream could be compensating for your sense of frustration or lack of productivity in a current job or hobby.

Watch

Dreaming of a watch or clock usually signals concerns with time issues. The watch in your dream may be prompting you to pay more attention to a deadline or reminding you that you haven't been keeping your eye on the passage of time.

Necklace

Traditionally, a necklace is associated with power, honour and riches. To some extent, this is true, as it can represent a deep emotion on the part of the wearer or the giver of the necklace. As it is a piece that has the capacity to hold the most jewels, the necklace makes a grand display, visible to all for admiration.

Fan

Ladies' fans symbolise sensuality and coyness. Dreaming of using a fan may suggest that you wish to bring out these aspects of your personality to deal with a current situation.

Glasses

Glasses relate to the way we see the world around us. Wearing glasses, particularly sunglasses, is a way of hiding oneself. Being 'long-sighted' suggests that you have a long-term vision of your future, whereas if you see yourself as 'short-sighted' you are only concerned about tomorrow. Apply these terms to whatever is going on in your life and pay attention to the dream. It may be telling you to change your viewpoint or shift your focus on things.

Crown

Dreaming of a crown denotes success and desire to achieve. Think about what you'd like to be crowned for.

Umbrella

Dreaming that an open umbrella is covering us relates to our coping mechanisms and need for protection in new situations. If you are fully covered by the umbrella, you probably feel secure in your ability to cope. However, if the umbrella leaks or is not effective, you may have to ask for help. Carrying an umbrella is a sign that you are prepared for any scenario. The umbrella, in the sense that we work 'under' a specific boss, also symbolises large companies or corporations.

Ring

Seeing a ring in our dreams reflects our 'wholeness', and therefore a relationship of some sort. An engagement ring symbolises the state of a present relationship—promise not yet fulfilled. A wedding ring, on the other hand, represents commitment and ownership. A family heirloom symbolises tradition and the influence of the family.

Gloves

A symbol of protection, gloves keep your hands clean. This can be a literal meaning, or it can also indicate that you want to avoid getting involved in any 'dirty business'. Expressions such as 'iron fist in a velvet glove' and treating someone with 'kid gloves' all have variations of meaning. Generally, however, it is about protection and covering up.

Jewellery/Jewels

Fan

Watch

Necklace

Glasses

Crown

Umbrella

Ring

Gloves

Cross-reference

For Jewellery/Jewels, see Gems pp.86–9
For Necklace, see Beads p.187
For Ring, see Wedding ring p.212, Engagement p.210

Metals

Metal

Any metal in a dream represents the restrictions that we feel society imposes on us as individuals. We may feel that the world is hard, cold and uncaring towards us and that we can't break out of the metal shell in which we are encased.

Silver

Silver represents something of value. We refer to those who lead privileged lives as being 'born with a silver spoon in their mouths'. Silver is also associated with the qualities of the moon. Is there something that's not within your reach at the moment? As a metal, silver is associated with emotions that are pure. To see silver or to wear silver in a dream can also suggest that the dreamer needs to tap into his or her emotional side.

Gold

The emphasis of this dream is on value—gold represents something precious and valuable to the dreamer. It may be the valuable part of ourselves so that finding gold means finding new aspects of others or ourselves. Gold does not tarnish and therefore stands the test of time. Think of the values you hold to as the most important in your life. Do you have a heart of gold or are you a gold digger?

Lead

Lead is heavy and so are our burdens. What is it that is weighing you down and making you feel heavy-hearted? Take note of all the symbols in this dream to help you understand its message. Don't forget that just as lead can be melted, so too can your present state, allowing it to be changed or transformed into a more positive one.

Steel

Steel is associated with strength, durability and inflexibility. When we say that someone has 'nerves of steel' we mean that he or she is a person of great determination who doesn't let his or her emotions get in the way. Depending on the context of the dream, it may indicate that you wish to possess some steel-like qualities. It could also be showing you parts of your self that are steely or impenetrable.

Metal

Silver

Gold

Lead

Steel

Quicksilver

Quicksilver

Quicksilver is mercury, and this substance can stand for the dreamer's own shifting or 'mercurial' emotions. Perhaps you or someone close to you is overly temperamental, or can't be relied on to provide emotional stability. This dream could be symbolising a stage of your life where emotional consistency is impractical, and you are being forced to adapt temperamentally to changing conditions. More generally, it may simply represent change or instability in the external circumstances of your life.

Cross-reference

For Gold, see Treasure p.221, Jewellery/ Jewels p.402

For Silver, see Treasure p.221, Jewellery/Jewels p.402

Tools & equipment

Hammer

Dreaming of a hammer can be a sign that a problem in your life requires a forceful or aggressive solution. Hammering in a dream can also be an indication that you are determined to 'nail' an issue or problem that has been bothering you.

Tools

The male organ is often described as a 'tool'. If the tool in your dream is used as a weapon, it may represent sexual violence. Generally, tools appear in our dreams to remind us of resources we have to help us keep things in order. If things in the dream are not in order and you are 'fixing' various items, take a closer look at what is broken and the tool you are using. A hammer, for example, may be telling you to 'hammer home a point'.

Anvil

An anvil is a symbol of a primal force—a spark of new life. Traditionally it implies that good fortune is ahead despite some obstacles. It may relate to how you use your energy and whether it can be used more effectively.

Hook

A dream involving a hook may indicate the desire to bring something closer to yourself. We talk about 'getting hooked with/on something'. It indicates our need to connect totally with someone or something, but in doing so shows feelings of dependency and immaturity.

Lens

What needs to be more closely examined? A dream of using a lens indicates a need to pay closer attention to detail.

Ladder

A ladder usually suggests a direction the dreamer is about to take. Climbing a ladder indicates success in a gradual manner, or in many stages (step by step), in order to achieve your goals (moving up the ladder). It may be highlighting your insecurities about opportunities that are not easily attained. Falling down or climbing backwards on a ladder will have the opposite meaning—that you feel that you have failed to achieve your goals.

Lance

A lance has a similar function to the knife—it cuts and penetrates. It is regarded as a symbol of sexual intercourse, the lance being a phallic/ masculine symbol. If you dream of lancing a boil or cutting something out such as a poison or foreign object, it may suggest that it is time to release some toxic feelings that have built up over some issue. Waiting for the body to expel it naturally may entail physical and emotional suffering that can be avoided.

Hammer

Tools

Anvil

Hook

Lens

Ladder

Lance

Cross-reference

For Lens, see
    Telescope p.380
For Ladder, see
    Falling p.257,
For Lance, see Knife
    p.393

Tools & equipment

Magnifying glass

When something is magnified in our dreams, and appears larger than life, it is a good indication that we need to pay attention to it. If you dream of using a magnifying glass, be more attentive to the small details in your life. It may also be that you are exaggerating a situation that need not be so huge; that is, that you're 'making mountains out of molehills'.

Magnet

A magnet has the power to attract or repel. This dream symbolises the effect or influence we have on others and vice versa. As it is a power, consider how you draw many things in your life—you may attract good things or you may be capable of drawing negative influences around you. Be aware that you have this energy. Focus on what it is that you wish to attract and what you want to repel.

Needle

A sewing needle in a dream may represent the power to mend, bring together or patch things up. To 'needle' someone is to irritate them and 'a needle in a haystack' is something that is impossible to find. Needlework is regarded as an image of what you've 'made' of yourself— your achievements and failures. If you are finding it difficult to thread a needle, it may be that you can't get started with a project. Discover what the source of frustration is. The needle that is used on our bodies for medical purposes denotes a sickness in the body in the negative sense, and healing power in the positive. Freudians would classify a needle as a phallic symbol.

Net

If you dream of being caught in a net, consider which parts of your life are being stifled, held back or trapped, giving you the feeling of being ensnared or overwhelmed. If the feeling in the dream was pleasant, that is, you dreamt of falling into a net, the dream may suggest security, either financial or in relationships. These days we refer to the Internet as 'the Net', so consider whether communication is the issue you are trying to resolve.

Pen/Pencil

These implements are used for writing or drawing, so they suggest issues of communication and self-expression. A pen is more likely to symbolise the former and a pencil the latter, although these meanings will depend on your own circumstances. Pencils are also associated with childhood, the period when we first begin to learn how to write and are anxious to prove ourselves. Freud interpreted the pen as a symbol for the male sexual organ. According to this reasoning, if you are a man and you dream either of losing a pen or being unable to write with one, the dream suggests that you are anxious about your potency or ability to perform adequately in a social role or relationship.

Magnifying glass

Magnet

Needle

Net

Pen/Pencil

Pitchfork

Pitchfork

A dream in which you are using a pitchfork suggests your desire to shift obstacles out of your way. It is a dream that symbolises the need for hard work if you are to achieve a desired goal or end.

Cross-reference

For Needle, see
    Sewing p.180
For Pen/Pencil, see
    Writing p.240
For Pitchfork, see
    Hay/Haymaking
    p.182

409

Tools & equipment

Yardstick

A yardstick is an instrument for taking measurements, and therefore it can symbolise our desire to 'measure up' to the expectations of others. Its shape also carries associations of correctness and 'upright' behaviour.

Nail

Dreaming about nails can mean a variety of things depending on the context of the dream. Dreaming of nails may suggest you feel cornered—'nailed against the wall' or 'nailed down'. It could also mean that you have had an insight or achieved a result: that is, you've 'hit the nail on the head'. Generally we associate nails with being 'bonded' and in that sense, we are holding together (particularly in a sexual relationship) or holding onto something. If you dream of being nailed to a cross, it suggests pain and sacrifice—once again referring to a relationship or your feelings towards some sort of critical situation. Perhaps you're feeling helpless, or see yourself as a martyr.

Screw

The word 'screw' has a variety of meanings depending on the context of the dream and the dreamer's culture. It stands for sexual intercourse as well as a prison officer. 'Having a screw loose' or 'missing a screw' means that you do not have full use of your mind or common sense.

Shovel

A shovel in a dream is used to dig deeper so as to reveal our innermost selves. You may need to dig into past experiences and pull out memories that will serve you at this time.

Tacks

In a dream, tacks represent the many small aggravations and problems in your life. Like pins and needles, they are symbolic of the things that annoy us and cause us irritation.

Whip

A dream in which a whip is being used may indicate your desire to speed up or hasten some process or event. Similarly, the expression 'take the whip hand' denotes a desire to take control. But the whip in your dream may also stand for something that inflicts pain, such as the critical remarks made by others. It may even by a warning to you to think about how your own actions or tendency to 'lash out' may risk hurting others.

Hoe

This common garden implement suggests the desire to improve one's physical or emotional environment by getting rid of issues or emotions that are no longer relevant, or that interfere with our growth. In general this dream is a positive one that signals our willingness to cultivate either ourselves, or the things that nurture or support us in our lives.

Yardstick

Nail

Screw

Shovel

Tacks

Whip

Hoe

Cross-reference

For Shovel, see
   Digging/Excavation
   p.171
For Whip, see Riding
   p.188
For Hoe, see Garden
   p.66

Tools & equipment

Pole

The meaning of this dream will depend on the type of pole that appears in your dream, and what it is being used for. Pole vaulting, for instance, suggests the desire to soar over your obstacles, while a flagpole can be a focus for our sense of identity or belonging. In Freudian dream interpretation, the pole is a symbol for male sexuality.

Plank

A plank is a symbol of support, often something that we use to create a bridge that will carry us from one situation to another. If, however, you are 'walking the plank' in your dream, it suggests that you are about to venture into an emotionally risky situation.

Cord

Generally, a cord represents ties that bind you to your family, friends or lifestyle. If you are trying to undo cords in your dreams, it is probably a sign that you feel tied down by the demands and responsibilities placed on you by others. If you are trying to hang onto a cord that someone else is pulling away, it may mean that you are worried about losing someone close to you.

Scissors

Scissors are used for cutting and are associated with sharpness, both concepts that occur in a range of idiomatic expressions. 'Cutting remarks' hurt us, as does a 'sharp tongue'. In a physical sense, this dream may suggest the feeling of being cut off from other people or certain feelings. It may also be telling you to cut out the things from your life that you no longer require.

Knot

Generally speaking, a knot stands for a problem or problems, something you are having trouble unravelling. It may suggest that you are experiencing emotional confusion, or can't work out how to solve a problem. If the knot comes undone easily in your dream, it is a sign that you should proceed with confidence. However, if you are tying a knot in a dream it suggests either that you're trying to remember something, or that you are afraid of losing a person or object.

Rope

A symbol of strength and power, rope can be positive or negative. If you are tied to a rope, something/someone is holding you back and the rope represents the restraints you encounter in your everyday life. If you are tied up to some object, you need to examine the relationship between you and what you are tied to. For example if you are tied to the kitchen sink, the dream is suggesting that you feel bound by domestic duties.

Pole

Plank

Cord

Scissors

Knot

Rope

Wedge

Cable

Wedge

Wedges are something we use to maintain an opening, whether in a door or a window. As a result, dreaming of a wedge may suggest our desire to open ourselves to a new situation or emotion. It may also signal the need for more openness or communication within a relationship. Don't let a wedge come between you and someone you love.

Cable

A dream with cables that you may have a desire for emotional security. This dream warns you to take steps to ensure that your life is properly 'anchored'. Don't take too many risks with your emotions.

Cross-reference

For Plank, see Bridge
    p.325
For Cord, see String
    p.387
For Rope, see String
    p.387
For Scissors, see
    Cutting p.171

413

Substances

Dye

If your clothes or bedding have become stained with a colour you can't remove, the dream symbolises your anxieties about being unable to control the process of change. It suggests that something is overwhelming you, or that you feel affected by someone else's actions, and that you are powerless to stop the process. If you are the one who is dyeing something, it is a sign that you are preparing to take charge of changes in your life.

Petrol

Petrol is the basic fuel we use to 'drive' ourselves from one place to another. If you dream that your petrol tank is empty, it could be a sign that your reserves of energy are low or that you lack the basic motivation to perform a task. If you are filling your tank with petrol, it's a sign of your desire to really 'go places'.

Incense

This fragrant smoke may suggest your desire to make contact with your more spiritual side. However incense may also stand for some awareness or pleasure that is short-lived, or in other words is likely to 'go up in smoke'.

Glue

Depending on the dream, glue is associated with permanence and fixture. Terms such as 'stick to me like glue', 'stick to it' or 'sticky situation' will help you work out the meaning of the glue in your dream.

Ammonia

Ammonia is a potent liquid and therefore to dream of such a pungent smelling product is to be warned of potential risks.

Liquid

Any liquid substance in your dreams represents 'flow'. Are you 'going with the flow' or are you resisting change?

Wax

Wax is a soft substance that can take many forms. For this reason it can stand for the capacity to adapt to different circumstances or to alter one's attitudes. A dream with wax in it may be prompting you to consider becoming less rigid in your approach to an issue or person. Alternatively, it may suggest that you are too pliable, and that you may need to offer some resistance to the attempts made by others to 'mould' you. Dreaming of waxing unwanted hair indicates your concern about beauty and image, while waxing the car or furniture is about pride and the need to 'show off' your best attributes.

Dye

Petrol

Incense

Glue

Ammonia

Liquid

Wax

Cross-reference

For Dye, see Colour
    pp.432–3
For Petrol, see Car
    p.262
For Wax, see Candles/
    Candlestick p.390

Substances

Grease

When we eat something greasy, we feel guilty that it's bad for our health. If we spill grease on our clothes, we are concerned about getting the stain out. Greasy dishes in the sink make us look like sloppy housekeepers. Generally, grease means that we aren't careful enough and that we aren't taking care of ourselves. A greasy or slimy character suggests someone who is not to be trusted. How does grease fit into your life?

Acid

Handling, observing or drinking acid has psychological overtones that suggest you have something weighing heavily on your mind and conscience. Feelings of anxiety, being placed in compromising situations and a sense that your general well-being is being 'eroded away' by external influences are all related symptoms. Although you may feel that these issues are eating away at you, there is the opportunity get rid of all 'poisonous' issues troubling you at the present time.

Oil

Oil is a lubricant, and for this reason its appearance in a dream suggests the desire to smooth things over or make them work more efficiently. The meaning of this symbol depends on the kind of oil that appears in your dream. For example, engine oil suggests efficiency, especially at work, while massage oil may convey the desire to ease your problems away. On the same principle, cooking oil symbolises your wish for things to be easier on your home front.

Poison

The poison in your dream is likely to stand for a harmful emotion or attitude, whether it originates in yourself, or comes from others. Interpreting the surrounding symbols in your dream will help you to decide what this is, so you can 'neutralise' it.

Dynamite

Some situation or emotion is in danger of 'exploding'. This may not be a negative dream—on the contrary, it could be a sign that you need to change some aspect of your life, or that an emotion you have been holding back from expressing can finally be released.

Drugs

Cigar

This is traditionally regarded as a symbol of the phallus, although as Freud is said to have once commented, 'Sometimes a cigar is only a cigar'. Cigars are associated with masculine power and prestige, so a dream of smoking one may suggest a desire for these personality traits, whether you are male or female.

Grease

Acid

Oil

Poison

Dynamite

Cigar

Cigarette

Marijuana

Cigarette

Lighting a cigarette in a dream is often a sign of anxiety, possibly about a social event or situation. If you are a smoker and trying to give up, however, or the people in your dream are reacting negatively to your cigarette, the dream is likely to be a reflection of your desire to smoke, or guilt about not being able to stop.

Marijuana

As a symbol, marijuana represents any illegal activity. Because smoking or inhaling it can prevent you from thinking clearly, dreaming of it can also highlight the risk of making unwise decisions. Alternatively, perhaps you feel the need to relax and tune out. Generally, this dream depends on the context in which you view the drug. If you are a user, it may just be routine, but if you have never tried it, you should focus on what the experience is and how you may be able to attain it without addiction or illegality.

Cross-reference

For Dynamite, see Explosion p.201, Bomb p.375

Mementos

Photographs

In dreams, photographs often stand for the dreamer's memories. If you are looking at family photographs, it could be a sign that you need to take stock of the influences of your family environment or childhood. Looking at a photo of yourself, or being photographed, is more likely to reflect your concerns with your self-image.

Keepsake

If you are presented with a keepsake in a dream it is probably a sign that you feel in danger of losing something. Alternatively, this dream may be forcing you to remember a person or event that you have been trying to put out of your mind.

Scrapbook

A scrapbook contains our most precious memories and mementoes. Usually the contents of the scrapbook are meaningful only to the dreamer. More generally however, this dream can suggest the process of holding onto an old memory. Perhaps it is time to close the book and move on in life on the principle that you can't go back to the past. A scrapbook can also give a distorted picture of the past, as it tends to project only the good. In this context the dream may be a warning that the dreamer is hanging onto the highlights of the past and not facing up to the whole truth of what really took place.

Cosmetics

Cosmetics/Makeup

A dream in which you are applying or purchasing cosmetics usually signals either anxieties about your age or appearance, preparation for a social event, or a desire to cover up something. Wearing makeup is about creating an image you wish to project to the outside world. Dreaming of applying makeup suggests that you may be trying to cover up your imperfections and/or create a beautiful image. The important message in this dream is that we all have the ability to change the effect or impression we make on others. Like sunglasses, makeup can be used to hide parts of ourselves we wish not to expose.

Photographs

Keepsake

Scrapbook

Cosmetics/
Makeup

Lipstick

Lipstick

Lipstick exaggerates the lips, making the sensual part of our nature a seductive one. Lipstick on a collar is associated with suspicion and distrust, particularly in a relationship. Reflect on whether it is your fears that are holding you back from expressing your sensuality.

Cross-reference

For Photgraphs, see
    Photography p.184
For Cosmetics,
    see Identity
    & appearance
    pp.310–11
For Lipstick, see Lips
    p.112

Musical instruments

Music/Musical instruments

Music is an expression of our inner selves and how we connect with life. Music, like life, has its discords and harmonies, its highs and lows. Hearing music in a dream can be interpreted either as 'music to my ears'—that is, pleasant words—or 'facing the music'—taking responsibility. If you are playing music you are expressing yourself in your own individual way. If the notes are harsh and discordant, there is an underlying conflict in your waking life. Pay attention to the rest of the dream so that you find its source. A musical instrument represents the way we communicate with others. If you were to play an instrument which one would you choose? Percussion instruments are associated more with the earthy rhythm of life, while the string and wind instruments are to do with the mind.

Cymbals

The crash of cymbals foretells some dramatic change or crisis in your life. It is a 'wake-up call' of some sort.

Gong

A gong is loud and demands attention. If you hear a gong in your dream, it suggests that you are being called for something, or that you need to pay attention to some issue in your life.

Music/Musical
instruments

Cymbals

Gong

Guitar

Drums

Guitar

The guitar, like all musical instruments, expresses our deepest feelings through its sound. Romantic, exciting and up- beat, the guitar represents these parts of our creative selves.

Drums

Of all the musical instruments, the drums are those most associated with fundamental rhythms and energies. Thus, playing them in your dream tends to be a sign of your need to release primal energy or aggression, or to make contact with the more basic and raw emotions.

Cross-reference

See also Music & dance pp.250–1

Musical instruments

Harp

This instrument can be a sign of your achievement of or desire for positive or harmonious 'vibrations' in your emotional or spiritual life. Alternatively, it may signal your desire to be more 'in tune' or harmony with others close to you.

Trumpet

The trumpet has traditionally been a symbol of triumph. In the Bible, the sounding of the trumpet is associated with joy, news (the Annunciation) and glory (angels with trumpets). However, trumpets are also associated with conflict. In war, the trumpet sounded the retreat or advance as well as playing a final goodbye. Depending on the dreamer's cultural background, age and experience, the sound of a trumpet will arouse various emotions and personal interpretations. It could just be a 'wake-up call' for you.

Flute

A wind instrument, the flute represents deep emotion. It evokes feelings of harmony, joy and lightness of heart and spirit. Therefore, dreaming of a flute symbolises your need or desire to express these feelings.

Violin

The sound of a violin appeals to our emotions, evoking passion and stirring the strings of our hearts. It is the sound of celebration and of love lost. What feelings are stirred in you when you hear the violin in your dream?

Piano

A piano is a symbol of creativity, although it suggests that accessing that creativity requires discipline and practice. If the piano won't play in tune, something in your life may be 'off key' or lacking in harmony. In Italian, piano means soft or gentle, so this dream could also be suggesting that you need to tread softly or carefully around a person or issue.

Organ

Organ music is associated with churches and religious ceremonies. It may suggest your desire to explore your spiritual or religious impulses, or it may stand for an activity that takes place in a church—such as a baptism, wedding or funeral. The word organ also refers to the different 'organs' of our bodies, such as our sexual organs, kidneys, heart, etc—see Chapter 4 for their individual meanings.

Bells

Bells in your dream signal the approach of an important event. If the bells are cheerful, it's likely to be a celebration. If they are mournful, you should be prepared for difficulties or sadness.

Harp

Trumpet

Flute

Violin

Piano

Organ

Bells

Cross-reference

For Organ, see Church/Temple p.149
For Bells, see Celebration pp.202–4, Wedding p.210

Material & fabric

Silk

Traditionally, ancient cultures regarded silk as a valuable cloth, which only those in high authority were allowed to wear. Today we still associate silk with things that are precious and sensual. Something that is as 'smooth as silk' is very pleasing to us. Think about what things around you are represented by silk and whether the dream is telling you that you need more indulgence in your life.

Velvet

Velvet is one of the richest and most sensuous of fabrics and has been around for centuries. In olden days, only the rich, the powerful and the clergy could afford to wear velvet. Consequently, it represented their status and wealth. Dreaming of wearing or touching velvet is a sign of the sensual and indulgent parts of yourself.

Wadding

Wadding is used for protection, so a dream involving this substance is likely to symbolise either a desire to protect yourself emotionally or, if you are removing the wadding in your dream, to come closer to the heart of a matter. Wadding can also be used as 'stuffing', and in this context your dream may represent a concern about overeating.

Lace

Lace is a symbol of the feminine and the delicate parts of our natures. If you are dreaming of making lace, it may suggest that you need to be patient.

Picture

Looking at a picture in a dream symbolises your attempt to examine some issue in your life or aspect of yourself. In this respect the dream is allowing you to take a more objective or detached view on a situation or feeling. Factors such as the colours and patterns in the picture will help you to determine the emotions that are 'colouring' your attitude to what is concerning you. Got the full picture?

Whistle

A whistle in a dream is a sign to pay attention to some situation, person or feeling. On the other hand, 'whistle-blowers' are persons who refuse to remain silent in the face of injustice, but draw public attention to an unfair situation. In this context your dream could be prompting you to think about a situation that is unfair to yourself or to others.

Ticket

A ticket represents the price you pay to get somewhere or to achieve your goals. If you dream of holding a ticket it probably symbolises admission to something. For example, it may represent your desire to be admitted into a new social or professional scene.

Statue

Tent

Sack

Wig

Picture

Whistle

Ticket

Cross-reference

For Statue, see
   Sculpture p.186
For Wig, see Hair
   p.113

CHAPTER THIRTEEN
Miscellaneous

As well as reflecting on what your dream was about, it is worth paying attention to some of the more abstract aspects of the dream. Try thinking about whether the dream was in colour or black or white. Was it set in the past or in the future? Did the dream take place in the dark or the light? These concepts can provide a whole new dimension to interpreting what the dream means. For example, the size of an object in your dream can give you a clear indication of how important it is to you in your waking life. This chapter also looks at type of dreams such as nightmares and recurring dreams.

& abstract

Colour

Colours

Most dreams are in colour, although we are not aware of this because we may find it difficult to remember our dreams. Colours can communicate emotion or states of energy. If the colour is unusual, it is there to draw your attention. If there are two or more clashing colours, these could denote aspects of your life that are out of balance or harmony. You should take particular note if this shows up in a dream.

Black

Black is devoid of all colour and light. It is not an actual colour but a shade, and can signal the need to explore the darker or deeper side of your nature—your subconscious mind. The blackness can represent depression or even death—not necessarily of a person, but of an idea, an aspiration, or a phase of your life. In olden times it was thought to represent the underworld, a deep space away from God where a person was said to be hiding. If you dream of black it is a good idea to ask yourself if your life is lacking warmth or colour, or whether you are hiding something. In general, the colour black suggests uncertainty about an aspect of yourself or your situation. At its most serious, it can signify grief or mourning. It can also suggest aspects of yourself which are undeveloped or hidden. In this way, the dream can be positive.

Blue

Blue can be both a soothing colour and one that suggests depression or sadness. Either way, it is associated with spiritual insight or wisdom. If a person is wearing blue in your dream it suggests that he or she has something intelligent, spiritual or truthful to communicate. You should listen carefully to these words, as they are likely to be valuable and to give you insight into your life.

White

Purity, birth, joy and enlightenment are all represented by the colour white. In cultures where white is worn at a funeral, white is seen as a new beginning rather than the end. Blinding white or bareness, however, can represent a lack of colour or activity in your life. Like black, white is devoid of colour. You need to make sure that you have balance in your life.

Yellow

The colour of the sun, it is seen as a positive colour that is associated with fertility, creativity and life.

Silver

Silver is the feminine equivalent of the masculine gold (the sun). It is associated with goddesses, queens and the moon. The colour silver represents magic, psychic ability and spirituality.

Gold

Gold is typically associated with wealth and royalty (gold crowns) as well as the masculine element. In ancient cultures it represented the sun and a higher knowing.

Dreaming of gold colours can mean that one is ambitious in accumulating wealth or that one has a 'golden opportunity' for knowledge and power.

Brown

Murky colours like brown tend to be associated with confusion or anxiety. To dream of these colours can also signal depression. Brown is an earthy colour and depending on

the dream can represent the stability and nourishment of the soil. The earth can either sustain in a positive way or be hostile and 'bog' you down in a muddy hole.

Red

The colour of fire and passion, red is also a symbol of masculinity. Depending on the rest of the dream, red can

suggest aggression, danger, violence, blood, or anger. Red screams out to be noticed— we need to heed the warning.

Green

This is the colour of nature and renewal. It can represent spring: the season of new beginnings. Harmony and nurturing are part of this season. This can translate to your own life, where new ideas that have been germinating are now suddenly sprouting.

Purple

Royalty, priests and people of rank have worn the colour purple throughout history. It was considered a unique colour, rich in texture and shade. Deaming of purple may mean you want to succeed in your job or are in search of esteem.

Colours

Black

Blue

White

Yellow

Silver

Gold

Brown

Red

Green

Purple

Cross-reference

See also Dye p.414

433

Shapes & patterns

Circle

The circle symbolises the self and personal identity. It may represent a female or, if the object is a ring, symbolise perfection and eternity.

Crescent

This represents the feminine and intuitive.

Cross

A cross suggests difficulties in aspects of our lives.

Diamond

This shape symbolises direction and choices.

Square

A square is a solid shape representing down-to-earth and practical matters.

Star

The points of the star are a reflection of your goals and aspirations.

Triangle

The nuclear family—mother, father, child—are suggested by a triangle. It is also a symbol of man's three parts—mind, body and soul.

Yin-yang

The traditional Chinese symbol of Yin and Yang stands for an ideal balance or harmony between the different potentials and parts of the self: between the intuitive or instinctive and the rational, 'masculine' and 'feminine', or active and receptive. If you dream of this symbol it is likely that you feel the desire or need for more balance in your life or personality.

Zigzag

When we travel in a zigzag we take an indirect, meandering approach to a destination, usually to avoid obstacles or to make the most of the view along the way. It's possible that your path through life may be 'zigzagging', or that you are required to solve a problem that can't be approached by a more straightforward path. More dramatically, the zigzag is associated with the path made by a lightning bolt. In this case the zigzag shape represents a powerful release of energy.

Kaleidoscope

Dreaming of a kaleidoscope may express your desire to achieve pattern and harmony. However, it can also reflect your feelings about how you view the world around you. Is the kaleidoscope broken up into many pieces or are different aspects of your life shifting too rapidly for you to be able to make a coherent whole? In childhood, a kaleidoscope has a magical quality, an altering perspective, which is extremely pleasant. The dreamer may wish to regain this type of feeling or to see the world with magic and wonder.

Circle

Crescent

Cross

Diamond

Square

Star

Triangle

Yin-yang

Zigzag

Kaleidoscope

Cross-reference

For Kaleidoscope, see Toy p.400

Time

Date

If a dream is drawing attention to a particular date, it is probably because you are anxious about an upcoming event or can't wait for a day to arrive. However, this dream could also be reminding you of some traumatic event in your past that you have not yet come to terms with. It might also be the numbers that are significant. If so, why are these numbers important in your waking life?

Late

Being late or running out of time is an indication that you do not feel totally in control of situations around you. You may feel the sense that you've left something too late and now you've missed out. This dream could relate to opportunities, personal choices, leisure or ambitions. If others are late, pay attention to your communications skills and avoid misunderstandings.

Future

Dreaming of future events are considered prophetic dreams. As yet there is no agreement from experts as to how one can foretell the future. If you dream of a future event take note of whether the dream recurs and analyse the symbols before you take the dream literally. The symbols in the dream may represent the needs you want to have fulfilled, or your fears of what the future holds.

Hourglass

The appearance in a dream of an hourglass is an indication of time concerns—perhaps eagerness for a particular date to arrive, or anxiety about an appointment that can't be put off. The dream may even be reminding you to hurry up and finish some project or activity. More symbolically, the hourglass can express our feelings about the passing of time or our own ageing process. In medieval art, for example, death was often depicted holding an hourglass, which was widely recognised as a symbol of mortality.

History

It's not uncommon for dreams to have historical settings. Generally speaking, these settings will stand for some aspect of the dreamer's self or his or her life. For example, a Western or frontier setting might represent the dreamer's sense of adventure or pioneering spirit, while a medieval one is more likely to be concerned with issues of romance or power. Interpreting such a dream requires you to think about the personal associations that these different historical periods carry for you.

End

Dreaming of an end or ending means it's time to move on; time for new beginnings. An ending can be either positive or negative. When change is inevitable, despite the dreamer's unwillingness, we need to decide what we need to take with us into our new phase and what we can leave behind. An end is usually felt in the dream as a loss, but it can be a time of renewal. If you dream of reaching an end of a cave or tunnel, it could mean that you have found a way out of a difficult time in your life.

Pendulum

Pendulums can indicate a concern with time issues. Perhaps you feel as if you are 'marking time', rather than making progress, or you are worried about time running out. But because pendulums swing from one point to another, they are also symbols of ambivalence or of not being able to make up one's mind—you may be suspended between one thing and another.

Date

Late

Future

Hourglass

History

End

Pendulum

Old

New

Old

Something old or ancient often suggests the desire to connect with or re-examine something in your past, whether a person, an emotion or a situation. This dream may also be challenging you to think about your attitudes to time, or even death. The old person or object in your dream could be a symbol of your own fear of getting old, or of becoming irrelevant (an 'antique'). Sometimes such a dream is a subconscious message that the dreamer can learn a lot from the past or hasn't yet learnt what lessons the past has to offer.

New

If you dream of 'something new', it usually indicates a new start or beginning. This type of dream can be inspirational for the dreamer as anything new brings hope.

Cross-reference

For Date, see
   Calendar p.396
See also Year p.439
See also Watch p.402

Seasons

Seasons

Seasons represent periods of our lives. Spring represents our childhood years, summer stands for our youth and young adulthood, autumn suggests maturity and middle age and winter symbolises old age and sterility.

Winter

Winter is the time of year when the earth lies fallow in preparation for the renewal of spring. Dreaming of winter may suggest that your own creative or emotional life is going through a period of relative inactivity or that you are waiting for more favourable circumstances to arrive and bring your ideas or emotions to life once more.

Spring

Spring symbolises new growth and new opportunities. The dream may be prompting you to make the most of them.

Summer

Summer represents pleasure, warmth and fertility. It is a positive time of your life in which the sun is shining down on you, so go ahead with your plans.

Seasons

Winter

Spring

Summer

New Year

Year

New Year

Unless you are having this dream close to New Year's Day, it usually represents your new plans for the future. New Year is a time of hope and resolutions, so dreaming of it indicates a new potential, project, phase or relationship in your life. It may mean a fresh start for you.

Year

If something in your dream draws your attention to a particular year it may be reminding you of an event that took place at that time. But this kind of dream could also be prompting you to think of an anniversary, or to assess the progress you have made recently.

Cross-reference

For New Year, see
  Celebrations
  pp.202–4
For Year, see Time
  pp.436–7

Times of the day

Sunrise/Dawn

Sunrise implies new beginnings, youth, hope and new realisations. We also describe a new awareness as something 'dawning on us'.

To dream of dawn is a symbol of new beginnings and hope. It can also be a sign of spiritual rebirth or of the dreamer's need to find new solutions or strategies to the problems in his or her life. The dream can also symbolise a successful transition out of a dark period in one's life. Generally, dreaming of dawn is seen as a good omen.

Morning

Morning represents youth or the part of our lives when we are most active. Dreaming of the morning is positive as we can still shape the day and its events through our thoughts and actions. It is a dream of vitality and optimism.

Noon

The hours of the day refer to age and our sense of responsibility and pressure. Noon represents mid-life and it is a time when we are fully responsible for ourselves. Usually it is a time of great pressure and decision making.

Sunset

Sunset is the opposite of sunrise. It represents an ending of the creative energy we had in our youth and, as a result, is associated with old age. To dream of a sunset denotes a need for closure in some aspect of your life. On the positive side, the ending of something can also be a release.

Evening

In dreams, evening represents wisdom and old age. It is also a time usually set aside for relaxation and quiet time. The dream may either be telling us that we should take more time to relax or to reflect or meditate. Peace and tranquillity is usually manifested as a starry evening sky, absolute darkness or a still night free of storms and clouds.

Night

The night is the ending of the day and as such can reflect the end of something in your life. It can represent our unconscious or the areas of ourselves that we don't wish to show to anyone else. It is also a time of rest, when the body and mind can be rid of expectations, physical activities and constraints. In one sense then, dreaming of the night suggests a longing for freedom, sometimes expressed by dreams of running away from the house at night or breaking into a new place. In general, the night represents the darker side of the self, which it is safe to explore during a dream state.

Sunrise/Dawn

Morning

Noon

Sunset

Evening

Night

Cross-reference

For Sunrise/Dawn, see Sun p.85
For Sunset, see Sun p.85
For Night, see Moon p.84, Stars p.85

Space & size

Weight

The weight in your dream could stand for the things that are 'holding you down'. This dream suggests your consciousness of being forced to take responsibility for others, or shoulder extra burdens. If, in the dream, you are having trouble moving, you need to think of ways to lighten some of these responsibilities.

Size

Size does matter in a dream. It indicates how important you see someone or something as being. If the object is large, the importance it has to you will be correspondingly great. In a relationship, we sometimes feel threatened if the other person has a 'big' reputation. If the object in our dream is small, on the other hand, it probably has little importance to us. However, it may also be an indication that you as the dreamer are vulnerable or 'feeling small'.

Nearness

If something is close to you in a dream, it means that you are close to achieving whatever 'it' is in reality. Being near-sighted, however, denotes that you are focusing your energies on a short-term goal rather than the future. Are you missing the 'big picture'? This dream may be asking you to pay closer attention not just to one objective but to the overall scheme of things.

Narrowness

When we think of a street as narrow, we often mean that it is restricted and secluded. Usually we avoid these streets, as they make us feel unsafe. Dreaming of being in a narrow space denotes feeling restricted or having limited choices or views (being narrow-minded). The dream may mean that you wish to be free of these limitations.

Space

If you dream of space around you or in a building, this space may represent your untapped potential. The dream may also express your need for space so that you can achieve your goals without being 'cramped' by any external pressures. Dreaming of 'outer space' in the sense of that which lies beyond the earth's atmosphere suggests that that you are searching for greater meaning or something bigger. This dream may be indicating that it's time for you to look for some sort of spiritual connection to provide that meaning.

Weight

Size

Nearness

Narrowness

Space

Cross-reference

For Weight, see
   Weighing p.174,
   Scales p.392
For Space, see Space
   & the planets
   pp.84–5

Numbers

Numbers

Numbers hold a different significance for each one of us. A number may refer to a date of birth, a house number, your family group or other events significant to you alone. The numbers below are generally regarded as universal symbols; however, you should interpret your dream with reference to all the numbers that have a special meaning to you.

One

One represents being alone; the self; unity.

Three

This number suggests a triangle and family unit—mother, father and child—and by extension, growth and fertility.

Two

Two stands for duality, such as male/female. Or it can symbolise communication or relationship.

Four

Stability and strength are signified by four: it is a solid structure and is associated with the four elements of fire, water, air and earth. It also represents the four seasons and, as a result, is both a balanced number and a cyclical one. The number four is often associated with logic.

Zero

Zero symbolises the female.

Five

Five represents the human body—five fingers, five toes and five senses. It can also denote impoverishment, whether mental or physical.

Six

The number six is associated with balance and with approaching your goals.

Seven

Traditionally a sacred number, it also suggests uncertainty and change, in which everything happens in cycles of seven.

Eight

Eight symbolises death and resurrection. The symbol of the number 8 on its side means infinity. This is a magical number that can denote significant lifestyle changes.

Nine

Representing pregnancy and childbirth, nine is also the end of the cycle and the start of something new.

Ten

Ten represents the male and female as one; a new beginning. This number is also associated with the public arena and with communication within groups.

Twelve

This number can stand for a full cycle of the year—twelve months, the twelve disciples or the twelve astrological signs.

Twenty-four

This is the symbol of the cycle of night and day (twenty-four hours).

Dreams & nightmares

Monster

A monster is a fear—one that is absolutely terrifying. The larger and more aggressive the monster, the greater our fear. The fear is usually one that we have allowed to sprout and grow out of proportion and which then comes back to frighten us. Fears depend on the individual and the image of the monster needs to be analysed by the dreamer. If this is a recurring dream, it is a good idea to try to work out what has you terrified. Also identify ways in which the monster gets at you and try to escape its clutches in the next dream. Perhaps this can free you from this fear. If you are feeling helpless, the dream is controlling your emotions. If you gain some power over it, you will slowly come to face the monster and shrink its size and importance in your life.

Nightmares

If we are overwhelmed by emotions of fear and anxiety in a dream, it's a good indication that it is a nightmare. In a nightmare you are usually trying to get away from a situation or feel stuck in a terrifying condition. It is the intensity of the fear that makes us remember this dream. There are typical nightmarish dreams that we all encounter but whose meanings vary for each individual. Understanding the cause of the nightmare can help us to deal with our real-life fears and obstacles.

Recurring dreams

It is common to have recurring dreams: dreams that perhaps start in your early years and then recur at different stages of your life. These dreams are always similar or have familiar outcomes. Unless the dreamer changes his or her method of handling a situation that is obviously causing emotional turmoil in waking life, this dream will continue to recur. Change your attitude, or the way you respond to certain emotional challenges that occur at regular periods in your life, and your recurring dreams will stop or change.

Curse

If someone curses you in a dream, it's a sign that you need to examine the sources of negativity that are affecting your life. Keep in mind that negative aspects in life will only have power if you let them.

Monster

Nightmares

Recurring dreams

Curse

Evil

Evil

If you sense evil or an evil presence in your dreams, accompanied by a feeling of foreboding and disgust, it usually indicates that something is going against your moral judgement. That something may well be your own urges—which, because they are uncontrollable, you judge as being unacceptable. When we fight against our own urges, it may feel like an evil force attacking.

Cross-reference

For Monster, see Fear p.161
For Evil, see Devil p.304
See also Dreaming p.118

Temperature

Heat

Dreams of being too hot often have a simple physical cause. You may just be feeling warm and need to throw off the blankets. More symbolically, hot climates or high temperatures in a dream can stand for the 'heat' of strong emotions or passions such as sexual or romantic love, anger or jealousy.

Cold

Experiencing cold in a dream is likely to be a reflection of your emotional rather than actual temperature. If you can't get warm, it is an indication that you need more protection or emotional support in some aspect of your life.

Warmth

In dreams, a feeling of warmth is associated with a need for emotional contentment or well-being. This dream could be either compensatory (providing something that is lacking in your waking life) or a reflection of a current situation in your life.

Thermometer

Usually, dreaming of a medical thermometer reflects the dreamer's concern over health matters. Check it out with your doctor. On another level this dream may indicate your emotional levels—hot, indifferent or cold.

Sounds

Siren

Like an alarm, a siren is a warning, usually of danger ahead. Sirens (alluring women) were also mythological sea nymphs whose singing lured sailors to their death. As a result, dreaming of a siren can also represent temptations that if acted upon, will cause upheaval and chaos.

Heat

Cold

Warmth

Thermometer

Siren

Silence

Silence

Silence in your dream indicates an absence of something and your inability to voice an emotional state. Just as absolute stillness and silence may proceed a storm, silence may represent expectancy and uneasiness.

Cross-reference

For Siren, see Mythical beings pp.308–9, Danger pp.196–201

Light & dark

Light

Generally, light indicates awareness, being 'switched on' to things, being seen and being active. It means illumination and consciousness. If the light is very bright in your dream, it suggests that you are being 'enlightened'. Pay attention to what is being revealed to you. Old-fashioned lamps are symbols of wisdom and guidance from a spiritual source. If you see a spotlight or light from a torch, focus your attention on what is shown to you. You may finally find the truth in a situation or the answer to a personal issue that you have been searching for. A flickering or dim light is symbolic of the life force being weakened. Take care of your health. It may also mean that you don't have the 'full picture' on some issue. Light at the end of the tunnel suggests hope is at hand, and if you 'see the light' you've finally understood something that was unclear before.

Darkness

Darkness in a dream may stand for something that you are unable or unwilling to properly see in your waking life. The darkness can also suggest depression, or symbolise your negative or pessimistic side. In this case, it is a sign that you need to take these emotions or doubts seriously, rather than trying to put them out of sight.

Radiance

Brilliance in a dream is asking the dreamer to look at something more closely with wisdom and 'clear' thought. Take note of what object on which the light is focused.

Shadow

Seeing a shadow in our dream is associated with our shadowy selves; any part of ourselves we don't like or are unable to express in our

waking lives. This shadowy part of ourselves remains hidden in our unconscious and only our dreams are able to express it. Normally in our dreams it follows us and we are inseparable. If it takes on an ominous and frightening aspect you should ask yourself whether you are 'afraid of your own shadow'? Delve deeply to find out what it is about your 'shady' nature that you are so afraid of letting out into the light. It may not be as scary as you think.

Directions

Left

The left is a symbol of our unconscious. It represents the hidden part of ourselves, our internal world of values, emotions and intuition. If we are right-handed, it is our left hand that supports the activity of the right hand. If you dream of being positioned on the left of a person or object, assess whether the dream is representing your 'leftist' attitude (unconventionality) or suggesting that you have been assigned a supportive rather than a dominant role.

Right

The right is our dominant, conscious and moral side. We 'have rights', can be 'the right hand man/woman', or 'start on the right foot'. These all relate to the external parts of our world in which there is action and activity. This is the opposite of the left, which represents our internal self.

Above

If you dream of something that is above you, it can suggest that some danger or mishap surrounding you is present. An object, or something hanging above you, may fall. If an object falls, but lands near you rather than striking you, it suggests that you will escape whatever hazard was meant for you, but that you must exercise caution.

West

The west is associated with the setting sun and, for this reason, dreaming of this compass direction may symbolise the end of something. The expression 'Go West, young man', associated the West with adventure and exploration, so dreaming of this direction may suggest your desire to explore something new.

Light

Darkness

Radiance

Shadow

Left

Right

Above

West

Cross-reference

For Light, see Lamp p.370
For Darkness, see Night p.441

CHAPTER FOURTEEN

Dreams inte

Once you have mastered the ability to remember your dreams and take notice of all the different elements that may occur in each dream, you can start to bring them all together to find a meaningful interpretation. To help you understand how to do this, some examples of typical dreams are presented in this chapter. As well as an explanation of what the elements of the dream represent, each one outlines how, by putting the dream in the context of your waking life, you can begin to decode the messages from your subconscious.

preted

Dreams interpreted

The following sample dreams and their interpretations will give you an idea of how to interpret your own dreams.

DREAM 1 I dreamed that I was on a bed and that my head was in a vice. Someone was turning the handle of the vice and my head was getting longer and longer, though I felt no pain. I could see myself from above, looking most peculiar with this long face. There was a row of red roses there too, and one that I was holding between my teeth. I asked the person what would happen, because I could tell that the squeezing of my head couldn't carry on indefinitely. He said not to worry; that I would be dead by the time the last rose disappeared. I could see that the roses were disappearing one by one. I felt relieved when he said this, and relaxed immediately.

What was happening at the time of your dream?
At the time of this dream I was at uni doing my honours thesis and I was under a lot of stress.
Interpretation
I felt that my brain was being squeezed and compressed. And the thought of dying (being relieved of this stress) was very attractive. The roses disappearing one by one meant that I was getting closer to the end (death) of my thesis. They were a symbol of congratulations and that I would succeed (which I did).

HEAD
The head is the thinking organ and therefore symbolises intellect, wisdom and power.

VICE
Represents some sort of constraint that has the dreamer in its grip.

TEETH
Symbolise aggression and the ability to withstand pain (grit your teeth).

ROSES
Traditionally associated with love, romance and the feminine.

REDS
Has the positive qualities of passion, vitality and strength but also the negative traits of force, aggression, danger and conflict. It is a colour that cannot be ignored.

DREAM 2 I was inside a house made with sand flooring and sand walls. It began to flood. I panicked and wanted to leave. It was obvious the whole house would cave in on me if I stayed. It wasn't stable. The neighbours advised me to stay, trying to convince me that it would be ages until it collapsed and there was no immediate danger. I felt trapped and knew that I wanted to leave for my own good. An older man appeared at the door. I ran to him and cried on his shoulder. He listened and let me sit on his lap.

What was happening at the time of your dream?
I was going through a crisis in my marriage at the time of the dream. I wanted to leave, but I felt trapped—I had two young children. I managed to pretend to be happily married, but in my heart I'd planned to wait till the children were older and then leave.

Interpretation
I knew that the marriage was unstable (sand), and that it was overwhelming me (flood). Others around me only saw the 'facade' of the public image as a happy couple and didn't believe me (neighbours in the dream). I stayed in the house (marriage) but planned an escape through the wisdom of the older man (my conviction and the legal system that would allow me divorce).

OLDER MAN
Jung's Wise Old Man is said to represent a combination of positive, masculine qualities such as strength, leadership and courage. He appears in dreams when the dreamer becomes aware that the only true guidance comes from within.

HOUSE
The house represents the dreamer and the soul. Being inside the house means going inside yourself and delving into your authentic self.

SAND
Shifts with the wind and as such is not stable or secure.

WALL
Indicates restriction and feelings of being trapped. It also suggests a blockage so that we can't progress or move on with our lives.

FLOOD
Symbolises a 'welling up' of emotion that needs to be released. It's uncontrollable and destructive. In the end, it can be cleansing and we can begin life again.

DREAM 3 I was driving along a road in my car, with the ocean on my left side. The water was coming dangerously close to the road, sending a spray of water. I was afraid of veering off. All at once I lost control of the car. I couldn't brake or steer. Instead it led me to the water's edge. The car drove into the water and I struggled to get out and save myself. I woke up frightened.

What was happening at the time of your dream?
I was feeling a low sense of self esteem at the time of this dream. I couldn't decide on what career path to follow and whatever came up as a suggestion seemed out of my depth. I felt inadequate.

Interpretation
The car and drive reflected my ambition, but the fact that I was veering into the ocean (unknown) was frightening. felt that I had no control in which direction I was heading as it all led to having to do further study or gaining more experience in a new field. This was out of my comfort zone (ocean) and I was feeling overwhelmed (fear of drowning). The dream was a mirror image of what I was feeling in real life.

DRIVING
Indicates our motivation and need for achieving our goal. Being the driver suggests independence and self confidence. Losing control of the car points to not having control over your direction in life.

ROAD
Like driving, a road indicates a sense of direction.

CAR
The car is a means of transport and as such is a symbol of where we are going on our life journey.

OCEAN
Symbolic of our emotional state. Being afraid of drowning in an ocean suggests a feeling of helplessness and fear of the unknown.

DREAM 4 There was a lion in my backyard. Obviously the fence was low enough for it to jump over. I scolded my husband for not making a higher fence. I wanted the lion to go as I was afraid of it. The lion began to stalk me and tried to attack me. I defended myself, still unharmed, but the fear woke me up.

What was happening at the time of your dream?
I enrolled to go back to university and gain another qualification in a field I was new at. My husband told me it would be too much for me to handle with full-time work, study and taking care of the family. He was unwilling to help and I felt vulnerable and at conflict, wanting to achieve my goal but not allowing it to consume me so that my family wouldn't suffer in any way.

Interpretation
The lion represented the ego (I wanted to achieve a new level of qualification) but at the same time I needed courage to do it on my own. The fact that I blamed my husband that the fence was too low meant that I wasn't taking responsibility for my action. I was happier to blame him if things went wrong, as he 'neglected' my needs (the low fence). The dream showed me that I needed to measure my courage and rely on my own instincts to reach my goals. The lion attacking me meant that I had a conflict to resolve and my ability to defend myself was a good indication that I would at least be responsible for my future direction.

LION
Symbolises pride and courage. Pride can be interpreted in a negative way, that is, that our pride is blocking us from expressing our animal (or basic) feelings.

LOW FENCE
Any fence suggests boundaries and enclosure for safety.

DREAM 5 My son was running away from me through a dark forest. I asked a group of people to help me, but they just looked on with blank faces. I ran on, out of the wood, and saw a narrow pier stretching out to a calm, grey sea. The landscape was very wintry and desolate. My son was running along the pier. I saw my husband there. He told me that our son was fine, that he was looking after him. Then we both turned and in the distance saw our son jump off the pier. I ran to where I thought my son had gone over and jumped straight in, feet first, and went down, down through the greenish water very fast. I thought I wouldn't find him, that he was lost forever. But on my way down I passed him coming up, paddling carefully. Bubbles were coming out of his mouth and he seemed quite relaxed. I was still going down when the dream ended. But I remember flapping my arms wildly to try and slow down, and feeling horribly embarrassed.

What was happening at the time of your dream?	Interpretation 1
My son was finding school very stressful, so I marched off to school to sort out the problem. He and I have a very close relationship and I think I don't distance myself enough from him. My husband is inclined to say, 'No, he's okay, he's managing. Give him some credit for coping'.	The car and drive reflected my ambition, but My response was actually an over-response. I jumped in to help him, but jumped in way too far. I was so caught up in what I thought was the right thing to do that I wasn't really thinking about the best way to help him. He was doing better than I thought (not sinking, but holding his own). The wintry landscape is to do with the slight emotional distance that developed between my husband's rational approach versus my emotional one over this issue. It could also reflect my son's feelings of alienation in a barren, wintry landscape. The people in the forest are probably the teachers in my son's life who didn't seem to help much at the time.
	Interpretation 2
	The dream could really have been about me and the stresses I was experiencing at the time. I could have been using my son as a symbol for this stress because I identify with him. I felt that I wasn't coping very well, but that dream suggests that I was coping better than I thought.

RUNNING
Suggests urgency to reach a destination or purpose.

FOREST
A dark forest represents sour intuition.

BLANK FACES
Represent an awareness of people around you who are emotionally removed from your purpose or problem.

PIER
A narrow pier is a symbol of the end of a journey.

GREY SEA
Points to our present emotional state. Although the sea is calm, it is grey, rather than a clear blue. This indicates that it is deep and perhaps dangerous, making us aware of our fear of the 'deep' and the unknown.

LANDSCAPE
A wintry landscape is desolate and lonely and mirrors our emotionally cold, distant and unproductive state.

GOING DOWN
Feet first suggests a cautious approach (jumping in feet first, rather than head first). However, going down too fast indicates a lack of control over a situation.

WATER
Jumping into the water symbolises an urgent need to delve into the subconscious with the aim of renewal of strength and conviction.

BUBBLES
In this instance indicates a sign of life.

DREAM 6 My brother was playing 'dare' with a huge snake-like dragon. It looked half-snake and half-komodo dragon with scaly skin and was purple/puce in colour. He opened the dragon-snake's mouth wide and put his head between its jaws. I was alarmed. I knew that the creature was poisonous. He just smiled and said, 'It's okay. I know what I'm doing'. He then released the dragon-snake's head and made me look at its tail. It was sitting in a bowl of ice-cream. On its tail, it had a few white suction caps with openings and was sucking the melted ice-cream through these.

BROTHER
Represents aspects of the dreamer's personality.

SNAKE/DRAGON
As a combination this creature becomes a powerful force in the dream. It represents trickery (snake) and the wild (dragon) aspects of ourselves which are kept in check.

ICE-CREAM
A reminder of childhood pleasures that we may have forgotten or have 'melted' over the years.

What was happening at the time of your dream?
I was having difficulty with my boss. He was undermining my authority and elevating himself as the only one responsible for the company's profits.

Interpretation

In real life, my boss put me on the defensive (my head in the creature's jaws) on most issues. I felt that I had to prove myself all the time. This could be why the creature looked like a dragon. I felt I had to be a knight and slay the dragon to prove that I was worthy and brave. The snake (cunning) put me on guard that I should not trust my boss' motives. The fact that it was my brother that I saw meant that I had to access another part of my personality to overcome my fear and distrust of my boss. When my brother showed no fear in the jaws of the creature, I was supposed to understand that once I took a stand, my boss would back down. He could see that I wasn't afraid of him and therefore not be threatened. Interestingly, the ice-cream took me back to the time when I was younger and reminded me that everyone was young once. Perhaps my boss wasn't so bad after all if I could connect with him on some other level. Perhaps on a more personal or leisure-based level? He could be 'fed' through the suckers and not the mouth. That is, he could show his vulnerability or human aspects in other ways, rather than the jaws, which represent his verbal prowess (venom). After the dream, I tried to communicate on a more personal level and was less defensive. It worked.

DREAM 7 I was climbing a hill, but the higher up I went, the more I couldn't see below. It wasn't just smaller; it was blurry. It felt as if there were fine silken sheets drawn like curtains below me. Looking from above I could see balloons sitting just on top of the sheets. The colours of the balloons were gold, yellow and orange.

HILL
Climbing a hill means that you are making an effort to overcome difficulties or achieve your goal.

GOLD
Associated with wealth, but can also mean the valuable part of us.

CURTAINS
Sheet-like curtains represent new ideas brewing in your mind and an expansion of vision.

YELLOW
The colour of the sun and seen as a positive colour. It is associated with the emotional self and with life, as well as the intellect.

BALLOONS
A search for the spiritual and doing what makes us feel uplifted.

ORANGE
A spiritual colour which enhances one's feelings of inner peace.

What was happening at the time of your dream?	Interpretation
I was searching for guidance on how I could advance with a career in writing. I was told that it didn't make money and that very few succeeded.	The hill required me to move upwards no matter what the effort. I was determined to follow my ambition to become a writer. The curtains were telling me not to look below where there was negativity. I was savvy enough to know the pitfalls of a writing career, but the sheer fabric of the sheets suggested that I not dwell too much on the negatives or I wouldn't keep climbing. The balloons were a sign that my higher self required me to pursue a creative career, so that my perspective could be challenged and new experiences learnt. Gold was the colour of my potential, orange was my search for inner peace and yellow was my mental power and positive attitude. I felt encouraged by the dream to go on further with my writing career despite the rejections and the instability of employment. The dream suggested that if I looked ahead, worked hard, followed my dreams and focused on the positive, the universe would take care of the rest.

DREAM 8 I have a recurring dream about being lost in a hotel. I usually lose the key, forget the room number, take the wrong elevator or stairs, or go into the wrong room. This is frustrating as I try so hard to remember where my room is located. Sometimes I end up sharing with strangers, other times when I've gone on tours the cab driver can't seem to find the hotel. As well as the room, I get lost in the car park and can't find my car to get home.

What was happening at the time of your dream?
I have to make new decisions.
Interpretation
The dream is set around a hotel so, whatever state I'm in, it's only temporary. I always seem lost as I can't remember where places are. I am searching for guidance from a previous experience so that I can make a good decision, but the problem is that these are new decisions to me. The 'newness' is emphasised by the tourist and the cab. It is a foreign place (my decision-making process) and I am looking for someone (cab) to help get me there (making a good decision). Where is the answer (key)? I look for clues so that I will be valued as a decision-maker (ambition/car park) but even there I am not certain of my direction.

HOTEL
Dreaming of a hotel indicates a short-term situation.

KEY
The key in your dream may symbolise your attempt to find a solution to a problem or situation that has been bothering you.

ELEVATOR/LIFT
Can suggest the aspect of ourselves with we are most in tune.

STRANGERS
Represents those whom we are not 'at home' or 'comfortable' with.

TOURIST
To be a tourist in a dream is to see things from an outsider's point of view, or with a fresh perspective. It may also indicate that the dreamer feels unfamiliar with his or her new surroundings.

CAB
A means of transport, indicates that you are going places or being taken somewhere.

CAR PARK
Like the hotel, this is a temporary place where the car (your means of moving forward) is stored, but is usually underground (intuition).

DREAM 9 I was walking in a large group towards a town. It looked like an earthquake had hit it. People there didn't seem to notice. I noticed that they were robots in human form. I warned the others not to arouse suspicion. I made the robots believe that my group had been brainwashed and that we were allies. Then I became careless. I looked down and I saw that I was carrying a book without the emblem of approval. The robots began to chase me.

What was happening at the time of your dream?
The school council made a decision that I didn't agree with. I felt that I was powerless to protest against the majority. I also felt that I had less respect for the school council as a group who were supposed to have the children's best interests at heart.

Interpretation
The town is the small mindedness—a closing of ranks and a definite pecking order. I may represent the silent majority (large group following) but they don't offer solid support. The council is represented by the robots—machine-like and de-humanised. They are perceived to go through the motions as if programmed, but do not have the community spirit to make choices that are beneficial to all. As I was part of the school council, I 'pretended' to be one of them, but really in my heart I was not part of their system (no emblem on the book). I didn't have the seal of approval, as I wasn't in agreement with their philosophy. Hence, the chase and my need to get away (fear of being found out or being 'brainwashed' into agreeing with the decision).

TOWN
Towns are places where there is a strong sense of community and a great deal of social interaction going on. If you see yourself in a strange town, it may mean that you don't yet feel comfortable in a new environment. The new town may also stand for a side of yourself that you haven't accepted yet or that others find hard to accept.

ROBOTS
Symbol of efficiency, emotional detachment and control.

BOOK
Associated with wisdom and a desire to find something out. It can also indicate a need to be recognised (published).

EMBLEMS
Similar to labels and uniforms. They can appear in dreams for identification and sense of identity.

Appendix

A good night's sleep is vital for us to re-charge our brains and organise our thoughts on a subconscious level. Over the centuries, and throughout different cultures, people have tried to enhance the sleep process with a range of charms, potions, herbs and crystals. Whether you are having difficulty getting to sleep, wish to protect yourself from bad dreams, or hope to have dreams which predict the future, this chapter outlines some of the most common methods for you to try.

Recipes for a good sleep

To charm something refers to enchanting something or someone. Words are spoken or sung in order to provoke an action of some sort. The words become a chant and are repeated until the desired result is achieved. When the object becomes charmed it then possesses magical qualities and is recognised as enchanted. The objects can be as ordinary as a horseshoe or a four-leaf clover to bring luck.

The North American Indians used a 'dream catcher' made from a net woven on a round frame which was decorated with feathers and beads. It resembled a manmade spider web and was hung over the bed. The net was believed to catch the 'bad' dreams, which then disappeared when hit by the early morning sun rays. The 'good' dreams were allowed to drift below to enter the sleeper's mind. This is a popular charm which is still used today in children's bedrooms.

Herbs and flowers

Herbs have been used over time to induce dreams, inspire you to dream, and have your wishes fulfilled through a dream. Before going to sleep, relax and then try repeating this affirmation:

'May my dreams bring me peace, happiness and success.'

By putting these herbs in a small sachet under the pillow, you will influence the types of dreams you wish to have.

Rosemary Wards off nightmares and brings restful sleep. Rosemary is excellent for dream recall and answering a particular question you wish answered. Also improves memory and helps to produce sleep.

Holly Nine holly leaves tied with nine knots and put in a scarf under your pillow allows you to have prophetic dreams.

Mugwort Promotes psychic ability and is thought to be useful in inducing prophetic-type dreams.

Cowslip Supposed to bring luck and encourage contact with departed loved ones whilst dreaming.

St John's Wort Protects against nightmares and bad dreams.

Valerian A great sleep enhancer. It will help you have a peaceful sleep.

Dried flowers If you want to be lulled to sleep with dreams of all things beautiful, this country garden mix will do the trick. Fill a small linen/cotton bag and leave it under your pillow. This is for a large quantity.

1 cup dried rose petals
1 cup any other dried and fragrant flower petals such as jasmine and lilac
1 cup dried lavender
1 cup dried lemon verbena
1 cup dried rosemary
6 drops bergamot essential oil

Dream crystals

Crystals, healing stones and charmed stones have also been known to contain healing properties and have their own inherent energies. Firstly, cleanse the crystal and dedicate it to whatever the intended purpose is. You must hold the thought for the purpose in your mind, while holding the crystal at the same time. If you wish to think on it, put the crystal by your bedside during the night.

Jade This is regarded as a dream stone, as it is believed to release built-up or suppressed emotions whilst dreaming. By unburdening oneself, it is believed to manifest your dreams in waking life, allowing you to be more confident and achieve your goals.

Lapis This is highly spiritual stone, once held sacred by the ancient Egyptians. It will help to give you spiritual insight into your dreams.

Opal This stone is said to induce happy dreams and boost self-confidence.

Ruby As a shielding stone, ruby protects you against nightmares.

Green sapphire Your dreams can be more easily remembered with the assistance of a green sapphire.

Star garnet Stronger than green sapphire, this is used to recall distressing dreams, with the aim that the dreamer will be able to solve the conflict once it becomes conscious.

Tunnellite This is believed to stimulate creativity whilst dreaming.

Dream potions

Only with a calming environment are you most likely to achieve a good night's uninterrupted sleep. It's best to take a warm bath beforehand, keep the lighting and colours in your bedroom warm and soft and tidy up any clutter. Avoid caffeine at least an hour before going to bed and have a soothing sleeping potion instead. Hot milk with honey is relaxing. Camomile tea or lemon balm help to unwind and restore the nervous system.

Aromatherapy essential oils are concentrated and only a few drops in a vaporiser or an oil burner are needed to evoke an ideal environment for sleep and dreams. Burn the oils an hour or two before sleeping and make sure the candle is out before you go to bed. The following oils are known to be ideal for sleep and sweet dreams:

Bergamot *(Citrus bergamia)* Can help to radiate happiness, particularly in times of grief. Its green colour has a calming and comforting affect. It is particularly good as a healing oil during times of agitation or when you are experiencing unhappiness.

Camomile (*Matricaria chamomila*) Calming and soothing properties, particularly if one is feeling overwhelmed with negative emotions such as anger or bitterness.

Clary sage (*Salvia sclarea*) Ideal for connecting with the dreamworld, which can help us to gain insight into ourselves. It encourages vivid dreams and dream recall. Before falling asleep, think on any problem or issue that you wish to clear up and repeat an affirmation such as 'I will remember my dream. My dream will have the answer'. Its association with predicting the future comes from its old name, 'clear-eye', and it may be this meaning of having a 'clear eye' or 'inner eye', which helps us see the future more clearly.

Cypress (*Cupressus sempervirens*) Refers to the evergreen leaves of the tree and has been used widely in cemeteries as a reminder of afterlife. As oil, it has comforting, warming and soothing properties and is particularly good at times of change and transition.

Jasmine (*Jasminium officinalis*) Believed to have spiritual properties. It is also thought to develop creativity and to stimulate appreciation for visual arts, music and beauty in general. Jasmine is good for meditation. It relieves stress and tiredness and is an ideal oil to unwind with before going to sleep.

Juniper (*Juniperus communis*) An ancient oil used by old civilisations world wide. It has cleansing properties that are useful to detoxify the body and mental state. Negative energies that have accumulated may be cleared by juniper oil, whether one is moving into a new home or a new work place.

Lavender (*Lavandula officinalis, Lavandula vera*) Helps with insomnia, tension and tiredness. It has balancing and healing properties, which will help guard against negative emotions. Both calming and energising, lavender oil has many uses—as a sedative, antiseptic and even as an anti-depressant. When used in an oil burner, it cleanses the room of negative energy and induces calm. You can massage some oil into the soles of your feet or sprinkle some drops on you pillow.

Neroli (*Citrus aurantium*) Induces peaceful sleep and is known for its purity, due to its white flowers derived from the orange-blossom. It de-stresses the mind and calms the body, and can enhance creativity when used with music and writing activities.

Rose (*Rosa centifolia, Rosa officinalis*) Renowned for its association with love. It is regarded as a soul fragrance, allowing us to connect with our spiritual energy. To induce dreams of romance, rose oil is ideal, as its own unique unfolding from bud to flower is similar to the unfolding of love.

Rosemary (*Rosmarinus officinalis*) Assists us with our sense of purpose and understanding of wisdom. It is known as a psychic protector, as it is best used in the morning in full strength. In an oil blend, use sparingly, as it is a stimulant. It was used in medieval Europe to drive away evil spirits from houses, and is widely regarded today as a mind stimulant. It can help with increasing the level of clairvoyance and intuition. Like clary sage, its properties are associated with clear-sightedness.

Sandalwood *(Santalum album)* Warming and soothing with purifying properties. It has been used as an incense for meditation for thousands of years because of its ability to quieten the conscious mind so that one can move into a deeper state of meditation. This action clarifies our thoughts and enables us to focus on inducing dreams, particularly if we are looking for direction or answers to some dilemma in our waking life.

Ylang ylang *(Canaga odorata)* A very sweet oil, balancing our physical and spiritual natures together. It is known as a sensual oil, due to its fragrance and its relaxing properties.

Blends for specific types of dreams
Make a blend, mixing the various oils to promote specific dreams. Use a few drops of each oil, depending on your personal preference, and use in an oil burner. Some oils may be harmful if you are pregnant.

Caution: Do not use oils if you are pregnant. Some people may develop a reaction when oils are used directly on skin. Generally, it is best to use oils in an oil burner rather than on your skin or in a bath.

Dreams of love
Rose	*heart warming*
Basil	*healing*
Bergamot	*comforting*
Ylang ylang	*sensual*

Dreams for good luck
Juniper	*cleansing*
Sandalwood	*clarifying*

Restful dreams
Lavender	*relaxing*
Camomile	*soothing*
Neroli	*peaceful*

Dreams for creativity and inspiration
Coriander	*warming*
Rosemary	*clarifying*
Cypress	*cleansing*
Lemon	*stimulating*

Dreams to predict the future
Basil	*healing*
Clary sage	*uplifting*
Bergamot	*comforting*
Jasmine	*invigorating*

General blend for dream enhancing
10 drops jasmine oil
10 drops nutmeg oil
3 drops clary sage

This is best burnt in an oil burner to promote a dream-inducing atmosphere in your bedroom.

Glossary

Anxiety dreams Dreams that reflect the person's waking anxieties. Being chased, not turning up ready for an exam, roadblocks and other such frustrating dreams indicate that one's insecurities are manifesting themselves in dreams.

Archetypes Symbols and characters that are commonly understood by everyone because they represent universal themes of life.

Collective unconscious Archetypal images/symbols/emotions shared by all people around the world.

Delta sleep This is a deep sleep stage where long brainwaves produce a deep but dreamless sleep.

Dream recall Being able to remember the entire dream, usually in sequence.

Incubation dreams A dream in which you ask the dream for guidance in solving an actual problem in your waking life.

Lucid dreaming Being aware that you are dreaming while still asleep in the dream. The lucid dreamer can learn to manipulate the dream to suit his or her wishes.

Night terrors A series of screaming and agitation that usually occur in young children during a terrifying dream.

Nightmares A distressing dream which causes the dreamer to partially wake.

Parasomnias Disorders of arousal of sleep, including sleepwalking, nightmares, night terrors and sleep talking.

Prophetic/precognitive dreams Accurate dreams predicting future events.

Psyche Our total personality.

Recurring dreams Dreams that are repeated.

REM sleep Rapid Eye Movement sleep, known also as dreaming sleep. The brain is in an active state like when we're awake, yet the movements are stilled so that we experience vivid dreams but can't move.

Bibliography

Pamela Ball, *The Complete Dream Dictionary*, Prospero Books, Canada, 1999.

Gregory J. Berry, *Dream Analysis: Thinking Beyond Jung*, Cranset, Hunter's Hill, NSW, 1995.

Tony Crisp, *The New Dream Dictionary*, Optima, London, 1990.

Russell Grant & Vicky Emptage, *The Illustrated Dream Dictionary*, Sterling, New York, 1996.

Geddes & Grosset, *Dictionary of Dreams*, 1997.

Georg Fink, *Dream Symbols A to Z*, Sterling, New York, 1999.

Sigmund Freud, *The Interpretation of Dreams*, Wordsworth, Hertfordshire, 1997.

Carl Jung, *Man and His Symbols*, Aldus, London, 1964.

Carl Jung, *Dreams*, Ark, London, 1986.

Jack Kerouac, *Book of Dreams*, City Light Books, San Francisco, 2001.

Peter Malone, *The Secret Language of Dreams: A Visual Key to Dreams and Their Meanings*, Pavilion, London, 1994.

Sandra A. Torson, *Cloud Nine: A Dreamer's Dictionary*, Avon, New York, 1994.

Kevin J. Trodeshi, *The Encyclopedia of Symbolism*, Berkley Publishing Group, New York, 1995.

Zolar, *Zolar's Encyclopedia and Dictionary of Dreams*, Fireside, New York, 1992.

F. & J. Zucker, *Dream Decoder: Reveal Your Unconscious Desires*, Simon & Schuster, NSW, 2000.

Web Sites
http://www.dreamcoach.com.au
http://www.sleeps.com/dictionary
http://www.lifetreks.com
http://www.sleepdisorderchannel.com/stages
http://www.dreamresearch.net

Index